Yours in Sisterhood

Amy Erdman Farrell

Yours in Sisterhood

Ms. Magazine

and the Promise of

Popular Feminism

The University of North Carolina Press

Chapel Hill & London

The paper in this book meets the guidelines for
permanence and durability of the Committee on
Production Guidelines for Book Longevity of
the Council on Library Resources.

Library of Congress
Cataloging-in-Publication Data
Farrell, Amy Erdman.
Yours in sisterhood: Ms. magazine and the promise
of popular feminism / by Amy Erdman Farrell.
    p.   cm. — (Gender and American culture)
Includes bibliographical references and index.
ISBN 0-8078-2424-0 (cloth : alk. paper). —
ISBN 0-8078-4735-6 (pbk. : alk. paper)
1. Ms.   2. Ms. (New York, N.Y. : 1990)
3. Feminism — United States — History — 20th
century.   4. Feminism — History — 20th century.
5. Women — United States — History — 20th century.
I. Title.   II. Series: Gender & American culture.
✓ PN4900.M77F37   1998
051'.082 — dc21   97-50228
                    CIP

02 01 00 99 98   5 4 3 2 1

To John *and to our children,* Nicholas *and* Catherine Ann

CONTENTS

Illustrations appear on pages 139–50

ACKNOWLEDGMENTS

As I complete *Yours in Sisterhood* it is a joy to acknowledge those who have helped me. Numerous institutions and funding sources have supported this project from its initial stages. A research grant from the Arthur and Elizabeth Schlesinger Library on the History of Women at Radcliffe College allowed me to travel to Cambridge and read the collection of unpublished and published letters readers wrote to *Ms.* magazine. The University of Minnesota supported my research with a McMillan Travel Grant, a Dissertation Special Research Grant, and an American Studies Dissertation Writing Grant. The School of American Research in Santa Fe, New Mexico, provided me with office space during the 1990–91 school year. An NEH Travel to Collections Grant and a Dickinson College Research Grant in 1992 financed my initial trip to the Sophia Smith Archives at Smith College, where the *Ms.* editorial files are collected. Finally, a generous grant from the Aspen Institute's Non-Profit Sector Research Fund allowed me to return to the Smith Archives and to take a full year's leave for writing the final manuscript.

I could not have done this research without the fine *Ms.* collections at the Schlesinger Library and the Sophia Smith Archives. I wish especially to thank Amy Hague, assistant curator of the Smith Archives, who guided me skillfully through the *Ms.* Collection.

A number of former *Ms.* editors and writers generously gave their time and thoughtfully answered my questions. I wish to thank Patricia Carbine, JoAnne Edgar, Jo Freeman, Marcia Ann Gillespie, Elizabeth Forsling Harris, Suzanne Braun Levine, Harriet Lyons, Mary Peacock, Letty Cottin Pogrebin, Gloria Steinem, and Mary Thom. Their multiple and often conflicting accounts of the *Ms.* project provided me with invaluable insight into the dynamic and contested nature of the magazine from its origins. I also wish to thank Mollie Hoben, copublisher of the *Minnesota Women's Press*, for sharing her taped interview with Anne Summers. My greatest debt goes to the thousands of women who wrote to the magazine, expressing quite eloquently their own stories of changed consciousness and their own hopes for and doubts about *Ms.* Their letters attest to both the strength of their attachment to this magazine as a resource for the women's movement and the formidable power of the women around the country seeking to change our country.

I have found it a pleasure to work with the editors of the University of North Carolina Press, particularly Kate Douglas Torrey, who first encouraged me to submit my manuscript, Barbara Hanrahan, who worked with me at the early stages, and Sian Hunter White, who saw it through to the end.

Many colleagues, friends, and faculty at the University of Minnesota helped me with the early stages of this research. Ruth-Ellen Joeres, Elaine Tyler May, David Noble, Riv-Ellen Prell, Paula Rabinowitz, Janet Spector, and, especially, George Lipsitz and Sara Evans, pushed me to define my questions, suggested important areas of inquiry, provided methodological guidance, and gave me their own models of fine scholarship. Betty Agee and Karen Moon steered me through the bureaucratic maze with ease and efficiency. I wish also to thank the members of the Feminist Studies Writing Group and the American Studies Writing Group, especially Michiko Hase, Mark Hulsether, and April Schultz.

My friends and colleagues at Dickinson College have been key to the completion of this manuscript. The list here is entirely partial; I could cast the net much farther to name all those who have supported me. I wish first to thank the members of the Birds, the women's writing group, particularly Mara Donaldson for organizing our monthly meetings. I wish also to thank Lonna Malmsheimer, the chair of American Studies, for supporting my research, Sharon Stockton, for "talking theory" with me, and Susan Rose, for being a companion extraordinaire on our inspirational trip to the Fourth World Conference on Women. I wish to thank the secretarial staff of Denny Hall, Anna McPherson, Elaine Mellen, and Vicky Kuhn, and, especially, Barbara McDonald for all her work in preparing the final manuscript. Finally, I wish to thank the director, Jane Seller, and the teachers of the Dickinson College Children's Center, most recently Katie Adams, Marsha Fraker, and Jody Geiling, who provided me with the peace of mind to know that Nick and Catherine were being loved and cared for while I was in my office.

I have been fortunate to have had many readers of my work. I wish to thank Myra Marx Ferree, Patricia Yancey Martin, Joyce Rothschild, and two anonymous readers, all of whom provided useful suggestions and commentary. Sharon O'Brien, another of my colleagues at Dickinson, read my manuscript in its entirety and provided the comments I needed to make my final revisions. Wendy Kozol has read numerous drafts of this manuscript, commented extensively, and bolstered me with her phone calls and friendship.

My family has been a source of strength, laughter, and love as I've worked on this book. Maxine Bloom, Sidney Bloom, the late Geraldine Aaron, and Jim Bloom have enthusiastically embraced my project and provided me with clippings from around the country about the changing status of *Ms.* I have shared in minute detail the many ups and downs of this project with my sister Ann Farrell Midgley, and I thank her for her unflagging sense of humor, warmth, and friendship. The entire Midgley family—my sister Ann, my brother-in-law Pat, and their children, Allison, Patrick, and Amy—and my brother Kirby Farrell, his wife, Laura Farrell, and their children, Jake and Griffin, gave me encouragement, love, and asked tactful questions about the status of my book. My parents, Lois and Jim Farrell, gave me the freedom to develop in my own direction from an early age. I wish to thank them both for their unfaltering love, my mother in particular for her quiet confidence in my work, and my father for his clipping service and cranky questions about my book. My husband and soulmate, John Bloom, cooked spectacular meals, read and commented on many, many drafts of this book, made sure I had the time to work, and buoyed my spirits when discouragement threatened. His companionship and love sustain me on a daily basis. Our son, Nicholas Farrell Bloom, now six, kept me on track with his regular inquiries about how my book was coming, and provided welcome distraction with his questions about life and sports. Our daughter, Catherine Ann Farrell Bloom, is now a year old and our chief family mischief-maker. An endless source of joy, Nick and Catherine inspire me to imagine a better future for all of us. This book is dedicated to John, and to our children, Nick and Catherine.

Yours in Sisterhood

INTRODUCTION

In the winter of 1972, the first issue of *Ms.* magazine hit the newsstands. The bright red cover, picturing a Hindu goddesslike woman dancing on a green plain, promised stories on sisterhood, abortions, children, sex roles, and living as a housewife. For some women's movement activists, the birth of this new magazine heralded the movement's "coming of age"; for others, it signaled the capitulation of the movement to crass commercialism. Whatever its critical reception, however, *Ms.* quickly gained national success, selling out in only eight days. Referred to as the "mouthpiece of popular feminism" and the "leading voice of feminist movement," *Ms.* almost immediately became the popular icon of the women's movement, synonymous, for many Americans, with the women's movement itself.[1] For one magazine to represent a movement so wide and diverse as the second wave of feminism meant that, inevitably, it would generate both extreme loyalty and seething resentment, and sometimes both.

The first commercial magazine in the United States to unambiguously claim a feminist perspective, *Ms.* magazine promised to be an "open forum; a place where women of many different backgrounds can find help and information to improve their lives."[2] With a circulation of 400,000–500,000 and an estimated readership of 3 million, *Ms.* magazine clearly worked as the popular, commercial expression of feminism in the United States.[3] Particularly for those women isolated by their familial, geographic, or cultural circumstances, *Ms.* acted as a lifeline, connecting them to a national community and discourse of feminism. Spanning two decades of great change in U.S. women's lives, from the early activism of the women's movement in the 1970s to the embattled but still vital status of the movement in the late 1980s, *Ms.* served as a crucial public arena where the implications of the term "feminism" and of the feminist movement were worked out.

This book explores the history of *Ms.* magazine, from its origins in 1971 to its final commercial issue in 1989. The story of *Ms.* magazine is a compelling one, for both those who lived through these decades as activists themselves and those who considered themselves onlookers or were too young to be part of the movement in those decades. It is a story of dedicated editors and writers, of courageous staff members who worked to convince large and small corporations to believe in a new kind of magazine, of articulate and stubborn readers who insisted that the magazine live up to its promise to be a resource for the women's movement. On a larger level, the story of *Ms.* is the story of the mainstreaming of feminism in the 1970s and 1980s, as the issues facing this magazine mirrored the dilemmas and advances encountered by so many feminist organizations in these decades. Moreover, the history of *Ms.* is about the creation of popular feminism itself, the experimental and daring attempt by a number of women's movement activists to engage a mass audience using the commercial media as their vehicle. As such, the history of *Ms.* is, in the end, about the possibilities and limitations of forging an oppositional politics within the context of commercial culture.

Throughout its two-decade history as a commercial magazine, *Ms.* worked as a resource for the feminist movement in two ways—as an actual organization, providing invaluable institutional sustenance to the movement, and as a discursive site, a locus point for the articulation and redefining of the meaning of the women's movement. I argue that the history of *Ms.*—as both an organization and as a discursive site—can be seen as a dialogue among the editors, writers, advertisers, and readers as to whom the magazine should speak, for whom it should speak, and to whom, literally and figuratively, it should belong. *Ms.* was contested terrain, a commercial feminist text struggled over by its various creators and users. This book highlights the major tensions that evolved as this magazine negotiated the multiple demands of its various constituencies.

Within the United States, scholars from diverse fields including history, sociology, political science, and American studies have completed excellent studies focusing on the organizational and grassroots origins of the second wave of U.S. feminism.[4] By tracing many of the major routes through which the feminist movement worked, and continues to work, these studies have been essential to our understanding of the growth of the contemporary feminist movement. Recent work on the origins, development, and survival of feminist organizations—from ones like the National Organization for Women to small, grassroots rape crisis centers—points to the critical importance of these institutions in allowing the movement to sustain itself and flourish.[5]

Ms. magazine was a particularly fascinating and important feminist organization, for it is one of the few to make a conscious attempt to harness the marketplace for its own purposes. That is, other organizations dealt with (and continue to deal with) state bureaucracy, the church, and the legal system in garnering resources for their work; other organizations continue to find they must, by default, deal with issues of finances and profit making in order to survive. *Ms.*, however, explicitly set out to make an alliance with the capitalist system, to use the financial resources of advertisers to fund the movement, and to forge a place for itself within Madison Avenue publishing. *Ms.*'s status as a feminist *and* mass media magazine gave the periodical the power to move in circles unavailable to smaller, more radical feminist periodicals, but it also created competing, conflicting demands. At the same time that *Ms.* promised its readers to be an "open forum" and to "work for a better world" it also had to survive in a media industry that dictated it attract as many advertisers as possible, many of whom were less than comfortable with its openly political perspective. Even in its years as a nonprofit organization (from 1979 to 1987), *Ms.* needed to attract sufficient advertisers to support its mass circulation. Both a "marketing opportunity" for advertisers and a resource within the women's movement, *Ms.* magazine was an inherently contradictory text. The first tension that characterized the history of *Ms.* emanated from the magazine's precarious union of feminism and capitalism, as the political ideals of its founders often clashed with the demands of the advertisers.

Prior to the building of any organizational base for the movement, however, comes the shift in consciousness necessary for women to perceive the need for new kinds of organizations. This transformation in consciousness (coming to an awareness of problems, gaining the power to name those problems, asking new sets of questions, and recognizing that one is not alone, idiosyncratic, or crazy in the new sets of perceptions) is a first, ongoing, and necessary part of any social movement, particularly for feminism, where women "live with the enemy" in personal and often intimate ways. As Mary Fainsod Katzenstein argued in her work on feminist movements of the United States and Western Europe, scholars must "identify the multiple networks through which feminist consciousness is purveyed and activism is promoted" if we are to understand both the history and the current status of contemporary feminist movements.[6] *Ms.* magazine was one of those key networks for the dissemination of feminist consciousness, providing a vital link to hundreds of thousands of women who could find cheap copies of the magazine at their grocery store or buy an inexpensive subscription. As Jane Mansbridge argues in her recent essay defining the feminist movement, however, those who articulated the goals and issues of the movement, in this case the writers and editors of *Ms.*, had to shape their words to resonate with the thoughts, experiences, and needs of their audience. The editors and writers of *Ms.* both entered into and helped to generate the "discursively created" feminist movement that both "inspires movement activists and is the entity to which they feel accountable."[7] For *Ms.*, the readers, as well as other feminist organizations, constituted that discursive community to which editors felt accountable. The second major tension characterizing the history of the magazine was this relationship among readers and editors, particularly as readers pushed, and expected, *Ms.* to be accountable to their own understandings of what a feminist magazine for women should be.

Part of this struggle over what a feminist magazine should be, of course, related to the dynamics of *Ms.*'s own articulation of feminism. When differentiating among the various branches of U.S. feminism (i.e., liberal feminism, cultural feminism, and socialist feminism) scholars and journalists frequently employ *Ms.* — and Gloria Steinem — as the most obvious and transparent example of liberal feminism. That is, after explaining that liberal feminism concentrates on the individual, and the need to eradicate sex roles, sex stereotyping, and legal inequities in order to break down barriers to full participation in the mainstream, they refer to *Ms.* as the example par excellence, as if the reader should at that point say, "aha, I understand" and have no more questions about this ideology called liberal feminism. Even a brief glance at the magazine, however, should dispel this easy categorization. One can open any *Ms.* from the 1970s or 1980s and find a clashing mixture of messages and representations — advertisements portraying women's liberation as an American Express card or a Benson and Hedges smoke, colliding with poems by Adrienne Rich, an editorial proclaiming the "sisterhood" of all women, an article bemoaning the housewife blues, Alice Walker speaking on the limitations and racism of white feminism, classifieds selling jewelry celebrating matriarchal culture, and letters from readers criticizing the magazine's advertising policies and sharing their own stories of discrimination or enlightenment. Considering this polyphony of voices — or sometimes what could more aptly be described as a cacophony of voices — one would be unwise to pigeonhole *Ms.*

Even if one focuses exclusively on the articulation of feminism by those primary voices in *Ms.* — through the "Personal Reports" or the essays by the key editors — one finds contradictions and complexities. In her germinal, and still very relevant, study *The Radical Future of Liberal Feminism*, Zillah Eisenstein points to the fundamental contradiction within liberal feminism:

the ideology emphasizes the importance of individual opportunity even as it must speak for all women on the basis of sexual class.[8] Indeed, *Ms.* not only negotiated this tension but also forcefully articulated an emphasis on the sisterhood of all women, the shared experience of both oppression and a unique female culture. The third tension that this book traces is the one stemming from the magazine's attempt to accommodate two strands of feminism, one emphasizing individual liberty, the other emphasizing shared sisterhood, otherwise known as cultural feminism. While the two kinds of feminism might be ultimately incompatible, like the other tensions characterizing *Ms.*, the magazine labored to make them coexist within the overall framework of liberal pluralism.

What makes *Ms.* magazine such a fascinating endeavor, I argue, is that it did indeed promise to create what I call a "popular feminism." I define "feminism" in its broadest sense: the commitment to improving women's lives and to ending gender domination. I purposively chose to use the term in this way in order to highlight how various constituencies attempted to refine and to elaborate on this definition within the discursive community of *Ms.* In speaking of a "popular feminism," I refer to both a feminism that is widespread, common to many, and one that emerges from the realm of popular culture. As George Lipsitz argues in his important work *Time Passages*, popular culture is neither high culture, where a "dogmatic formalism privileges abstraction over expression" and makes it accessible only to those highly trained in its intricacies, nor is it "folklore," a pure expression of cultural meaning emanating from the grass roots. Rather, popular culture is the realm of commercial culture, where "images and icons compete for dominance within a multiplicity of discourses," where the dominant ideology and interests of commercial producers clash with the needs and desires of its consumers but also must "engage audiences in active and familiar processes."[9] Unlike its sister feminist publications like *off our backs* or *No More Fun and Games*, which refused the territory of commercial publication as contaminated, or its sister mainstream publications like *Good Housekeeping* or *McCall's*, whose purpose was to market to women, not to change their lives, *Ms.* promised to claim this territory of commercial popular culture for feminism.

Despite the centrality of popular culture in twentieth-century America, scholars have paid little attention to the role of popular culture in forming a collective oppositional consciousness among women during the 1970s and 1980s. Part of the reason for this is the lack of popular culture texts that claim a feminist perspective or that clearly promote feminist ideas. I would argue, however, that part of the reason also stems from a belief that all mass media are corrupt and unable to construct anything but the most dominant of stereotypical images. As one historian of the 1970s wrote, "Attempts to alter popular consciousness through the mass media . . . greatly underestimated the ability of the established order to absorb dissent while offering mere appearance of change."[10] What this study illuminates, however, is that the struggle of the established order to "absorb dissent" is a complicated process in which the losses and victories are not always so clear-cut. Moreover, as recent work in cultural studies and poststructuralist theory demonstrates, the whole notion of corruption masks the ways in which knowledge industries and political struggles work in the late twentieth century, the ways in which all texts, knowledge, and political practices are constructed within competing social, political, and economic contexts.[11]

Much feminist scholarship within the last twenty years has focused extensively on commercial media—from women's magazines to television programming—as significant forums for constructing and disseminating ideal images of womanhood, femininity, and gender identity. In addition, recent scholarship within the field of cultural studies explores not only the representations of women in popular culture but also, more extensively, the ways subordinated groups resist and negotiate power relations, particularly through social practices connected with popular culture and mass communications. Cultural studies scholars have focused on such seemingly disparate practices as fan-identification with MTV stars and romance reading as evidence of protofeminist impulses within the lives of girls and women.[12] This book takes these works on women's and girls' popular culture and uses their approaches to examine a magazine that promised not "pleasure" (although the editorial perspective was not antithetical to creating a pleasurable reading experience) but a feminist community.

From its origins in 1972, *Ms.* worked as a fascinating hybrid, bridging the genres of mass circulation women's magazines and feminist periodicals. As a crossover magazine, in many ways it looked and sounded like any women's magazine one might find on the newsstand—a glossy cover photograph, an ad on the back cover, a rhetorical style that emphasized a personal tone, and a table of contents filled with titles of self-help articles. Editors of *Ms.* explained in publicity notices that it was to be a "service" magazine, as the publishing industry euphemistically terms them, but one with a twist. With articles like "How to Be a Troublemaker" and "Stories for Free Children," it suggested that the way to improve one's life was not to keep one's man but to reject patriarchy, to foster independence, and to fight sex roles. Its early editorials claimed an oppositional stance, promising to be an "open forum" and to "push the philosophical boundaries that brave and radical feminists are trying to explore."[13] Commercial women's magazines consciously seek to speak to women as a group, to foster a gender consciousness so that they will have a ready audience for their products. In her work on mass media for girls and women in the baby boomer age, Susan Douglas argues that this marketing to women did not "co-opt rebellion, but . . . actually helped to create it," as girls who had grown up thinking of themselves as a consumer generation found it rather easy to begin thinking of themselves as a cultural and political generation.[14] Significantly, *Ms.* latched onto women's magazines' expert ability at fostering gender consciousness, and promised to use that gender consciousness not to forge a marketing cohort but to foster an oppositional gender consciousness, speaking to a "group called women" who recognized and resisted androcentric culture.[15] Thus, *Ms.* did not so much repudiate the genre of mass market women's magazines as try to revise it; a rhetorical move from "us girls" in the mainstream women's magazines to "we sisters" in *Ms.* marked this transformation.

Despite the inherent complexity and contradiction that characterized *Ms.* from its initial issues, many scholars and critics refer to the magazine in static and unified terms, either as a direct reflection of the movement or as a magazine that had little to do with the "realities" of the 1970s and 1980s. To be fair, *Ms.* magazine has not been the exclusive focus of their studies, but the magazine emerges frequently as a source for analyses, historical interpretations, and cultural critiques. Indeed, the magazine *Ms.* evokes such emotionally charged responses in scholars that these generalizations need to be addressed before it is possible to examine *Ms.* as a contradictory and complex text.

Winifred Wandersee, for instance, refers to *Ms.* rather extensively in her history of women in the 1970s. While she argues that most mass media "profited immensely from 'women's liberation' but managed to redefine it in individualistic, market-economy terms," she describes the *Ms.* of the 1970s as a "barometer of the women's movement in its popular form."[16] This description suggests she sees the magazine as almost a transparent reflection of the 1970s feminist movement. Other critics have dismissed *Ms.* as a corrupt forum that had nothing to do with the concerns of real women. Displaying her contempt for the "masses," both as a reading public and as a magazine industry, Adrienne Rich, for instance, wrote:

How shall we ever make the world intelligent of our movement? I do not think that the answer lies in trying to render feminism easy, popular, and instantly gratifying. To conjure with the passive culture and adapt to its

rules is to degrade and deny the fullness of our meaning and intention. . . .
For many readers the feminist movement is simply what the mass media
say it is, whether on the television screen, or in the pages of the *New
Yorker*, *Psychology Today*, *Mother Jones*, or *Ms.* Willful ignorance, reduc-
tiveness, caricature, distortion, trivialization—these are familiar utensils,
not only in the rhetoric of organized opposition.[17]

For Wandersee and Rich, their respective interpretations of *Ms.* depend on
whether they see *Ms.* as having been co-opted by that "corrupt" commercial matrix or as having been able to survive and subvert that context. That
is, while Wandersee and Rich seem to be far apart in their analyses, their interpretations stem from the same basic assumption. In general, both view
mass media as vehicles for communication in which images and ideas are
constructed and then transmitted directly to the viewer, listener, or reader,
who receives intact, already formed messages. The difference between their
analyses is located in their understandings of who constructs the meanings:
Wandersee perceives the images and ideas in *Ms.* as truthful because she
sees the control of the magazine in the hands of feminists; Rich perceives
the images and ideas in *Ms.* as reductive and distorted because she sees the
control of the magazine in the hands of less-than-trustworthy mass media
journalists.

As recent work in semiotics, textual theory, and cultural studies demonstrates, however, the communication process is more complex than analyses
that allow for only a "positive" or "negative" reading would suggest. Julia
Kristeva, for instance, sees language as a "heterogeneous signifying process";
there is no one, fixed meaning for any utterance but rather a multiplicity
of meanings. Those meanings are constructed, as John Fiske argues, at the
"interface" of the textual signifiers and the everyday lives of those who use,
experience, and come into contact with those texts. Janice Radway's work
on the reading of romance novels and the Book-of-the-Month Club further
illuminate the ways that editors, writers, and readers form interpretive communities in which cultural meanings are shared and mapped out.[18] If reading
texts is as complicated a process as Kristeva, Fiske, and Radway suggest, and
if meaning is not located solely in the text itself, then it becomes impossible
to determine whether *Ms.* created a transparently "good" representation of
feminism or a transparently "bad" representation of feminism. Above all, to
define the portrayal of feminism in *Ms.* as either good or bad demands asking
whether the representation reflects "real" women's concerns. This assumes

that there was (and is) an identifiable, unified feminist perspective rather than a plurality of feminist perspectives. In addition, to label the representation of feminism in *Ms.* as either "good" or "bad" assumes that within *Ms.* there is one static meaning rather than multiple meanings and perspectives constructed within the text and in relation to the readers and the context. The goal of this study, therefore, is neither to condemn nor to praise *Ms.* as a realistic or unrealistic reflection of feminism in the 1970s and 1980s nor to set out to uncover its errors, as if there is some clear conception of a better road taken. Rather, the goal is to examine the feminism(s) that were constructed within the competing tensions of *Ms.* What were the choices the founders and editors made? What was the significance of these choices? The consequences? What lessons might we learn from the roads that *Ms.* did choose?

There is yet another common perception of *Ms.* that also obscures the complexities that always characterized the magazine. This view combines the optimism of Wandersee with the pessimism of Rich, constructing a jeremiad in which *Ms.* underwent an extreme transformation from a magazine untainted by marketplace demands when it began in the early 1970s to a magazine thoroughly enmeshed in a consumer, individualistic ideology by the time it was sold to Fairfax, Inc., in 1987. In a scathing editorial prompted by the magazine's decision to sell to Fairfax, for instance, Maurine Christopher traced what she saw as the continual downfall of *Ms.* since its inception.[19] Describing the history of *Ms.* as "co-optation" is one of the most common interpretations of the magazine, as well as one of the most problematic, for it poses an illusory "golden age," divorced from the very real complexities that have always surrounded *Ms.* That is, while we can certainly trace changes in *Ms.* since 1972, it must be clearly understood that *Ms.* was always a "corrupt" form, in that it was always firmly enmeshed in a commercial, mass media matrix. Furthermore, the notion of "co-optation" suggests that feminism itself, as a social and political movement, exists as a pure space, uncontaminated by struggles among its participants for power and resources until it comes into contact with commercialism. Certainly we know that this is not true.

The complex and contradictory nature of *Ms.* as a political and a commercial text make it impossible to discuss the way the magazine constructed an oppositional stance to patriarchal values without simultaneously confronting the ways in which a capitalist market engulfed that patriarchy, as well as the fight to disrupt it. Thus, this project focuses not only on how *Ms.* as a text represented feminism but also on the economic and political conditions that shaped, and sometimes determined, what *Ms.* could or would publish, the conditions for publication, and the symbolic and material "ownership" of the magazine. That is, this project is based on the assumption that a text in isolation cannot "speak for itself"; we must always look at the text in relation to material conditions and political contexts. It is particularly important to emphasize the connections among the apparatus of *Ms.*, the political context in which the magazine was situated, and the codes of representation in *Ms.*, since these connections were often masked and difficult to identify.[20]

The questions that have driven my research and my writing focus on the production, representation, and reception of this magazine within the context of the 1970s and 1980s. How did this mass circulation, feminist magazine — as both an organization and as a discursive site — work as a resource within the women's movement of the 1970s and 1980s? What did it mean for Gloria Steinem and her cofounders to attempt to create a "popular feminism," one that would speak to a multiplicity of women? What were the consequences of using the genre of the mass media women's magazine to "speak feminism?" How did it negotiate the tensions emerging from forging an oppositional space within a patriarchal and capitalist context? What tensions emerged from its competing imperatives to be simultaneously a "marketing opportunity" and a "cause" magazine? How did the various tensions outlined above — between advertisers and editors, between readers and editors, and within the articulation of feminism itself — develop over time and influence one another? For instance, what was the relationship between readers and advertisers? How did advertising imperatives shape the articulation of feminism?

Methodologically, these questions translated into a focus on three aspects of *Ms.* magazine — the organizational structure of editors, publisher, and writers; the magazine itself; and the readers. Theoretically, the questions coalesced around a materialist focus on the conditions of publication (including the relationship of the magazine to the Ms. Foundation for Women and the Ms. Foundation for Education and Communication, under whose auspices the magazine became nonprofit in 1979); a poststructuralist emphasis on the language of the text and the semiotics of photos and visuals; and a cultural studies emphasis on reception, on readers as key agents in the production of meaningful representations of feminism within *Ms.*[21] This book at certain points focuses on the implied reader, the woman to whom *Ms.* was trying to speak. Equally important, considering that the production of meaning requires the active interpretation by users of the text, this book considers the reception of *Ms.* in "real" readers' lives — how they read and understood the magazine and the feminism(s) articulated within it. How do we explain their responses as more than idiosyncratic reactions? How did the dialogue they developed with the editors and with other readers affect the magazine?

As sources for this project, I drew from a wide range of materials, ranging from the text of *Ms.*, to interviews with former editors, to an examination of letters and editorial files. In terms of the magazine issues themselves, I was interested in all aspects, including the covers, the articles, the editorials, special columns and features, the ads, the letters, and the "No Comment" section, to which readers submitted ads (from other periodicals) that they found offensive. In writing this book, I chose to discuss certain themes and issues that highlighted the process of dialogue and debate within the interpretative community that surrounded *Ms.* A strict content analysis, in which the researcher counts and categorizes stories and issues, certainly would have revealed the diversity of topics and issues, but it would not have illuminated the engendering of a discursive community that propelled my own study.

Given the focus of this study, my sources had to go beyond the text itself to the creators and the consumers (though these categories sometimes blurred in the history of the magazine). In the early 1990s, I interviewed, in person or by phone, many of the former editors of *Ms.*, including Gloria Steinem, Patricia Carbine, Elizabeth Forsling Harris, Marcia Gillespie, Mary Peacock, Mary Thom, JoAnne Edgar, Letty Cottin Pogrebin, Suzanne Braun Levine, and Harriet Lyons. I also examined the editorial files of the magazine and the minutes from the Ms. Foundation, located at the Sophia Smith Archives at Smith College. Finally, I read the unpublished letters written to *Ms.*, which are collected at the Schlesinger Library at Radcliffe College.

The decision as to how to organize this research proved to be a difficult one. As I began writing I realized that two organizational strategies were obvious choices, each with its own strengths and weaknesses. The first, with a section on the editors, the advertisers, and the readers, highlighted the strength of each member of the *Ms.* "discursive community" to shape the magazine. While this approach clarified the demands and power of each segment to mold the magazine, it failed to illuminate the powerful dynamics among the editors, writers, advertisers, and readers. For this reason, I chose the more accurate route of a chronological approach, which would elucidate these dynamics as well as provide an understanding of the changes over time in political, economic, and social climate that clearly affected the magazine. The one exception to this chronological approach is Chapter 4, "Readers

Writing *Ms.*"; while the readers' perceptions can be found throughout the narrative, I chose to highlight their voices in one chapter in order to emphasize the way they created a powerful bloc of "accountability" for the editors.

Chapter 1 considers the organizational and editorial origins of *Ms.* within the context of debates surrounding the media in the early 1970s women's movement. Through a close examination of the 1972 preview issue, this chapter also outlines some of the early tensions characterizing *Ms.* as a political and commercial text. This chapter also discusses the extensive public debate provoked by the creation of *Ms.* This magazine clearly challenged both those in the publishing industry and women's movement activists to consider the possibilities and potential consequences of a mass media forum that blurred commercial and political boundaries. Chapter 2 analyzes the dynamics of *Ms.* in the 1970s, focusing particularly on the conflicting philosophies of sisterhood and egalitarianism discussed by the writers and editors, and on how the focus on personal transformation dovetailed with a consumer ethic. Moving from the optimism of the early movement, Chapter 3 considers the textual and organizational changes in *Ms.* during the conservative 1980s. A narrowing of feminist perspectives and an increasing reliance on images that deflected attention from *Ms.*'s political position characterized this period, as editors and staff worked to preserve the gains they had won in the 1970s. At the same time, however, *Ms.*'s new status as a nonprofit magazine pulled it away from the commercial realm, as it needed to emphasize its "educational" forum. Redirecting the perspective taken in earlier chapters, Chapter 4 focuses entirely on readers' responses to the magazine — the way readers used it as a space in which they could articulate their changing identities, create ties with other women, and employ the marketing promises espoused by editors to buttress their own claims and to resist the power of advertisers. The dialogue that these readers developed with the magazine is an extremely important one for us to understand, for it was not only radical women within grassroots organizations who created the feminist movement, but also women across the country — like *Ms.* readers — whose ties to the movement were often mediated through commercial texts. Chapter 5 examines the magazine during a period of volatile ownership, focusing on how the need to build circulation and to please advertisers pushed the magazine to deflect "politics" and to close down reader interaction with the magazine. This chapter concludes with a discussion of the lingering power of *Ms.* even in these later years, illustrated by the notorious "It's War" issue, which reminded advertisers of the magazine's political roots and rekindled readers' belief in a mass media feminist periodical. Finally, the conclusion considers the historical legacy of the *Ms.* experiment, contrasting the commercial *Ms.* to the current promises offered by the new advertising-free *Ms.* By tracing the changes in *Ms.* from its origins in 1972 to its final sale in 1989, this project dramatizes how *Ms.* worked as a powerful yet contradictory channel for the women's movement, torn between articulating and advancing a bold vision while at the same time mediating, controlling, and sometimes undermining its initial promise to be a mass media resource for women across the country.

A note on my own position regarding this magazine is in order before we embark on this exploration of *Ms.* and the promise of popular feminism. Indeed, one of the enduring legacies of the feminist movement is the insistence that critical self-examination is crucial to any scholarly undertaking. I do not come to this work as one who was an avid reader of *Ms.* magazine herself. When *Ms.* first came out in 1972 I was in elementary school; my mother never bought or discussed the magazine. We read the *Akron Beacon Journal*, *Time*, *National Geographic*, and an occasional issue of *Vogue* or *House Beautiful*. When I first closely read *Ms.* in graduate school, finding it on the tables outside the Feminist Studies offices, I considered myself familiar with it. *Ms.* was simply part of the cultural landscape in which I grew up, a staple in the grocery store and in the lists of magazines available through Publishers' Clearinghouse Sweepstakes, helping to create the backdrop that made us laugh when a family friend bought my father a "male chauvinist pig" tie and that encouraged my parents to imagine all sorts of future possibilities for their youngest daughter. That "easy familiarity" I felt with the magazine, however, gave me my earliest impressions of the magazine—as a transparent example of "liberal feminism," as a magazine that had undergone a jeremiad of sorts, from its early "radical" origins to its corrupt commercial status in the late 1980s. Quickly, however, those early, false impressions gave way to a more complex understanding as I read issue after issue of the magazine.

I came to this project not as one who read and interacted with the magazine during the 1970s and 1980s but as a member of the next generation. In exploring the history of *Ms.*, I refused the position of the daughter who ignorantly takes for granted the work of her feminist foremothers. Perhaps I have chosen a more dangerous position, particularly when those mothers are still engaged in the work of their lifetimes: that of one who casts an eye simultaneously thankful for and critical of what her foremothers created. My own vision in approaching this research was shaped by both the early assurance that *Ms.* was there for me as well as the emergent critiques within feminist historical writing and feminist popular culture studies that have informed my own activism and scholarship.

The story of *Ms.* magazine is a narrative neither of decline nor of success. Indeed, this study differs sharply from both the dismissive essays written by media critics and from the celebratory tone of *Ms.*'s histories of itself.[22] Significantly, I have refused to characterize the *Ms.* experiment as solely re-formist—which some critics argue must describe any endeavor that remains within a capitalist framework—or revolutionary. This reformist/revolutionary split, I argue, creates a dichotomy that pigeonholes and dismisses important elements of social change. The choice by the *Ms.* founders to create a feminist mass media periodical, to take the commercial resources available in twentieth-century culture and attempt to harness them for the feminist movement, was a bold experiment, one that created layers of contradictions and compromise. Its history teaches us about the gains and losses inherent in creating a popular feminism.

CHAPTER 1

Like a Tarantula on a Banana Boat
The Origins of *Ms.* Magazine

I n a 1972 review of *Ms.*, Onka Dekkers, a writer for the feminist periodical *off our backs*, pinpointed the unique nature of this new magazine for women:

> *Ms.* is making feminist converts of middle class heathens from academia to condominium ville. A slick, reputable looking magazine breaks down defenses and lets the word worm its way into the brain. *Ms.* is almost in violation of Truth in Packaging laws. There is a female mind-set on those glossy pages slipping into American homes concealed in bags of groceries like tarantulas on banana boats. Curious girl children will accidentally discover feminism in *Ms.* the way we stumbled onto sex in our mother's *Ladies' Home Journal*. . . . In the August issue of *Ms.* Del Martin and Phyllis Lyons matter of factly explain how ladies do it together. That paragraph alone could revolutionize slumber parties for generations.[1]

As Dekkers so ingeniously explained, *Ms.* promised to maintain its place on news racks, grocery store counters, and coffee tables while offering a feminist message. In this sense, *Ms.* was the quintessential reformist endeavor, for it attempted to transform the institutions and industries of advertising and women's magazines, to work within consumer culture. Rather than eschewing advertisers' dollars, it sought to reform their messages and to use their money to communicate a political message. Rather than rejecting the format of the women's magazine, it attempted to create a magazine for the "new woman" out of the genre. It promised readers that there was no need to reject Madison Avenue, or the pleasures of consumer culture, in order to identify oneself as a feminist. For activists like Onka Dekkers, its greatest promise —

indeed, its revolutionary promise—was that it could potentially weaken women's resistance to feminism and make them rethink the stereotypical images they had previously known in mainstream media.

While activists like Dekkers applauded *Ms.*'s attempt to create a popular feminism, the commercial matrix in which *Ms.* existed, which prioritized profit and marketability, threatened to undercut the revolutionary possibilities inherent in the creation of *Ms.* Many women in the early 1970s resisted this threat by moving outside the mainstream publishing industry and beginning their own alternative periodicals. These activists believed, in the words of author Audre Lorde, that the "master's tools will never dismantle the master's house."[2] These activists wanted to dismantle the house, not to rebuild it, which, they argued, is what a mass circulation feminist magazine was attempting to do. In contrast, the founders of *Ms.* attempted to create a new house with the master's tools. *Ms.* magazine worked to disrupt cultural hegemony from the inside, to fashion a new representation of women, and of women's magazines, within the context and the constraints of the commercial market. The strength of this "new magazine for women" was its ability to be both a women's magazine, which had a place on the battlefield of existing women's magazines, and a resource within the women's movement, a mass circulation text that could connect women to a national community of feminism. This dual identity, of course, was also its weakness, for the price exacted by the commercial market to maintain legitimacy and solvency often seemed to exceed what was gained by capturing a position on those newsstands. The hopes for revolutionary change that *Ms.* represented—as well as the fears that it inspired—originated with the birth of the magazine itself and the movement that generated it.

The Resurgence of Feminism

At the time when *Ms.* began, a resurgence of the women's movement had already been going on for nearly a decade, challenging the cultural and political restrictions of the feminine mystique. While most historians would date the birth of a widespread women's movement in the late 1960s, the stirrings of change had begun earlier. In 1960, President Kennedy appointed Esther Peterson, the former recreation director of Bryn Mawr Summer School for Women Workers, to the Women's Bureau. Peterson pushed for the creation of the Presidential Commission on the Status of Women, to be chaired by Eleanor Roosevelt. In 1963, the commission's report came out, assessing the quality of women's lives and the existence of extensive discrimination and women's "double burden" in the economy, the family, and the legal system. Two concrete results emerged from this report: the civil service was not to discriminate in hiring on the basis of sex, and the Equal Pay Act of 1963 mandated that workers performing the same job must be paid on an equal pay scale. Perhaps more importantly, however, was the activism the Presidential Commission initiated among a whole generation of professional women. Within a year of the report, most states had established women's commissions, which went on to compile their own more localized studies and to lobby at state and national levels against discrimination.[3]

Representative Martha Griffiths propelled the women's movement forward even more when she pushed to have added to Title VII of the Civil Rights Act the category of "sex" in addition to race, creed, and national origin. While many of her congressional colleagues snickered over the apparent absurdity of protecting rights on the basis of sex, Griffiths forcefully lobbied and won enough votes to pass the act with the word "sex" added. As a result, the Equal Employment Opportunity Commission (EEOC), established by the act, immediately began receiving grievances from women. Significantly, however, the commission failed to respond to complaints, and even passed loopholes allowing newspapers to continue the practice of advertising jobs by sex. The concern that many delegates brought to the 1966 Third National Conference of State Commissions on the Status of Women about the EEOC's lack of action changed to outrage when they realized that the conference would allow no resolutions or official discussion concerning the problem. According to oral histories from the time, during the final lunch of the conference, the angry whispers among delegates turned to action when Betty Friedan called upon her colleagues to form an organization that would fight the inertia of the EEOC. Women each donated a $5 membership fee on the spot, and thus was born the National Organization for Women. At the same meeting, Friedan drafted the new organization's statement of purpose, which emphasized the need for parity between men and women: "To take action to bring women into full participation in the mainstream of American society now, assuming all the privileges and responsibilities thereof in truly equal partnership with men."[4]

By the time *Ms.* began publishing, women had won a number of legal and legislative victories, thanks to the work of NOW and its offshoot, the Women's Equity Action League, formed in 1968 to focus on legal and economic issues affecting women. The National Women's Political Caucus, established in 1971 by Bella Abzug, Betty Friedan, Representative Shirley Chisholm, Gloria Steinem, and others, also increased the visibility and participation of women in political circles. Most significantly, after fifty years of lobbying by feminists, the Equal Rights Amendment finally passed both the House and the Senate. Supported by both the Republican and Democratic Parties, twenty-two of the needed thirty-five states had ratified the ERA by the end of the year. (The battle to win the ERA had not yet been won, of course. Indeed, the first decade of *Ms.*'s life was marked by the ongoing struggle to pass the amendment. It was finally defeated in 1982.) Title IX of the Educational Amendments of the Civil Rights Act also passed, barring sexual discrimination in any educational program receiving federal funding, a law that would hold particular significance for the future of women's sports. Barbara Jordan of Texas and Elizabeth Holtzman of New York were elected to the House of Representatives, soon to become major figures in the Watergate impeachment hearings. Shirley Chisholm ran for the Democratic presidential ticket, with Frances "Sissy" Farenthold as her running mate; their defeat did not lessen the impact they made on a nation never before confronted with an all-female ticket or a black presidential candidate. Women's rights seemed to be supported as a matter of "common sense" in Congress. Representative Bella Abzug, for instance, spoke of 1972 as a "watershed year. We put sex discrimination provisions into everything. There was no opposition. Who'd be against equal rights for women? So we just kept passing women's rights legislation."[5]

While the growth of national organizations like the National Women's Political Caucus and the National Organization for Women signaled obvious expansion within what has become known as the "egalitarian" wing of the movement, these organizations focused primarily on battling discrimination in legal and economic circles, not in creating a grassroots movement. Soon after the founding of NOW, however, a new social movement began to ferment, one that engaged women on the basis of their daily lives and experiences. These women challenged not only legal and economic restrictions to women's freedom but also the very definitions of womanhood, femininity, marriage, and sexuality, anything that constituted the reality of women's lives and existence. Initiated by a cohort of women younger for the most part than those involved in NOW or the NWPC, these women were mostly white, middle-class, and well educated. Many had been active in the Civil Rights and/or student Left movement of the 1960s, such as the Student Nonviolent Coordinating Committee (SNCC) or Students for a Democratic Society (SDS), where they had honed their organizational skills and gained experience organizing women in poor or urban communities. By the middle of the sixties, however, both these movements proved less hospitable to women, as the Civil Rights movement moved toward an ideology of Black Power, one that emphasized separatism and the centrality of black manhood, and the student movement began to emphasize primarily the antidraft movement, which positioned men as the heroic resisters and women as their helpmates.[6] Women involved in these movements increasingly began to recognize the subordinate role they played in these movements and to analyze the way their own oppression was structured into the fight for others' liberation. Stokely Carmichael's by now infamous remark that the "position of women is prone," when he was asked to comment on the role of women in SNCC, came to represent the unwillingness of most men in the New Left and Civil Rights movement to support, or even to recognize the validity of, women's growing discontent.[7]

By 1967, a number of women's liberation groups had independently sprung up across the country in response to the anger women felt at their roles in leftist organizations or at their lives as housewives and mothers. By 1970, the mass media (and the FBI, as *Ms.* would report in the late 1970s!) had begun to report on the phenomenon of "women's liberation." The activities of the bigger, more radical groups such as Redstockings, New York Radical Women, and the Chicago Women's Liberation Union received the most media attention, stemming in large part from the "zap actions" that these groups performed to highlight the oppression women faced: the hexing of Wall Street, the speakouts where women told their own stories about illegal abortions or rape, the demonstration against the 1968 Miss America Beauty Pageant. Scholar Rivka Polatnick points out that African American women participated in this early stage of feminist activism, though the media and historical scholarship has largely ignored them. The Mount Vernon/New Rochelle (New York) group of black women, for instance, mostly from the lower working class or on welfare, fought against sexism within the black movement and racism in the larger world, forcefully articulating the political roots of their individual problems, the importance of their roles as mothers, and their right to reproductive self-determination through access to the pill.[8] By the early 1970s, the women's movement had also established itself in cultural and academic circles: *Sisterhood Is Powerful*, Robin Morgan's anthology of writings from the women's movement came out in 1970, the same year that Kate Millett published her best-selling *Sexual Politics* and that the first women's studies courses were offered in colleges and universities. In 1972, Marge Piercy published her feminist novel *Small Changes*, the Feminist Press began circulation of the *Women's Studies Newsletter*, and the Cal Arts Feminist Art Program in Los Angeles designed the *Womanhouse*, an abandoned house "decorated" by feminist artists with jarring murals and displays.[9]

Perhaps most importantly in terms of the wildfire spread of a national women's movement was the growth and explosion of consciousness-raising groups. These groups could be formed and could meet anywhere — in an office, a neighbor's house, a church basement — and they formed the basis for the essential grassroots activity of the movement. At the foundation of these groups was the act of consciousness-raising, the dynamic conversations that started at the point of women's personal experiences and left no aspect of female existence unexamined. Most central to these conversations was the point of view that the personal is political; that is, one's own personal life is politically structured with inherent power struggles. Moreover, as women began to talk to each other they began to recognize connections among their disparate experiences, a larger pattern that framed many of their lives, and, in particular, their problems. Women began to see themselves as part of a sisterhood, and, because women could fight in solidarity with one another, they began to recognize that, in the words of writer and activist Robin Morgan, "sisterhood was powerful."

As the women's liberation movement took hold, many of the new activists wanted to stay connected to the economic and racial struggles that had propelled them into activism in the first place. They saw gender oppression as one part of, perhaps more important or perhaps less important, the oppressions people faced within a racist and capitalist society. These activists viewed skeptically any emphasis on the ways that women differed from men, whether culturally or biologically, as women's "difference" had historically been used as a weapon to keep women in a subordinate place. Other activists, however, rejected in particular the economic analysis that framed much of the New Left, seeing gender as the primary problem from which racial and economic oppression resulted. These activists felt comfortable emphasizing the ways women differed culturally and biologically from men; their analysis was central to an understanding of "women as a group," which would provide the basis for much feminist activism surrounding rape, violence against women, eating disorders, and other "women's issues" in the 1970s and 1980s. As we are to see very clearly in the history of *Ms.*, however, this significant emphasis on the sisterhood of all women would prove to be a complex issue, as it legitimated much of the activism of the new women's movement but also raised difficult questions about which women stood as the "norm" of the group, and how women were to deal with and understand differences among themselves.[10]

Feminist Media History

Whatever differences characterized the women who made up the early women's movement (and there were many), what connected many of them was an anger that they targeted at the mass media. Beginning with the publication of Betty Friedan's *The Feminine Mystique* in 1963, many activists pointed to the way that mainstream media, in particular women's magazines, had perpetuated stereotypical images of women as housewives, mothers, and brainless consumers interested only in pleasing the men in their lives. Simultaneously, they also recognized the power of the media to define the women's movement for the American public; at its most extreme, the media could either suffocate the movement by giving it no coverage, or the media could breathe life into the movement by spreading its word over an entire nation. Ironically, activists saw media as both a root of women's problems and a potential solution.[11]

The 1970 *Ladies' Home Journal* sit-in was one of the most distinctive examples of the way activists targeted the mass media as both a source of women's oppression and as a source for feminist opposition. On March 8, over two hundred female writers, editors, and activists took over the main editorial office of the *Ladies' Home Journal*, one of the major women's magazines of the twentieth century. For eleven hours, they sat in editor John Mack Carter's office, calling for day care for *Journal* employees, higher wages for its women workers, and an all-female editorial staff. This sit-in clearly expressed the frustration many women felt toward mainstream women's magazines, both as workplaces that exploited women employees and as texts that reproduced stereotypical images of women as mothers and wives. As a consequence of the sit-in, the *LHJ* published an eight-page supplement in the August 1970 issue covering some of the major topics of the new women's movement — motherhood, sex discrimination, culturally dictated standards of beauty. Perhaps most importantly, the supplement exposed hundreds of thousands of American women to consciousness-raising and the burgeoning feminist movement.[12]

While the sit-in forced the magazine industry in general to take notice of women's dissatisfaction, anger, and demands, most activists viewed the *LHJ* supplement as a token response. Since the inception of mass circulation magazines in the late 1800s, women had been targeted as an important audience, primarily because of women's roles as consumers. That is, publishers could sell space to advertisers by offering them a lucrative, female audience. From *Godey's Lady Book* in the 1800s to *Family Circle* in the 1960s, the editorials and articles in these magazines maintained an ideological atmosphere supportive of women's roles as homemakers and household consumers. Magazines like *Cosmopolitan* and *Vogue*, which began publication in the 1960s, targeted women not as housewives but as single women, conscious of style and of their relationships with men; importantly, however, the emphasis on women as consumers remained unaltered. The publishing industry saw women as potential consumers; editorials, articles, and cover stories never promised to inform their readers to create an informed citizenship, as they did in general interest magazines like *Time* or *Life*. Indeed, the only media research specifically designed to ascertain women's opinions was a 1940s study, funded by a woman's magazine, that rated influences on women's consumer habits.[13] An eight-page women's liberation supplement in the *Ladies' Home Journal* constituted a step in the right direction, but it fell far short of changing substantially the women's magazine industry that so clearly depended on women in the role of the primary consumer for their families.

At the same time that women's movement activists criticized the women's magazine industry, they also recognized the importance of the communications industry for reaching a national audience. The *LHJ* sit-in notwithstanding, activists found they had little access to the mainstream media; their difficulties reflected the problems most marginalized groups in the United States experience in relation to the dominant press. Far from being a "marketplace of ideas," to use the lingo common in many journalism histories, the press has generally represented the interests of those with power within the culture. Marginalized groups generally have found their ideas misrepresented, ridiculed, or ignored in the mainstream press. What's more, marginalized groups have often found their literal access to mass media, as employees and writers, obstructed because of discriminatory employment practices and other problems.

Many women's experiences as activists in the Civil Rights movement made them particularly wary of the power of the media to distort. One observer from the 1970s argued that this was especially true for young white women, who grew up believing that the media would "objectively" report and represent their interests; young black women harbored no such illusions.[14] By the late 1960s and into the 1970s the mass media did publicize the women's movement quite extensively (though not in women's "consumer" magazines), generally focusing on "zap actions" by radical feminist groups, demonstrations that provided titillating television coverage. In 1968, for instance, the New York Radical Women staged a counterdemonstration to the Atlantic City Miss America Pageant, part of which included a Freedom Trash Can, into which they tossed bras, girdles, copies of *Ladies' Home Journal*, and other icons of women's oppression. The press seized on this demonstration, providing the movement with much-needed publicity but also trivializing it by referring to the participants as a bunch of "bra-burners" in the process.[15]

In addition, the press demanded spokeswomen for the movement, women upon whom they could rely for interviews and photographs, activists whom they could use to "represent" the movement. Radical feminist groups, such as Redstockings and New York Radical Women, attempting to eliminate hierarchies and individualism within their own ranks, refused to supply spokeswomen for what they saw as a media charade. As a result, the media created is own "star system" of feminists, with women like Gloria Steinem, Kate Millett, and Betty Friedan as the recipients of the media's attention. While these women were all in their own right activists and powerful articulators of the movement, the media's focus on these individual figures obscured the broad-based and diverse nature of the movement. In a sense, the media had the power to "create" the movement through the attention they gave it, but they also had the power to destroy it—by turning their cameras and their reporters' attention elsewhere.[16]

As a result of this media "misattention," activists began a policy of granting interviews only to women journalists, hoping that this would both push women reporters, writers, and editors out of the women's pages and provide more sympathetic coverage. One significant effect of this policy was that many female journalists found themselves transformed by those on whom they were supposed to be "objectively" (i.e., "skeptically") reporting. Indeed, Gloria Steinem herself reports that it wasn't until she was reporting for *New York* magazine on an abortion rights rally sponsored by Redstockings member Kathie Sarachild in 1969 that a "lightbulb" went off in her regarding women's rights. Listening to the twelve women speak out about their abortions, Steinem recalled her own abortion as a young college graduate and how she and other women were forced to deny and hide the reality of their own lives. As a result of this watershed event, Steinem wrote "After Black Liberation—Women's Liberation" for *New York* and began the life for which she is best known, that of women's movement activist.[17]

During this same period, activists began to take hold of the media itself, beginning their own women's movement newsletters and journals. By 1970, there were over 500 feminist periodicals, newsletters, and magazines being published in the United States, most of them with extremely small circulations and small, volunteer staffs. These periodicals played a crucial role in organizing women, providing a forum for debate on philosophical and political issues, and sustaining interest and courage. As one NOW member from Pittsburgh so aptly put it in 1966, "You can't have a revolution without a press."[18]

Many activists were so angry and distrustful toward the mass media that they urged a total blackout, avoiding any mainstream media or even male-dominated alternative media. They advocated the creation of separate, small media forms controlled by women. *Off our backs*, for instance, founded in 1970 by Marilyn Webb and some of her friends, contained national news items relevant to feminism, as well as political satire and commentary on popular culture and advertising. Its circulation grew to 15,000 by 1977 and continues today as a Washington, D.C.–based national feminist newspaper. The women who founded *off our backs* focused on the way the mainstream media system misrepresented and co-opted feminist concerns. Webb and her colleagues pushed for feminists to develop their own media channels, uncompromised by either patriarchy or capitalism. Their initial statement of purpose read, "It is time to call a halt to all dealings with the mass-media — no more interviews, no more documentaries, no more special coverage. We don't need them and we don't want them. In the interests of self-defense and honest communication we have begun to create our own papers and our own magazines. Our energies must turn now to the strengthening and expansion of our own media."[19] While the attempt to remain completely separate from commercial channels proved impossible (even journals like *off our backs* found they had to contend with concerns about money and readership), activists who founded alternative media provided an important space for women to articulate relevant issues, to connect with other feminists, and to critique the role of the commercial mass media. The founders of *Ms.*, however, chose a different route, attempting to transform, rather than to avoid, the mass media.

Indeed, the contrast between those who began *off our backs* and those who began *Ms.* is one that speaks to a longstanding debate among feminists, one that has prevailed since the women's movement of the nineteenth century and the inception of mass publication technology. In the nineteenth century, women activists published a number of periodicals, such as *The Woman's Journal* and *The Revolution*. Most of these had relatively small circulations and sponsors who supported the magazine financially. Some, like Susan B. Anthony's *Revolution*, spoke without compromise about women's rights; radical in its approach, the *Revolution* was not particularly popular among the general public, or even among most women. Public officials, in particular the postmaster general, argued that these journals challenged standards of "respectability," and they attempted, sometimes successfully, to censor these publications. During the late nineteenth and early twentieth centuries, numerous suffrage journals were published, including ones local and national in perspective. In contrast to a journal like *The Revolution*, these spoke primarily to women, acting as important organizing tools for the suffrage movement. Other journals of the same time, like birth control activist Margaret Sanger's *The Woman Rebel*, faced extensive censorship; federal charges against Sanger and her journal even forced her to leave the country.

During this same period of suffrage publications, there was a parallel development of the mass circulation women's magazines, like *Godey's Lady Book*, designed to attract a large female audience, but as consumers, not as political participants. These two genres, the suffrage journal and the mass circulation women's magazine, were far apart in their format, audience, and purpose. Yet at least one activist in the early 1920s clearly saw the potential for combining the two, envisioning a mass circulation women's movement magazine. After the passage of the Nineteenth Amendment in 1920, suffrage activists questioned the direction of the "woman movement" and the future of the institutions, journals, and organizations developed during the height of the fight for suffrage. Freda Kirchwey, writing for the journal *The Suffragist* in 1921, called for a "new sort of women's magazine," one that would work to "spread the feminist revolution." The existing women's magazines (in the tradition of the *Ladies' Home Journal*) were not up to this challenge, for as Kirchwey put it, "Have you ever read one? Undoubtedly you have. They differ from each other sufficiently for circulation purposes—and yet essentially they are all the same. One has more fashions, another more stories, another more helpful hints for housekeepers: but they are all imbued with one deep purpose—to make a domestic career endurable to all married women." Kirchwey called for a national magazine that would compete with popular ones like *Ladies' Home Journal*, one that could speak to a broad range of women, not just to a select group of women active in suffrage and other political movements. Women were discontented, she argued, "whether they have worked for the vote or whether they have stuck steadfastly and unquestioningly to their dinner dishes." [20] Not until the 1960s, with the revitalization of the "woman question" and a growing tide of discontent among women, did activists in any significant way begin to echo Kirchwey's criticisms of mainstream women's magazines and her call for a new kind of "cross-over periodical."

Imagining a New Kind of Women's Magazine

In 1970 and 1971, Gloria Steinem began to talk to writers and activists in the New York area about her desire to start a women's movement newsletter. Like the activists who staged the sit-in at the *Ladies' Home Journal*, Steinem not only recognized the serious problems women faced in the mainstream media but also saw the need for national communication among women. Already a prominent media figure by the late 1960s, Steinem had been writing a political column for *New York* magazine and speaking regularly at rallies, political meetings, and marches. As a journalist and activist, Steinem was aware of the discrimination and trivialization women faced in the media. Many feminist writers found their work published only if an "anti–women's movement" piece could be found to be published next to it, and many had their articles rejected because editors said they "already had" a feminist piece. Their work as writers and their lives and identities as women were, usually by no choice of their own, separated. In speaking about this splintering of lives and work, Gloria Steinem refers to the times the editor at *Ladies' Home Journal* would hand her an article and say, "Pretend you're a woman and read this."[21]

It was a fortuitous friendship between Steinem and Brenda Feigen Fasteau, a recent graduate from Harvard Law School, that triggered the process that would eventually develop *Ms.* magazine. Steinem met Fasteau, then the national vice president for legislation of the National Organization for Women, in 1970. Working together on behalf of the Equal Rights Amendment, they saw the need for an organization that would deal not only with national issues, as NOW did, but also with the daily concerns and experiences of women; as a result they began the Women's Action Alliance in 1971. An outgrowth of the National Women's Political Caucus, of which Steinem was a founding member, the WAA acted as a "switchboard" among the various women's groups, coordinating activities among women's movement groups, serving as a resource for public education, and replying to requests for information.[22] From their work with the WAA, both Steinem and Fasteau saw the need for some kind of women's media to link women nationally and to raise money for the movement, particularly since foundations rarely funded women's groups at the time. According to Steinem's biographer, Carolyn Heilbrun, Fasteau imagined a glossy feminist magazine, but Steinem doubted that such a marriage of advertisers and the feminist movement would ever work. She envisioned a newsletter, not a crossover, mass media, feminist publication.[23]

Steinem quickly connected with the two women — Elizabeth Forsling Harris and Patricia Carbine — who were to become her partners in the original parent company of *Ms.*, Majority Enterprises. According to Harris, who had been active in the publishing world, she and Steinem were introduced through a mutual friend at *New York* magazine, Armond Erpf. According to other sources, it was Fasteau who first introduced Harris to Steinem, after learning of Harris's attempt to form the national newsletter *Women — The Majority Report* and after hearing of her fund-raising skills. Regardless of who introduced the two, soon after being approached about this new endeavor, Harris left California to come to New York, convinced that women needed a national forum. In 1971, Carbine had just become the editor of *McCall's* magazine, after leaving her position as executive editor of *Look* magazine. Steinem had been a regular contributor to *Look*, and the two had sealed their friendship when Carbine threatened to quit her job if *Look* bowed to advertiser pressure and refused to publish a piece Steinem had written on Cesar Chavez's United Farm Workers crusade.[24]

Wanting to focus her attention on the WAA, Fasteau soon dropped out of the picture, leaving Steinem, Harris, and Carbine to pursue the dream of a mass-distributed feminist magazine for women. When Steinem began working with Harris and Carbine, she imagined launching a newsletter for women activists, not a crossover mass media periodical, one that was both political and commercial. Together Harris and Carbine persuaded Steinem that she should transform her goal from a newsletter to a magazine, one that would compete on the newsstands with general interest magazines and, in particular, with other popular women's magazines. From their own experiences in the magazine industry, they knew that a magazine drawing on the extensive financial resources of advertisers could actually make money for the movement, one of Steinem's goals; newsletters had no access to this financial reservoir. In addition, as Carbine expressed it, if a "forum" for women was the objective, a mass circulation magazine, not a newsletter, was the way to go. She considered a magazine to be an "extraordinary medium" through which to communicate to women, because it was portable, easy to read, and visually pleasing.[25] Unlike a newsletter, or even a smaller periodical like *off our backs*, a women's movement magazine could offer a mass circulation voice for feminism and could push more mainstream women's magazines — and the industry surrounding them—to change. Steinem finally acquiesced to their persuasive points about the power of a mass media magazine for women. It was a daring move, particularly considering the history of women's magazines, which were clearly designed from their origins as magazines for consumers, not for politically minded women wanting to change the world.

Throughout the first part of 1971, Steinem, Harris, and Carbine made numerous, unsuccessful attempts at financing the project. Katharine Graham, publisher and chief stockholder of the *Washington Post* and one of the few women in publishing in the nation, provided seed money by buying $20,000 worth of "stock" in a company that didn't even exist yet.[26] The real break for the magazine, which by the fall of 1971 had the title *Ms.*, came later that year when Clay Felker, the editor of *New York* magazine, made a surprising offer, rare in the publishing industry. Steinem had worked closely with Felker for many years, helping him to launch the new magazine *New York* and writing a regular political column for him. (Indeed, Felker gave Steinem her first break by assigning her to these political writings rather than the celebrity shots that editors usually saved for her.) He proposed to publish a short preview issue of the magazine in the year-end issue of *New York*. *New York* would solicit the advertising and pay all printing and publishing costs, *Ms.* would provide the writing, and the two would split evenly the newsstand profits. (*New York* would keep all advertising profits.) He offered the same deal for the "stand-alone" preview issue of *Ms.* that would be published in January. For Felker, this move made sound business sense. Publishing a special double issue including *Ms.* would allow *New York* magazine to attract the women's advertising they had been trying to gain. As Felker said in an interview with *Newsweek*, "We owe Gloria a great deal, and wanted to help her get started. It isn't all altruistic, of course. We're going to make a lot of money out of it."[27] In an early editorial, however, the founders of *Ms.* dismissed Felker's "business" talk, contending that he too had been persuaded by the urgency of the movement. "Clay had begun to believe, like us, that something deep, irresistible, and possibly historic, was happening to women," they wrote.[28]

With the immediate sellout of the preview issues and the overwhelming response from subscribers, financial investors began to look seriously at *Ms.* However, most were quickly put off by the founders' requirements that the *Ms.* staff retain financial and editorial control and that the magazine would refuse advertising that contradicted its editorial policy. By the spring of 1972, Warner Communications had offered to invest $1 million in the magazine. While this amount clearly made Warner the major investor in *Ms.*, the communications company agreed to take only 25 percent of the share of the stocks. Both Carbine and Steinem explained that Warner had originally offered to invest only if they could maintain majority control of the stock, but *Ms.* refused. Steinem insisted that the magazine be woman controlled, and finally Warner acquiesced. It was an excellent public relations move for Warner, particularly during this time period when the women's movement was considered, by some at least, "fashionable," bringing in much free advertising through interviews and news bulletins. While most national magazines needed at least $3 million as start-up money, Warner's investment in *Ms.* separated this new magazine from the underground, regional, and often more radical periodicals that were run on a shoestring budget.[29] The funding also assured editors that *Ms.* could run for at least a year even with a poor response from advertisers.

The Preview Issue

Once the offer came through from Clay Felker and *New York* magazine, the *Ms.* founders acquired offices on Lexington Avenue, in the heart of midtown Manhattan. The offices were furnished with more enthusiasm and energy than official furniture; editors found themselves sitting at boxes set up as desks.[30] *New York* magazine "loaned" many of its employees to work on the preview issue, particularly in the areas of layout and advertising. *Ms.* had its own masthead of editors, but Felker maintained the final say in which articles were to be printed in the inset. He was particularly concerned about obscene language, having just lost advertising dollars because of publishing a picture of a woman with unshaved armpits.[31] Like the woman's movement journals of the nineteenth century, *Ms.*, from its origins, had to work to maintain that veneer of respectability.

Most of the editors and writers on the first issue of *Ms.* came to the magazine with ties either to *New York* magazine or personal or professional connections with Steinem. Alice Echols, in her far-reaching history of the radical feminist movement of the late 1960s and early 1970s, suggests that "a number of feminist writers were especially angry when *Ms.* formed and went outside the movement for its writers and editors." (This quote illuminates as much the animosity some felt toward *Ms.* as it does the debates over who was "in" and who was "outside" the women's movement.) According to Echols, Susan Brownmiller, Nora Ephron, and Sally Kempton were already working to establish a mass circulation feminist magazine, *Jane*, when they met with Elizabeth Forsling Harris to suggest merging the two endeavors. Harris apparently refused. Brownmiller, in her recollection of one meeting she had with Steinem, even implied that Steinem was surprised by the suggestion that a feminist women's magazine would include feminist reviews of books and movies.[32]

While it may be true that Steinem had not explicitly considered feminist book reviews, Brownmiller's insinuation that Steinem did not know what a feminist magazine would look like is not quite true. Like many of her journalist cohorts, Steinem knew she wanted a magazine that would allow women writers to write about their lives with truth and honesty, to "write for a magazine that one would actually read." Harris reported that the magazine would "communicate the commonality of feeling among women around the country. It will attempt to show them they are not alone in their anger and frustration and that the same feelings are being experienced by all sorts of women."[33] Steinem described the magazine as a "how-to magazine for the liberated female human being—not how to make jelly but how to seize control of your life." In addition, these publicity articles reemphasized the advertising policy, which called for ads that "respect[ed] women's judgment and intelligence."[34]

This "new magazine for women," as its masthead read, resembled many of the women's magazines already on the newsstand. As a "how-to" magazine for women, it fit with the basic genre of women's "service" or "consumer" magazines, as those in the publishing industry describe the traditional women's magazines filled with advice columns and informative articles. In an interview on the marketing potential of *Ms.*, Carbine explained the similarity of *Ms.* to mainstream women's magazines and the relevant differences:

> The strength of women's magazines in the past has been, in most part, the how-to approach. They have dealt with the woman's life inside the home. For instance, how to prepare hamburger 101 ways.
>
> I'm not suggesting that kind of information has not been a service. *Ms.* is as well going to be a how-to magazine. The difference is that *Ms.* will address itself to the question of how a woman can change her life and what the ramifications of that change might be—in terms of one's self and one's relationship with husbands, lovers, children, other women, one's job and the community in which one lives. *Ms.* will be very focused on this type of service question, and, in truth, it will become the cutting edge of the women's magazine field. It will make it more possible for other women's magazines, perhaps, to also change and address themselves to these questions.[35]

The blueprints for this new magazine would, in fact, closely resemble the type of magazine that Freda Kirchwey had envisioned fifty years earlier.

This resemblance to mainstream women's magazines was also important because it was this chameleonlike quality that allowed *Ms.* to infiltrate mainstream culture. In general, *Ms.* looked like a conventional women's magazine, with lots of color, bold headlines, glossy paper, and dozens of bright advertisements. Most importantly, *Ms.* spoke in a language familiar to readers of traditional women's magazines, in an intimate voice promising personal transformation. Janice Winship describes mainstream women's magazines as a mixture of self-help and fantasy, a blend that offers both "survival skills" within a patriarchal culture and "daydreams" that these skills really do work.[36] The *Ms.* editors renounced these skills and assurances as outdated, sexist myths, scorning the self-help articles on housekeeping and makeup, the escapist romance stories and the futile advice columns. Significantly, *Ms.* did not need to transform radically the editorial construction of women's magazines but could work instead to redefine what constituted a woman's daily life and self-help. *Ms.* replaced articles on cooking and makeup with articles on car mechanics and equitable marriage ceremonies. Inspirational articles about the "*Ms.* Woman of the Year" replaced romantic reveries about a handsome man and a plain young girl. Regular columns like "Money," "Woman's Body/Woman's Mind," and "Populist Mechanics," for instance, focused on specific changes each woman might make.[37] Like many of its sister publications, *Ms.* focused on the transformation of each reader's personal life, but from a feminist perspective. Significantly, the reliance on a how-to, self-help formula cemented the magazine's emphasis on an individualistic, liberal feminism.

At the same time that the first issue of *Ms.* blended with the other women's magazines on the newsstand, however, it also broke with many of the conventions of its sister magazines, like *McCall's*, *Good Housekeeping*, and *Cosmopolitan*. As one early reader of *Ms.* recalled, "It was a magazine that made a statement."[38] Most obviously, *Ms.* broke with the standard conventions of cover art. Rather than displaying a photograph of a woman's face — looking beautiful, sexy, and satisfied — this cover portrayed a drawing of a woman's entire body on a shocking red background. Significantly, *Ms.* rejected Western imagery in its portrayal of the new woman of the 1970s and turned to an image of a Hindu goddess, Durga or Kali. In traditional Hindu mythology, Kali represented the female side of the male deity Siva; her role was both reproductive and destructive, and she carried in her ten arms various weapons designed to slay demons.[39] Rather than swords, the hands of the *Ms.* cover woman contain the "weapons" of a woman's daily life—from iron to dust mop to typewriter. The cover celebrated women's reproductive power at the same time it critiqued the patriarchal culture surrounding it. The woman danced on a green, fertile plain, her womb illuminating the growing fetus, while the sell lines (as a magazine's cover captions are known in the publishing industry) about sex roles and abortions suggested more than a certain ambivalence about women's lives as mothers and housewives. Not only did this cover critique patriarchal culture, it also refused to construct a definitive image of the "*Ms.*" woman: the woman's hands were filled with the accouterments of a housewife—the role primarily of a white, middle-class Western woman—but the woman herself suggested a Hindu goddess, indicating that this magazine intended to speak to all women, to transcend differences created by race or class. The cover signaled an early feminist recognition of diversity at the same time that feminists imagined the possibilities of a more fundamental underlying unity among all women.

The title itself—*Ms.*—acted as an educational device, publicizing the women's movement with a one-syllable word. The title required readers, advertisers, and publishers to pay attention, to learn the meaning and the pronunciation of this word previously familiar only to secretaries who needed a title for a woman with unknown marital status. Flaunting the reader as an "unknown woman," this title was particularly provocative considering that advertisers demand detailed reader profiles. Indeed, the title of this new magazine was so little recognized as a title of courtesy for women that editors included a short explanation under the masthead, similar to the ones that had appeared in publicity notices and news pieces. The article described the history of "Ms." as a term used by secretaries, the increasing tendency for women to use it who didn't want to be identified by their relationships to men, and the proposed bills in Congress that called for all federal employees and applicants to be identified with "Ms." only. The article further explained how to pronounce it and how to use it. "In practice, Ms. is used with a woman's given name: Ms. Jane Jones, say, or Ms. Jane Wilson Jones. Obviously, it doesn't make sense to say Ms. John Jones: a woman identified only as her husband's wife must remain a Mrs." Adding a somewhat premature suggestion that "titles were going out of style altogether," the editors concluded with an argument as to why the change in title was important: "The use of Ms. isn't meant to protect either the married or the unmarried from social pressure—only to signify a female human being. It's symbolic, and important. There's a lot in a name." The subscription advertisement for *Ms.* contained in the preview issue included a similar but even more poignant description of the new title: it juxtaposed the "form of address meaning whole person, female," with the derogatory forms of address used for women—from dame, bitch, and chick, to wench, babe, and doll. The choice was clear—either be referred to as an object of men, or be referred to as a "whole person," a "female human being." [40]

This theme of feminism as a humanizing force prevailed throughout the preview issue. It covered a wide range of topics, including articles on raising children without sex roles, creating marriage contracts, the sexual revolution and women's liberation, language and feminism, the women's movement and politics, the physical and emotional cycles of men, and lesbian love. A number of the pieces went on to become minor classics within the movement, or at least among the avid readers of *Ms.*: Vivian Gornick's piece on women's fear of success, Judy Syfer's "I Want a Wife," Gloria Steinem's "Sisterhood," and Jane O'Reilly's "The Housewife's Moment of Truth." Some of these articles became standard features in the subsequent issues, such as "Stories for Free Children," a monthly nonsexist children's story printed with a perforated edge so readers could easily tear it out. While most of the articles were written by and primarily for white women, black women wrote two articles, "The Black Family and Feminism," an interview with Eleanor Holmes Norton by Cellestine Ware, and "Welfare is a Women's Issue," by Johnnie Tillmon. In addition, Dorothy Pitman Hughes, the child care activist in New York City, cowrote a piece on the how-to's of starting child care centers. Her article emphasized the importance of racial diversity among both the children and the staff.

As did the article on child care centers, many of the pieces focused on readers' own involvement with the movement. Barbaralee Diamonstein's "We Have Had Abortions" listed fifty-three American women who acknowledged having abortions and included a coupon for readers to add their names to the petition. *Ms.* editors then forwarded the names to national and state legislatures and to women in other countries forming similar petitions for abortion reform laws. "Heaven Won't Protect the Working Girl," written by Louise Bernikow, included information on fighting job discrimination through federal legislation. And the final article, "Where to Get Help," listed over fifty national women's groups, from political organizations like the National Organization for Women to ones focusing on the needs of women in the academy, women on welfare, and lesbians. While these articles covered many seemingly disparate topics, what linked them was a sense of boundless optimism about the possibility for women to change the world. Nearly every article—from ones on nonsexist architecture to nonsexist child rearing—

ended by discussing how the changes might at first appear utopian or even impossible but merited our belief, since our entire culture was at stake. As Letty Cottin Pogrebin phrased it in "Down with Sexist Upbringing," "If we win, human liberation is the prize."[41] By no means was the women's revolution portrayed as a selfish revolution, one with only women's needs in mind. Rather, it was portrayed as a "humanizing" revolution, in which all people — women, men, and children, would be freed.

Clearly, in this preview issue the editors attempted to construct an inclusive women's movement magazine.[42] As readers were to point out quite vocally in their responses to this issue, though, many women felt left out — both older women and young, teenage girls, for instance. Moreover, even in this conscious attempt to be inclusive — or perhaps because of it — obvious contradictions and discrepancies emerged among articles. The interview by Anne Koedt with a woman who had recently fallen in love with another woman, for instance, portrayed love between women as a natural extension of caring about women in the movement, even if the blurb about the two women assured readers that both had previously had only heterosexual relationships. In "Down with Sexist Upbringing," on the other hand, Pogrebin, in an attempt to show that allowing boys to play with dolls would not cause them to be gay, quoted an authority who claimed that "boys become homosexual because of disturbed family relationships, not because their parents allowed them to do so-called feminine things."[43] Many of the articles could speak to only certain women; for example, O'Reilly's piece "The Housewife's Moment of Truth," in which she discussed that "click of recognition" among women, particularly housewives, when they realized they were oppressed, strongly resonated among women across the country, as their letters indicated. But the scarcity of responses among women of color, lesbians, or working-class women suggests that they experienced a much weaker connection with O'Reilly's vision.

The range of topics addressed and perspectives expressed in this issue contradicts many of the stereotypes about 1970s feminists — and Ms. in particular — as homogeneous and single-visioned. Nevertheless, part of the underlying problem within Steinem's inclusive approach was the way the magazine subtly suggested that all women's identities were equal and could easily coexist. Steinem's piece entitled "Sisterhood" most explicitly constructed a women's culture that obscured all differences among women. "The odd thing about these deep and personal connections of women," she wrote, "is that they often ignore barriers of age, economics, worldly experience, race, culture — all the barriers that, in male or mixed society, had seemed so difficult to cross." The belief in sisterhood that Steinem articulated certainly approached the potential for connections among women from a white, middle-class, heterosexual perspective, and it was clearly too hopeful. The promise of sisterhood within *Ms.*, however, made it a unique periodical among mass media women's magazines. Even the ad for *Ms.* in the preview issue explained that "*Ms.* is written for all women, everywhere, in every occupation and profession — women with deep, diverse ambitions, and those who have not yet had a chance to formulate ambition — women who are wives, mothers, and grandmothers, or none of these — women who want to be fully a female person and proud of it. In brief, women who want to humanize politics, business, education, the arts and sciences . . . in the home, the community, and the nation." [44]

In writing a magazine "for all women, everywhere," however, the editors of *Ms.* also had to write a magazine that would attract sufficient advertisers. All three of the original founders of the magazine — Gloria Steinem, Patricia Carbine, and Elizabeth Forsling Harris — recalled that they envisioned *Ms.* as a magazine that would be able to change the publishing/advertising industry. Beginning with their first "regular" issue, referring to the first issue *Ms.* would publish without the help of *New York* magazine, the staff would refuse all sexist advertising, a judgment to be made by editors, and would refuse all advertising that required complementary copy. They would reject food advertising, for instance, as those advertisers require their magazines to include recipes, food articles, and so on. The editors and publisher hoped that they could set new standards for advertisers that would then translate to other women's magazines as well. The advertisements in the preview issue were solicited by *New York* staff, so the *Ms.* staff's new criteria were not yet in effect. Still, in the preview issue we can begin to see the ways advertisers could colonize — and commodify — the women's movement, and the magazine, through the types of ads they created.

Many of the ads solicited for the preview issue by the *New York* staff, particularly ads for liquor and cigarettes, were similar to the ones to be found in subsequent issues. A few ads were ones that would clearly offend the *Ms.* staff, and would later be rejected under their "nonsexist" ad policy. An ad for a beauty salon, for instance, read, "Guys Dig Flabby Girls. Guys Blindly in Love." Many of the ads were more for New York–based companies and were more "upscale" than the ads in *Ms.* would be. The department store Bloomingdale's, for example, illustrated its newest Ralph Lauren outfit for women, available at all New York area stores. The approach this ad took, however, resembled that in later *Ms.* advertisements. The woman in the ad, dressed in pants and a tie, was "Ms. Bloomingdale," a "great looking girl dressed by a man who knows."[45] Clearly, this ad used the women's movement as the raison d'être for buying new, masculine, "hip" clothes. Like many of the advertisements, however, it portrayed the new "Ms." woman as simply another fashion trend who is to be dressed by a man; it did not portray the new "Ms." woman as a "full human being" as the articles in *Ms.* portrayed her.

The advertisements also drew on some of the most compelling themes evoked by feminism — equality, freedom, personal transformation, and sisterhood — to justify a consumer ethic. For instance, a common tactic in these advertisements was to acknowledge the women's movement, then to offer some specific consumer product as the solution to women's problems. In the preview issue, for example, an ad for the Redactron Company, which sold typewriters and word-processing systems, suggested that the "dead-end secretary was dead." The ad encouraged women to send for "Free the Secretary" buttons and then ask their bosses about the new machines. This transformation of feminism into consumerism was not a new trend. As Nancy Cott demonstrated in her study of the first wave of feminism, in the 1920s women's magazines frequently sold household products in the name of "freedom" for women.[46] Like the 1920s ads, the Redactron ad spoke to women's new identities, encouraged their resistance through the offer of a free button, and channeled that collective movement among secretaries into a demand for a product — in this case a new word processor. Readers of *Ms.*, however, would hardly accept this "channeling" without some resistance of their own. With the publication of the preview issue of *Ms.*, the constant negotiation and conflicts among readers, writers, editors, and advertisers, were set into motion.

With its first issue, *Ms.* initiated themes that would resonate throughout its history: a focus on the transformation of the person; a conviction in the importance of pluralism, of including the voices of "all" women; and, finally, an emphasis on the ultimate "humanizing" quality of feminism. Most of all, what the magazine initiated in the first issue was a shift in perspective from its sister magazines, a new angle from which to write that began with O'Reilly's "click of recognition."

Creating a New Kind of Women's Magazine Organization

The founders of *Ms.* wanted to create a new kind of magazine organization as well as a new magazine. That is, they attempted to blend the philosophies of egalitarianism emerging from the women's movement, particularly as they applied to organizational strategies, with the demands of putting out a mass circulation magazine. They wanted to pressure the publishing and advertising industry to recognize the qualifications of women writers and business staff; to create an organization in which everyone felt "equally close to the magazine"; to assemble a diverse group of writers and staff, all of whom could share in the creation of this new magazine. The idea of an "open forum for all women" extended beyond the boundaries of the text, to apply to the way the magazine's organization ran as well. Implementing this more egalitarian organization was neither as easy nor as successful as was originally imagined, but the experimental attempt to forge a new mode of operation was pathbreaking within the context of the New York commercial publishing world.

The period immediately following the preview issue brought some major changes to the leadership of *Ms.* magazine. According to the original plan, Elizabeth Harris was to be publisher and chairwoman, Steinem was to be editor and president, and Patricia Carbine was to be a consultant and major stockholder. Because of Carbine's position at *McCall's*, however, she did not want her name to appear on the masthead. While Carbine and Steinem worked together quite well from the beginning, Steinem and Harris found they differed sharply on a number of major issues. Both Carbine and Steinem were disappointed in Harris's ability to raise money for the endeavor. Equally important, Harris and Steinem differed dramatically as to their vision of what the magazine should be and how it should be run. Harris explained that she was "pretty shocked" at some of the articles in the preview edition, especially the "lesbian issue." In addition, Harris objected to Steinem's goal of creating a writer-centered, nonhierarchical magazine. "Unbeknownst to me," Harris reported, "Gloria was meeting regularly with women writers" and "plotting to set up a magazine that would be run by editorial people." In summing up her differences with Steinem, Harris commented, "Gloria prided herself on being a radical feminist. A radical feminist is someone who is hell bent for action who is going to go out and make change her way. . . . I don't believe you have to tear down the fort." By the time the financing from Warner came through, Harris had left *Ms.*, maintaining her share of the stock and sharing the profits from the preview issue.[47] Within a few years, Harris's name even disappeared from the masthead's list of founding editors, and, when it was brought to Steinem's and Carbine's attention that Harris continued to refer to herself as "founder of *Ms.*," Steinem wrote a note to her colleagues: "Can we do anything to get her to stop using [her] name? even *former* co-founder??!"[48]

While Harris accused Steinem of wanting to "tear down the fort," the origins of *Ms.* more closely resembled "rebuilding the master's house, using the master's tools," to return to the title of Audre Lorde's well-known essay.[49] Patricia Carbine's personal history illustrates this attempt to reform, not to "tear down," as Harris put it, the magazine industry. Carbine explained that she moved from her position at *Look* to take the editorship at *McCall's* because she wanted to use her experience as journalist, editor, and woman to make "course direction changes" not "radical change" in the women's magazine industry. Moving to *McCall's* in the fall of 1970, she started to talk with Steinem in early 1971. While she had initially planned to stay and "fight it out" at *McCall's*, by the fall of 1971 she told the *McCall's* management she was dedicated to this new magazine; by winter of 1972 she had been released from her contract. She chose to go to *Ms.*, Carbine explained, because, "perhaps once in a lifetime one gets to take the most activist of steps within one's field"; she wanted to do something about the fact that for much of her journalistic career she had been the only woman in the room. By "training and inclination an editor and writer," Carbine commented, it was "by default" that she became not just editor-in-chief but publisher. With the exception of Katharine Graham, there were no women at the time who had experience as publishers of major magazines or newspapers. Insisting that the magazine be woman-run as well as woman-controlled, Carbine and Steinem concluded that Carbine had as much experience in the management and production sides of the magazine industry as any other woman.[50] As the *Ms.* founders' brief career histories demonstrate, their agenda was not to eschew the mainstream publishing industry entirely but to place women into significant positions within the industry and to highlight the concerns of the women's movement.

The question of what constitutes a feminist organization has been a central issue among scholars and activists since Jo Freeman wrote her pathbreaking article on the origins of the contemporary women's movement in 1973. Some researchers, like Patricia Martin, have defined feminist organizations as ones espousing "feminist ideology, values or goals"; that is, an organization is feminist if its purpose or philosophy is feminist. Using Martin's definition, an organization's goals are more significant than how that organization happens to be run in determining whether or not it is feminist. As Marilyn Crafton Smith reminds us in her overview of women's movement media, many feminist organizations, particularly national ones like the National Organization for Women, adopted traditional, bureaucratic, top-down management styles. The adoption of alternative organizational styles was not central to many of these organization's definitions of themselves as feminist.[51]

Nevertheless, in general the ideology of inclusiveness and democratic participation has been a major tenet of feminist activism and organizing, at least since the 1960s. Indeed, in *The Feminist Case against Bureaucracy*, Kathy Ferguson argues that, by definition, feminist organizations are those that value and seek to implement at least some forms of egalitarianism and inclusivity. In their studies of rape crisis centers, women's health clinics, and lesbian-feminist collectives, researchers like Joan Acker, Sandra Morgen, Verta Taylor, and Nancy Whittier have argued quite persuasively that feminist organizations oppose patriarchal standards through their alternative, antihierarchical organizational strategies. For these researchers, not all organizations that exhibit characteristics of participatory democracy are feminist, but all feminist organizations, by definition, do exhibit qualities of a collective-democratic workplace.[52]

In her study of alternative organizations, sociologist Joyce Rothschild provides a framework for understanding collective-democratic organizations, contrasting the characteristics of collective-democratic workplaces with those of hierarchical ones. Most importantly, within a collective-democratic workplace, authority resides within the collectivity as a whole rather than with an individual, as it would in a bureaucratic organization. Collective-democratic organizations seek to eliminate hierarchies, circulate knowledge among all its members, equalize rewards (of both the financial and prestige sort), and place value in personal relationships. The members' "substantive values," rather than remuneration or organizational rules, motivate the workers. As Rothschild writes, "Personalistic and moralistic appeals ... provide the primary means of control." In her study of a free school, an alternative newspaper, a free health clinic, a food cooperative, and a legal collective, Rothschild found that neither money nor status was the most important incentive for the workers; rather, the desire for meaningful work and a fair workplace provided the fundamental encouragement.[53]

Drawing from this range of definitions, the commercial *Ms.* magazine can be defined as a feminist organization from a number of perspectives. Using Martin's definition about goals and purposes, *Ms.* magazine was clearly a feminist organization from its inception; the founders created *Ms.* to both disseminate information about and raise money for the women's movement. *Ms.* was also a "qualified" feminist organization when one applies Ferguson's definition of an antibureaucratic, collective-style organization. The founders wanted to provide meaningful work for feminist writers and editors, and they attempted to implement a less hierarchical, more fair, and more inclusive management style within the workplace. *Ms.* was never explicitly a collective in terms of ownership, however. Gloria Steinem, Patricia Carbine, Elizabeth Forsling Harris, Katharine Graham, and Warner Communications held the original stock in *Ms.* The Ms. Foundation for Women later held the stock in *Ms.* Finally, three different corporations, Fairfax, Matilda, then Lang held the stock. In other words, the workers never co-owned *Ms.* Moreover, *Ms.* was never explicitly a collective in terms of its organizational style. Gloria Steinem was the Editor, and Patricia Carbine was the Publisher. In its last two years as a commercial magazine, Anne Summers and Sandra Yates held these key positions. In addition, *Ms.* adopted a bureaucratic style within the business side of the magazine. Those with the most contact with advertisers and corporations worked in a much more rationalized structure, where chain of command and rewards were more clearly delineated. In contrast, the editors, those with the most contact with the women's movement, incorporated an inclusive, democratic style of management.

At the same time they wanted to claim part of the women's magazine territory for *Ms.*, Carbine and Steinem also wanted to build an organization in which responsibility and power were more dispersed than in traditional organizations. Steinem, in particular, wanted to transform the publishing industry into a more humane and more democratic workplace. Clearly, the widespread criticisms of hierarchal organizations and their role in reproducing a patriarchal system articulated by women's movement activists influenced Steinem in her attempt to create a more egalitarian organization. "The hierarchical form doesn't work any more at home or in the office," Steinem said in an interview with *Time* in December of 1972. "We have tried to find a workable new solution that reflects the opinion of the majority."[54] Carbine described the organization not as a pyramid or ladder, but as a circle, with the magazine at the center. Her goal, she said, was to "make everyone feel equally close to the center of that circle."[55] The *Ms.* experiment with a more open form of governance, however, applied more directly to the editorial than to the business end of the operation. The founders of *Ms.* attempted to foster equality among editors and between readers and editors by downplaying status, providing access to information, increasing their influence within decision-making processes, and eliminating a "pink-collar" ghetto. Material incentives were much less tangible than were offers of meaningful work and social change.

One of the first tasks for Steinem and Carbine after the preview issue was published was to assemble a complete, independent magazine organization. One year after the preview issue, a *Time* magazine article reported that Steinem and other staff editors were "scouring the country for women journalists."[56] While the *Ms.* staff may have looked nationally, and did develop extensive national contacts, most editors, writers, and contributors came from the New York area. This was particularly true of the editors whose names appeared on the first masthead, including Bina Bernard, JoAnne Edgar, Nina Finkelstein, Nancy Newhouse, Mary Peacock, Letty Cottin Pogrebin, and Gloria Steinem. Moreover, most of the staff that came to *Ms.* soon after its initial publication had previous connections with Steinem, Carbine, the other editors, or someone who knew one of these people. In describing the early group of editors, which included herself, Harriet Lyons described it as a "self-selected staff." Those who were part of the earliest discussions about *Ms.* that took place in Steinem's living room were "known to each other . . . from their college days. We're talking Smith, and Wellesley, and Vassar, and white and privileged."[57] Many of the editors recall the formation of the original group differently from Lyons, and often their accounts conflict. Not all of the editors met through college, for instance; Lyons herself came to *Ms.* with an introduction by Dorothy Pitman Hughes, a day-care advocate whom Steinem knew well. In addition, Carbine and Steinem have pointed out that they were one of the only staffs of mass circulation publications that was in any way diverse by age or race. As numerous women's groups were to argue in the years to come, however, the *Ms.* staff was by no means representative of the women involved in the movement. It was a group that formed primarily through ties that already existed — writers who knew each other from previous work assignments, women who knew each other from college, or activists who had connections with Steinem or with someone who knew her. By no means explicitly closed to outsiders, the reliance on previous connections made this organization implicitly closed.

Many radical feminists were clearly angry about the way *Ms.* assembled its staff. One member of the Redstockings collective later wrote that she was "shocked that *Ms.* had compiled a whole staff who we had never heard of." Another wrote, "Now the radicals have been cut off from the media because there are so many more 'respectable' feminists around."[58] To discuss the homogeneity of the editors' roots in *Ms.* is not to suggest that they all came to *Ms.* for the same reasons or viewed this fledgling magazine in the same way. Some, like Letty Cottin Pogrebin and Suzanne Levine, came to *Ms.* with a background in writing or editing for women's magazines. Pogrebin, for instance, had been writing the "Working Woman" column for the *Ladies'*

Home Journal, John Mack Carter's long-term concession to the feminist sit-in at this office. Others, like Mary Thom, came with research experience and a background in women's movement activism. While the writers and editors I interviewed all described themselves as part of the movement in some way, Lyons remembers the early group as being "not that smart about radical politics or about feminist history," adding that she was the only woman who had been in a consciousness-raising group before *Ms.* began.[59]

For some of the founders, feminism symbolized what they called "the intelligent woman" and a vehicle for career advancement. Mary Peacock, who served as the editor of all the columns and regular features from 1972 to 1977, was the editor who most clearly fit the description of a "career feminist," as defined by Ferree and Hess in *Controversy and Coalition: The New Feminist Movement*. Peacock remembers that she "sort of considered [herself] a feminist, as it came floating through the air." Formerly the editor of what she described as the "hippy-politico" magazine *RAGS*, Peacock explained that she felt *Ms.* was "not a trade journal for the already committed." Rather, she perceived it as a magazine that was to "fight with the other women's magazines on the newsstands and be the one that says I'm for the more intelligent woman, I'm for the woman who knows where her own self-interest lies, I'm for the woman who is putting this name of feminism on an idea of self-esteem and independence." Peacock felt vaguely a part of the feminist movement, which she associated with increased self-esteem, independence, and intelligence among women. Her goal was to make *Ms.* the most successful and most interesting women's magazine on the market.[60]

The other founding editors put more emphasis on the role of *Ms.* in articulating and popularizing feminist writers and feminist ideas. Editor Suzanne Levine, for instance, was recruited primarily because of her experience as a managing editor. She described herself, however, as "temperamentally prepared" for the movement, of which she felt *Ms.* was a part. After reading the preview issue, for which she hadn't worked, she filled out the "I've had an abortion" coupon. By the time these were opened in the *Ms.* office, she was working there and opened up her own envelope. She said she knew at that point that she was in the right place and felt very anxious to get the material on the women's movement "out there."[61]

Gloria Steinem articulated the most idealist vision of *Ms.* as a vehicle for the women's movement and as a magazine that would change the publishing industry, the advertising industry, and the genre of the women's magazine. But the women who made up the editorial and business staff also came with their own visions and hopes, often working for little money. "We weren't exactly volunteers—we were paid weekly, when there was money," Mary Thom remembered.[62] Salaries, set high for a radical publication but much lower than for a traditional women's magazine, ranged between a low of $12,000 for researchers like Thom, and a high of $20,000 for Steinem.[63] In exchange for low pay and extreme dedication, the women who came to work at *Ms.* found they gained experiences and handled responsibilities that rarely would have been available to them at mainstream presses. Most importantly, *Ms.* provided an opportunity for women to combine their employment with their beliefs, to participate in the women's movement through their work. They were motivated by what Rothschild termed "substantive" values. In the words of editor Harriet Lyons, they hoped to "revolutionize women's lives," through *Ms.*[64]

Ideas of sisterhood did extend to making the workplace more egalitarian and inclusive. Part of Carbine and Steinem's method for dispersing power was to have a masthead with no titles, in which staff was listed in alphabetical order. To facilitate a sense of inclusivity, Carbine and Steinem installed bleachers and floor-to-ceiling carpet in the editorial meeting room. By choice, neither Steinem nor Carbine sat at the center conference table, in order to avoid dominating the discussions. Everyone was encouraged to have a voice in these editorial meetings. Both Carbine and Lyons refer to Lyons's initial meeting at *Ms.* as an example of this open policy. Lyons first went to *Ms.* as a volunteer and sat in a corner of the room answering phones while the editorial meeting was going on. The discussion centered on ideas for future cover stories. Lyons, who said it was "so open and egalitarian it was no problem for me to butt in," suggested Marilyn Monroe. The room fell to a dead silence as the editors nodded in agreement. After the meeting, Steinem approached Lyons and asked, "So what are you doing with the rest of your life?" Lyons responded, "So make me an offer." She began to work at *Ms.* for whatever petty cash was available.[65]

From its origins, the business side of *Ms.* was run in a much less egalitarian fashion than the editorial side. Carbine described a "hierarchy of responsibility" in the business offices of *Ms.* As she put, "My mistakes were more expensive than anyone else's." Rather than transforming the business procedures within publishing, Carbine's goal was to use *Ms.* to train women to become publishers themselves. *Ms.* had no trouble finding qualified women to serve as editors or writers, but when the magazine began few women had held major positions in the publishing end of the magazine industry, including the advertising departments, the business departments, and circulation. Carbine refused the advice of colleagues who encouraged her to hire sympathetic, qualified men and hired the first all-female sales staff in the country. Her goal, she said, was to transform the entire "landscape of publishing." *Ms.* was to be a "training ground for women of whatever experience, including none, whatever age and color and ethnic background." When asked if her decision to hire an all-female business staff hurt *Ms.* financially, Carbine responded that it may have helped *Ms.* in the early years to hire men who "got it," who could use their friendships and contacts to acquire advertising. But that was not her purpose, she said.[66]

The founders of *Ms.* never rejected the institution of the mainstream women's magazine. Rather, they sought to reclaim and revise it, to make it a resource for women in the movement. Likewise, they never rejected the Manhattan publishing industry but attempted to infiltrate it, to stake out territory for feminists within the commercial publishing world and to shake it up a bit, make it more egalitarian, more answerable to women as writers, editors, publishers, and readers. Both Carbine and Steinem felt strongly that *Ms.* should be taken seriously by the publishing industry and by women themselves. Thus, they chose offices in midtown Manhattan, where all the major publishing houses were located; they created official titles of editor-in-chief and publisher; and they selected expensive, glossy paper for the magazine, making it blend in with the other periodicals on the newsstand. At the same time, they hired the only black, female-owned company in New York to do the carpeting; they had a feminist carpentry class build the bookcases; and they had children from the West 80th Street Day Care Center paint the desks in bright colors.[67] This was to be a "real" Madison Avenue magazine, but one that was woman-centered, woman-controlled, and run in a fashion as egalitarian as possible.

With the former editor of *McCall's* as publisher and a women's movement writer and activist as editor, *Ms.* was poised for recognition and legitimacy in two worlds—that of mainstream publishing and that of the women's movement. In essence, *Ms.* magazine existed in dialogue with both the dominant magazine industry—whom the founders wanted to challenge and influence—and the alternative feminist press—which the editors attempted to popularize, by both exposing it to a broader audience and reframing it in a consumer orientation, a "self-help" format familiar to that broader audience. While the mainstream women's magazines worked as primary cultural articulators of femininity—as the protesters at the *Ladies' Home Journal* clearly proclaimed—*Ms.* promised to work as the cultural articulator of feminism.

Initial Reactions

Even before *New York* magazine published the inset, *Ms.* received widespread media attention; Steinem's fame (in that same year she had appeared on the covers of *McCall's*, *Newsweek*, and *Time* magazines) as well as the media's curiosity about a feminist women's magazine brought in numerous offers for TV talk shows, interviews on radio programs, and stories in print journalism. Importantly, all of this publicity was free, since it took the form of "news" rather than advertising. In thinking about the period prior to the publication of the first issue, Harris remarked, "I can't think of a magazine that's gotten more [publicity and media attention]."[68] Of course, not all of the attention was positive; many of the articles took a decidedly skeptical view about the longevity of a women's movement magazine and an even more doubtful tone about its contents. For instance, a *Newsweek* article published in November 1971 explained that "predictably enough, the magazine will dwell constantly on the changing role of women in U.S. society, both inside the home and outside it."[69] However skeptical much of it was, though, this publicity proved invaluable since it provided name recognition, a "commodity" that publishers seek avidly. Moreover, this publicity helped to explain to a broad audience the project of a magazine that broke with traditional women's publications and promised to be a resource within the women's movement.

The passion associated with the magazine was demonstrated most palpably by the letters that poured into the *Ms.* offices. The *New York* inset brought in 85,000 subscription cards, often with a check and letter of congratulations enclosed. Most strikingly, the preview issue drew in 20,000 letters from readers, echoing the shift in consciousness that the writers described, berating the editors for the sexist advertising, sending support, and seeking information. This was an amazing number of letters, considering that only 300,000 copies of the issue were published. Magazines with four times that publication rate average only 400 letters per issue.[70]

In the creation of *Ms.* was the possibility of constructing a mass-based feminist movement through the media; a much less favorable possibility, however, was that *Ms.* would fail, making movement organizers appear foolish, or, worse, that the movement itself would be co-opted by commercial interests. As a commercial, feminist, mass media magazine, *Ms.* challenged both those in the mainstream publishing industry, who believed politics had no place in the marketplace, and women's movement activists, who argued for separatism.[71] But some activists and journalists envisioned in *Ms.* a new genre that could speak to women across the country, crossing boundaries of lifestyle, education, class, and race. Importantly, when *Ms.* emerged on the newsstand, it served not only as a consciousness-raising device for readers across the country but also as the spark to much dynamic debate about the role of mass media within the women's movement.

Many women in the publishing industry voiced skepticism about the project, arguing that the movement was too ephemeral to sustain a magazine. "I fear that, because they may have vastly overrated the national impact of the women's movement, they may be in for a grave disappointment," argued Mary Breasted in a 1972 *Saturday Review.*[72] Others doubted that the magazine could last, not because the political movement would die out but because feminism would hinder its profit-making potential. Pamela Howard, also a writer from *Saturday Review*, argued that *Ms.* might not survive economically because of these contradictory demands: "Basically the new [women's movement] magazines grew out of a movement, which leads people to quickly label them 'cause' magazines. *Ms.* is the most vulnerable in this respect because it is carrying the ideology into its advertising policy. Difficulties could quickly arise if the 'cause' begins to interfere too much with the day-to-day business of the magazine."[73] While the cause did indeed "interfere" with the day-to-day business of the magazine, and the day-to-day business with the cause, *Ms.*'s initial success suggested that these two demands were by no means incompatible. The enormous returns on the early subscription notices, coupled with at least some advertising executives' and investors' perceptions that this was a "hip" new magazine, indicated that a feminist, mass media magazine could work, both economically and as a resource for women in the movement.[74]

Some women considered *Ms.*'s economic success equally as important as, or even more important than, its editorial goals. It is crucial to remember that at the time *Ms.* began there were few women's businesses in existence; certainly there were no mainstream media organized on feminist principles and run by women. In 1972, Anne Jardim, a Harvard Business School lecturer, wrote that "it is vitally important that *Ms.* should succeed as a business — first, because business success will justify and confirm the relevance of the ideas and convictions which brought it into being; second, because business success will mean an unmistakable crack in the stereotyped belief that women cannot organize and manage a business." Jardim went on to reflect on the danger that failure would pose:

If *Ms.* were to prove a business failure, the impact of that failure would inevitably be reflected in some highly damaging assumptions: 1. that its ideas were too far out; 2. that they were not shared by the great majority of women; and 3. that its organizers were a group of fanatics at odds with the real biological, psychological, and social position of women. These assumptions would then simply reinforce the belief that women, with a few rare exceptions, are useless when it comes to business management. I don't have to tell you just how severe a setback this would be to everything that has so far been achieved.[75]

Not just a gauge of national interest in the women's movement, *Ms.* also carried the burden of proving that women could succeed in business.

Many women active in the movement, however, questioned the intentions of the *Ms.* founders, the implications of the magazine for the movement, and the consequences of linking feminism to a commercial context. In 1972, a woman from the magazine collective *Up from Under* described her anger and doubts about *Ms.*: "When I see these fancy-shmancy types moving in, it really disgusts me. It's so exploitative and cynical. All those things that people went through in the early years of the Movement — discussions about abortions and breaking up with men. Those women who are in the spotlight now don't have any feeling. Gloria Steinem should really demand that a woman from the Telephone Company go on the *Dick Cavett Show* instead of appearing herself all the time."[76]

While many voiced skepticism and outright anger about the project, others responded optimistically to the offer of a feminist magazine in a commercial package, and placed faith in the ability of *Ms.* to win advertisers' dollars while it spread the feminist word. In 1972, one writer for the underground feminist periodical *off our backs* reported a rather humorous yet chilling anecdote about the prevalence of the magazine: "*Ms.* sure caught on fast. Today when the Breather called the *oob* office he moaned, 'Mzzzzzzz' into the phone."[77] For many activists, the early issues did suggest that this new magazine could provide the popularizing force needed by the movement. Writing for the *Saturday Review*, Pamela Howard argued, "What better way is there for getting across the message of the Women's Movement than to use communications as a tool?"[78]

Even observers skeptical of the commercialism embedded in *Ms.* viewed the magazine as a useful resource for the movement. In her review of the new magazine, Onka Dekkers wrote, "Every month as many women read *Ms.* as read the rest of us put together. The rest of us being papers and journals like *oob*, *Goodbye to All That*, *Mountain Moving Day*, *The Ladder*, *Aphra*, *Everywoman* and roughly 30 other publications — products of love and conviction by mostly unsalaried staffs. Believing a strong women's media to be a major component of a feminist revolution, I could love it for that reason alone." [79] A writer for *Northwest Passage*, a Leftist underground periodical, echoed Dekkers evaluation of the magazine's worth: "Until recently, the only place we could read about the feeling of women involved in changing their lives on a day to day basis was in underground publications. . . . Feminism has left its incubator to enter the big world." [80] While Redstockings and other activists perceived *Ms.*'s entrance into the "big world" as a co-optation, some recognized how *Ms.*'s dual status as both a commercial and political text could work as a revolutionary device. Activists based this faith in the magazine on more than a hope that *Ms.* could reach thousands more women than the underground press; they recognized the power of a magazine that could mask its "real" intentions and speak to women who were expecting the pleasure of reading a mainstream, consumer-oriented women's magazine.

That *Ms.* became the source of so much debate for women active in all spectrums of the burgeoning feminist movement suggests the hopes that many invested in the magazine as well as the threats many perceived it to pose. The founders of *Ms.* created a magazine that could enter into unsuspecting homes like "tarantulas on a banana boat," offering feminism in the guise of a consumer women's magazine. That specific strength, however, also was its greatest weakness, for the commodification of feminism often threatened to overpower the construction of a pluralistic, inclusive political philosophy. While this commercial context may have undercut *Ms.*'s ability to be as openly radical or confrontational as smaller periodicals like *off our backs* or *No More Fun and Games*, its place on the racks with the other mainstream magazines provided it with an excellent position from which to invert and to negotiate the dominant codes of representation in women's magazines, to construct a feminism compatible with the genre of the consumer-oriented women's magazine. Yet, *Ms.*, maintaining a position on the commercial magazine stand, raised a complex set of questions about what a feminist representation of women would look like and if a feminist magazine was even possible within a commercial context.

CHAPTER 2

Self-Help and Sisterhood
Ms. in the 1970s

In remembering the beginning of the 1970s and the early days of *Ms.*, editor Suzanne Levine explained that it felt like a "great wave was building," a universal recognition of the rights and importance of women.[1] Indeed, optimism and a sense of endless possibilities characterized the early years of the *Ms.* publication. When the Equal Rights Amendment passed Congress in 1972, no organized group of activists existed to support its ratification, an indication not of lack of support but of a confidence that states would ratify the amendment quickly and as a matter of course. The legalization of abortion with the Supreme Court's *Roe v. Wade* decision in 1973, coming on the heels as it did of the legislative and cultural gains women had made in 1972, made many women's movement activists feel extremely optimistic about the potential of the movement, and, in particular, about the ability of established institutions — from the family, to the workplace, to the law — to transform according to the needs and demands of women. Events like Billie Jean King's defeat of Bobby Riggs in the 1973 tennis match bolstered women's spirit that feminism was a winning movement. By 1975, the number of women's movement rallies and demonstrations taking place reached an all-time high, with more than 300 nationally reported feminist events.[2] The National Organization for Women's change in their statement of purpose, from "into full participation in the mainstream of American society" to "out of the mainstream and into the revolution," captures the essence of the hopefulness and confidence that characterized the early 1970s.

Thanks to both a changing culture in which women found encouragement to enter nontraditional fields and the ongoing litigation sponsored by organizations like the Women's Equity Action League (WEAL), the 1970s saw a tremendous increase in the number of women professionals. By 1979, 23 percent of medical school graduates were women, compared to less than 9 percent in 1970. Similarly, by 1979, nearly 29 percent of law school graduates were women, compared to less than 6 percent in 1970. The women's movement transformed the entire field of higher education, as 150 women's studies programs and departments were established by 1975. Interdisciplinary journals such as *Women's Studies* (established in 1972), *Feminist Studies* (established in 1972), and *Signs* (established in 1975) challenged the academic paradigms in various fields, and two major conferences, the Berkshire Conference on the History of Women, begun in 1972, and the National Women's Studies Association, begun in 1977, allowed women's studies scholars from across the disciplines to share their new research on women. By the 1970s, feminists had also begun to build a wide network of women's businesses, organizations, and institutions such as rape crisis centers, battered women's shelters, coffeehouses, bookstores, and health clinics. The publication in 1973 of the Boston Women's Health Collective *Our Bodies, Ourselves*, a detailed work giving women information and feminist perspectives on their own health care, marked the centrality of a concern for women's health care in the new movement, and the beginning of an important new genre of feminist publishing.[3]

While the growth of national organizations like the National Women's Political Caucus and the National Organization for Women in the early 1970s signaled obvious expansion within what has become known as the "egalitarian" wing of the movement, scholars such as Alice Echols have pointed to the splintering and decline of the radical feminist movement by the time *Ms.* was published.[4] This fragmentation within the women's movement, however, can also be viewed as indicative of the expansion of the movement among many different groups of women. Organizations formed by lesbian separatists, black women, socialist feminists, and domestic workers, to name only a few, could each articulate the concerns of women not clearly addressed in the more mainstream national organizations. This proliferation of groups developing organizations and newsletters built a broad-based, grassroots network of feminism; in expressing their concerns and ideas, they also each developed particular theoretical understandings of feminism. Together, the various feminist organizations and philosophies created a complex web into which *Ms.* entered and from which *Ms.* would, and often did, draw.

To understand the context in which *Ms.* published in the 1970s, it is essential also to recognize the incipient backlash that characterized the decade. Even as the women's movement created new institutions and challenged patriarchy in legal, economic, social, and familial circles, the antifeminist movement gained steam. Two of the major victories of the 1970s women's movement—the ERA and the legalization of abortion—proved to be the rallying points for a growing antifeminist movement, raising, as they did, core issues about what it meant to be a woman in twentieth-century America. Almost immediately after the Supreme Court legalized abortion in 1973, the Catholic Church founded the National Right to Life Committee (NRLC), a national organization designed to coordinate the activities of anti-abortion activists.[5] Phyllis Schlafly, a right-wing activist who, prior to the 1970s wave of feminism, had been best known for her anticommunist activism, became the best-known symbol of the antifeminist backlash, with her STOP ERA campaign founded in 1972. Significantly, the activists of the backlash identified *Ms.* as the "feminist movement"; Schlafly, for instance, attacked the ERA by connecting it with the new magazine, which she described as "anti-family, anti-children, and pro-abortion. It is a series of sharp tongued, high-pitched, whining complaints by unmarried women. They view the home as a prison, and the wife and mother as a slave. . . . Women's lib is a total assault on the role of the American woman as wife and mother, and on the family as the basic unit of society. . . . They are promoting Federal 'day-care centers' for babies instead of homes. They are promoting abortions instead of families."[6]

After its initial momentum, the push for ERA ratification slowed considerably, affected significantly by the anti-ERA campaigns such as the one championed by Schlafly in her periodical, the *Eagle Forum*. Thirty states had ratified the amendment by early 1973; although the amendment needed only eight more states to ratify, proponents found the remaining states to be difficult to move. Four states actually voted to rescind their earlier ratification, an action that few legal scholars thought would stand up in court but that nevertheless proved an important blow to the push to get the needed additional votes.

Just as the feminist successes had generated a backlash among conservative activists, the growth of STOP ERA and Right to Life mobilized feminists on a national scale. The National Abortion Rights Action League (NARAL, which had changed its name from the National Association for the Repeal of Abortion Laws after the legalization of abortion in 1973) proved to be the most vocal supporter of abortion rights in the 1970s, primarily because activists thought that the Supreme Court decision provided adequate assurance of a woman's right to reproductive freedom, and because activists were becoming increasingly caught up in the ERA campaign. Indeed, with the election of Eleanor Smeal to its presidency in 1977, NOW refocused its attention on the ERA battle. Organizations like the National Federation of

Business and Professional Women's Clubs channeled part of their dues to the ERA battle, helping to finance the ratification campaign.

The dual conferences that took place in 1977 in Houston exemplified the simultaneity of the growth of the women's movement in the seventies and the birth of a powerful backlash. In November 1977, nearly 20,000 women gathered in Houston, Texas, for the First National Conference on Women, chaired by Jimmy Carter appointee Bella Abzug. Funded and organized by the National Commission on the Observance of International Women's Year, the conference marked the crescendo of the liberal mainstream women's movement of the 1970s. For four days, women who came together as participants and as observers debated topics ranging from abortion and the Equal Rights Amendment to sexual preference and minority rights. Despite divisions among the women, by the end of the conference a majority of participants had passed resolutions supporting each of these issues. Moreover, the public discussion of issues that only ten years previously were considered private or perhaps taboo and would have been silenced marked this as an extremely significant event. The torch relay, begun in Seneca Falls, New York, and concluding at the welcoming ceremony of the conference, created a symbolic display of the power and breadth of the women's movement. With over 2,000 participants, wearing T-shirts proclaiming "Women on the Move," the torch relay inspired thousands of onlookers — either on the streets, or, more vicariously, on their television sets — who cheered the runners on their way. The Houston conference, however, coincided with an event that signaled a significant warning bell. Across the city from the conference, conservative activist Phyllis Schlafly staged a counterconference, marked not by debate, as was the National Commission's conference, but by a clear commitment to anti-abortion and anti-ERA activism. Schlafly's conference marked one of the first nationally visible signs of the growing political threats to the gains women had made earlier in the decade, and it certainly tempered the enthusiasm expressed by the torch relay. Despite the fact that public opinion polls continued to show that the majority of Americans supported both abortion rights and the ERA, it was clear that the well-organized, well-financed backlash touched on many people's fears about how feminism challenged the family, daily life, and what it meant to be a man or a woman.[7]

Ms. magazine emerged on the cultural scene at a critical moment, one marked by both the victories of the new women's movement and the birth of a powerful backlash. The magazine existed squarely in the center of this national debate about the significance and meaning of feminism, simultaneously mirroring and defining the crucial issues. Significantly, it came to represent "mainstream feminism" for a range of feminist activists as well as for proponents of the burgeoning antifeminist movement.

Covering Feminism

In their attempt to create a popular feminism, *Ms.* editors had to think carefully about the cover, the primary definer of *Ms.* and of mass media feminism. When describing how they chose covers, editors explained that it was generally a "gut level" decision as to what would sell, what was visually appealing, and what would capture readers' attention. They argued that they never consciously attempted to shape a certain kind of feminism on the covers.[8] As the magazine is examined further, however, we find that the covers are much more than a "natural" outcome of editors' personal opinions; they illustrate the complex relationship among the political and economic concerns that shaped *Ms.* In addition, they constructed visually—in condensed, multilayered fashion—the philosophical perspectives that *Ms.* represented. The covers acted as the initial site of signification, where the meaning of *Ms.* was first constructed and first seen by readers and by advertisers. Moreover, the covers challenged the hegemonic defining power of other women's magazines, as they redefined other women's magazines' portrayal of "news" and "womanhood."

Stretching, inverting, and breaking the semiotic codes of popular women's magazines, the *Ms.* editors attempted to construct oppositional representations of women that served the interests of women and of feminism rather than the interests of patriarchy. In order to maintain their place on the marketing battleground of the newsstands, particularly as advertising became more difficult to solicit and readers more difficult to reach because of the competition from the new magazines for working and executive women, *Ms.* needed to blend with the other women's magazines. The eighteen years of *Ms.* magazine covers are marked by what John Fiske terms "semiotic resistance," the attempt to forge oppositional meanings, and by what he terms "evasion," tactics used to avoid capture, in this case boycotts by readers, librarians, or, most importantly, advertisers.[9] In the 1970s, we see *Ms.* primarily engaged in "semiotic resistance"; by the 1980s, "evasive" tactics take center stage.

Six months after the spring preview issue was published, the first regular edition of *Ms.* appeared on the newsstands. Featuring a cartoon portrait of the 1940s comic book figure Wonder Woman, this July 1972 issue stood in sharp contrast to its neighboring women's magazines. Dressed in her red, white, and blue sparkling outfit, emphasizing pointed breasts, powerful hips, and high-heeled boots, Wonder Woman stepped forcefully over a miniaturized city below her. Her momentum, her strength, and her size expressed the enthusiasm and energy of the early women's movement; she represented the figure of "womanpower," the public relations slogan used by national women's organizations to communicate the potential of women, economic and otherwise. As well as illustrating the ascendant hopes of the movement this cover also revealed the uneasy role *Ms.* played as vehicle for a political movement and for a marketing venture. While *Ms.* often drew from the various strands of the women's movement, the choice of this cover design clearly privileged certain tendencies within the movement—in particular the valorization of the individual—and meshed well with the magazine's economic imperatives.

Considering the year of publication, as well as the editors and writers who made up the staff of *Ms.*, it is no surprise that a cartoon of Wonder Woman would find itself on the cover of the first regular issue. Besides illustrating the enthusiasm that many of the staff felt about the women's movement, Wonder Woman resonated with some of the most dominant and most powerful beliefs about the way the women's movement would transform the culture. Like women from the first wave of feminism in the nineteenth and early twentieth centuries, feminists in the 1960s and 1970s drew powerfully upon national rhetoric concerning democracy, equality, and freedom to express and to legitimate their demands. In addition, many activists in the 1960s and 1970s viewed electoral politics as both the key to and the best evidence of women's improved status; that is, getting women into local, state, and national offices could serve as both the origins of and the proof of women's success. Dressed in her red, white, and blue, a figure whose original purpose was to fight for national freedom, and now carrying the sign "Wonder Woman for President," Wonder Woman reflected the use of democratic ideals by many women activists. The choice of Wonder Woman, a figure from the 1940s, to represent the 1970s women's movement was not atypical either. Feminist scholars, writers, filmmakers, and artists across the country were reclaiming the histories of "strong" women to serve as foundations for the new movement; in particular, the "Rosie the Riveter" working woman from the 1940s became a popular figure. The introduction to the Wonder Woman cover story emphasized her links to the 1940s: "Wonder Woman had feminist beginnings, but like many of us, she went into a decline in the fifties. To celebrate her reincarnation, now in the making for publication in 1973, *Ms.* presents one of the originals here; the true forties version of how WW came to America."[10] But the cover story refigured the nationalist, freedom-fighting Wonder Woman to become a more pacifist figure, a strong heroine, but nevertheless a nonviolent one; the words under her read: "Peace and Justice in '72." The sell lines on the cover echoed the philosophy of the Wonder Woman presentation. Concerns with the vote ("Gloria Steinem on How Women Vote"), work ("Money for Housework"), and a reclaiming of feminist figures ("New Feminist: Simone de Beauvoir") dominate the page.

On a commercial as well as ideological level it is also not surprising that *Ms.* chose to picture Wonder Woman on its July 1972 issue. Warner Communications, the primary financial investor in *Ms.*, owned National Periodical Publications, which published and was then planning to begin republication of Wonder Woman comics. The editors' decision to highlight Wonder Woman on the cover was a fortuitous one, both because she was a figure that would resonate with the women's movement and because featuring her would please their major investor. The Wonder Woman cover exemplifies the way *Ms.* straddled and merged the worlds of the women's movement and the commercial publishing industry. The choice of a figure that reflected the concerns of the burgeoning women's movement while at the same time pleased the financial investors was not simply "natural" nor "good business sense" but rather an example of the kind of strategic thinking that shaped the format of the magazine and construction of the movement within *Ms.* Indeed, the competing commercial and political demands placed on *Ms.* created tangled threads that are often difficult to separate. Yet these are extremely important threads to untangle, for they illuminate the broader problem of how commercial concerns influence political movements within U.S. culture and of how, in turn, politics shape and push our economic system. Moreover, by sorting out these threads, we begin to see more clearly both the possibilities and the limitations of constructing oppositional politics within a commercial matrix.

After its preview issue, *Ms.* experimented with its covers and refused to construct a definitive image of the *Ms.* woman. This was a particularly significant move considering that the cover serves as a covert advertisement, acting not only to attract readers but also to convince advertisers that the magazine will provide the best vehicle for reaching those readers. In general, advertisers look for consistency in the covers, seeing that as a tangible sign that the magazine is speaking to the desired audience.[11] The desire for cultural change in the representation of women, however, propelled *Ms.* editors to refuse the commercial imperative to paint a definitive picture of the *Ms.* reader. Early covers ranged from close-up shots of well-known women —

Bella Abzug, Cicely Tyson, and Bette Midler—to cartoons and illustrations representing women's relationships to money, motherhood, and men. In subtle and sometimes obvious ways, *Ms.* also played with traditional symbols, inverting their use and suggesting new meanings—Marilyn Monroe represented a new heroine for the women's movement rather than an object of male sexual desire (August 1972); Madge the hairdresser became a symbol of the pink-collar ghetto (March 1977); the Statue of Liberty ironically questioned women's status in the United States (July 1976).

In the early years, *Ms.* did sometimes use images of successful and famous women, but it frequently attempted to portray those women in a more "realistic" and less glossy fashion, such as the April 1973 Judy Collins cover, which pictured her with little makeup or styling. Many readers responded enthusiastically to this new vision of women:

> How lovely it is to see Judy Collins on your cover looking for all the world like a human being. How beautiful are those heavy eyebrows; thin, uncovered lips—slightly parched and more than slightly crooked; and skin replete with shine, shadows, and faint lines. A face that lives—almost a mirror (though our faces are entirely different.) May we never again compare our faces to "cover-girl perfection," the perfection of plastic surgery and camouflage cosmetics, tactics to make each of us just so many flaws to compete with. Programmed neurosis. Down with the cover girl. Up, up, up with the Uncovered Woman.[12]

Interestingly, these "realistic" covers were not always a result of a conscious decision on the part of editors; they resulted just as much from the magazine's low budget for photography, props, makeup, and so on. In addition, many editors disliked these "realistic" covers, such as the November 1980 issue featuring four Soviet women and the May 1977 issue featuring a homemaker, as they considered them unflattering portrayals, becoming caricatures of ugly feminists within the context of a newsstand of beautiful women.[13] Many readers, however, expected *Ms.* covers to contrast sharply with those of the other women's magazines; if the covers blended too closely, they perceived *Ms.* to be a failure, a look-alike to the other women's magazines they scorned.

During the 1970s, *Ms.* published covers that broke most with the conventions of popular women's magazines. Pathbreaking in their attempt to represent the unrepresentable, these covers articulated visually that which previously had no name—abuse against women, child pornography, and sexual harassment, for instance. The power of these covers came from their ability to name what had been unnamed, to challenge viewers to reconsider what had appeared to be "natural" or hidden aspects of women's lives. The August 1976 issue featured a close-up of a white woman on the cover, her right eye bruised and her entire face swollen. She looks directly at us, pulling us into her world, just as the faces on the other women's magazines do, but the close-up shot and the bruises shock us into recognizing her pain. This cover story brought the subject of battered wives into the open, available for discussion, analysis, and resistance. It drew an overwhelming response from readers who shared their own histories of abuse.[14] Within the context of the 1970s, on the stands next to the smiling women of *McCall's* and *Vogue*, this representation of a battered woman shattered a significant visual and cultural silence. Many readers, however, wrote to *Ms.* to object to this portrait of a battered woman, arguing it was simply a sensational, voyeuristic cover used to sell magazines. Indeed, while this cover demystified male power within the family, it also used this sense of danger to compel the attention of potential buyers. In their cover story on sexual harassment (November 1977) editors attempted to avoid accusations of "sensationalism" by featuring a photograph of dolls rather than one of "real" people. Like the portrait of an abused woman, this cover represented a concept that did not exist previously because it had no name—"sexual harassment." This cover pulls our eyes toward the "woman's" chest, where we focus on the huge hand of her presumed boss, groping inside her shirt. She has a paralyzed look on her face, her back appears rigid, and her mouth is tightly shut. The focus of this portrait is on the hand and her look of outrage, not on the grin of the man, as it would be in a *Benny Hill* episode or *Animal House* prank. Yet many newsstand operators and librarians refused to display the issue, and numerous readers argued that this issue reminded them of *Playboy*. For many readers, the fact that the "shock appeal" of this cover sold issues suggested editors were simply using the victimization of women to sell magazines. Despite the use of dolls, others found the cover degrading, demonstrating that the use of "real people" in photographs is not a necessary ingredient to creating disturbing representations. Indeed, some readers even wrote that *Ms.* should represent no women visually, arguing that all images of women were inherently voyeuristic and served patriarchy.[15]

To report the range of responses these covers evoked is not to suggest that reception of texts is simply relative, but to highlight how these confrontational covers caused readers to question any visual representation of women, particularly within a commercial context. Indeed, even these covers that most clearly broke with the prevailing codes of commercial representation common to women's magazines were enmeshed in their own marketing context, designed to grab readers' attention. Within a commercial matrix a fine line marks the distinction between articulating that which previously had no name and using such "exposure" as a titillating marketing device. Indeed, any "exposure" of women within a commercial, patriarchal context runs the risk of exploiting the very women it was ostensibly meant to serve.

As much as we might debate the ultimate implications of these covers, what remains clear is that editors did not shy away from the controversial in the 1970s but worked to give it the most publicity possible. In contrast, the 1980s covers shifted away from controversy, although they continued to play with the symbols of commercial magazines and to articulate concepts that spoke to the changing conditions of women's lives, such as the February 1985 "blended family" issue. From its early years, *Ms.* had faced repercussions from newsstand operators, librarians, and advertisers who believed its covers too outrageous or radical. That the half-clothed models of *Cosmo* were positioned within easy sight and reach suggests that it was not nudity or sexuality per se that made the *Ms.* covers offensive. Rather, librarians and newsstand operators censored and boycotted covers that clearly challenged prevailing codes of race and gender. The publisher of *Ms.*, Patricia Carbine, reported that newsstands across the country refused to display the January 1973 issue, which pictured a close-up shot of the presidential candidate Shirley Chisholm with her running mate, Cissy Farenholdt. By placing an African American woman next to a white woman it broke a taboo; that Chisholm was an African American woman with power and national status probably made this cover even more threatening.[16]

Because of this fear of censorship and advertising boycotts, editors often masked the more "controversial" stories behind a less threatening cover. Editors acknowledge this tradition of masking, although they also re-emphasize the ways *Ms.* worked to thwart advertisers' power.[17] Articles on lesbian mothers, on Andrea Dworkin's theories on heterosexuality, or on African American midwives, for instance, might merit a short sell line but were often hidden behind less controversial covers. Ironically, commercial periodicals usually place their most provocative, sensational story on the cover in order to gain readers' attention and, with some luck, their money. *Ms.*, however, had to mask, to downplay, differences in order to maintain its legitimacy and its position on the racks with *McCall's* and the *Ladies' Home Journal*. In many cases, then, the price for maintaining a position on the newsstands was a silencing—or at least a masking—of significant and possibly threatening feminist issues. From its origins, *Ms.* had to negotiate the competing and often contradictory standards of readers, advertisers, newsstand operators in its creation of covers. As with many other aspects of the magazine in the 1970s, however, from advertising practices to the formation of a national foundation for women, the editorial decisions regarding covers showed a marked optimism about the magazine's ability to create a popular feminism.

Promising to Be a Mass Media Forum for Feminism

From its origins, *Ms.* promised to be more than a reflection of a movement in progress; the founders saw the magazine as a vehicle for social change, one that would resonate with the experiences of women across the country. Part of *Ms.*'s strategy for establishing itself as a mass media voice of feminism was to position itself as an "open forum; a place where women of many different backgrounds can find help and information to improve their lives."[18] Importantly, its official discourse explicitly espoused a pluralistic feminism, one that could speak to and include the differences inherent in a mass audience. Their first "Personal Report from *Ms.*" (a semiregular feature of the magazine) stated,

> If you asked us our philosophy for ourselves and for the magazine, each of us would give an individual answer. But we agree on one thing. We want a world in which no one is born into a subordinate role because of visible difference, whether that difference is of race or of sex. That's an assumption we make personally and editorially, with all the social changes it implies. After that, we cherish our differences. We want *Ms.* to be a forum for many views.[19]

In their selection of articles and their editorial philosophy editors promised a perspective that would recognize female and racial subordination and would oppose that subordination, through social change. Unlike the feminist groups springing up across the country, and unlike the women behind many of the smaller periodicals, editors named no explicit theoretical perspective from which they were working. *Ms.* was to be a "forum for many views," a magazine that welcomed individuality and difference.

Despite the claim of variety, however, a close examination of the editorials, articles, and covers does reveal a pattern, an overall approach to understanding and framing "women's issues" and "feminism." *Ms.*'s presentation of feminism was significantly shaped by the imperative to be both "timely" and (at least somewhat) "reasonable," necessities if they wanted to maintain a place on the newsstands next to the other women's magazines. Moreover, their editorial perspective was much more defined than the amorphous quality of their editorial statement indicates. (Indeed, one must immediately recognize that the claim that they had no theoretical perspective was in itself a theoretical perspective, one rooted in an individualistic understanding of how ideas are created and social change happens.)

Any analysis of the articulation of feminism in *Ms.* must take into account the context in which it was working. *Ms.* set out to popularize feminism within a genre and format already in existence, that of women's magazines. From its origins, *Ms.* resembled conventional women's magazines, with lots of color, bold headlines, glossy paper, and dozens of bright advertisements. While its smaller size suggested a newsmagazine, like *Newsweek*, more than a woman's magazine, its non-time-bound cover stories, its catchy sell lines, and the covers that borrowed many of the visual techniques from women's magazines placed it into the genre of women's magazine. The title, *Ms.*, as well as the subtitle, "For a Better World," identified it as a *feminist* women's magazine. By the end of 1972 the editors had established the general format of the magazine. Regular columns included a number of self-help pieces, ranging from articles on revised manners and child raising (Manners for Humans and Stories for Free Children), to a column on self-help in the health field (Women's Body/Women's Mind), to pieces on mechanics (Populist Mechanics), and a column "How to Make Trouble," which carried articles on subjects ranging from how to start one's own consciousness-raising group to how to begin a nonsexist, racially diverse child care center. Other regular columns focused more specifically on the work and lives of both historical and contemporary women; they included *Ms.* on the Arts; Lost Women, a column featuring historically significant women; Found Women, a column highlighting the lives of contemporary feminist activists; and the Gazette, a "tear-out" section printed on newsprint with national news, how-to information, and the names and addresses of local women's organizations across the country. The Forum, a less-frequently published column, focused on the theoretical statements of mostly nationally known feminists. Two regular columns featured the words and ideas of readers—the letters section, and the "No Comment" section, to which readers sent clippings of offensive advertisements, brochures, and headlines. Every six months to a year *Ms.* also included a "Personal Report from *Ms.*," a piece written by Gloria Steinem or a staff member discussing the finances, successes, and problems facing the magazine. The feature and cover stories changed each month, focusing on a range of topics, from the lives of individual women to major feminist issues on topics like body image, women and money, women and voting, sexuality, and work.

As was discussed in Chapter 1, *Ms.* editors appropriated the "self-help" focus of traditional women's magazines, redefining it in ways relevant to an audience of women interested in self-improvement, autonomy, and changing the world. As editors sought to "get the word out" about feminism within the format of a commercial women's magazine, they not only had to redefine self-help, but, ironically, they also had to redefine "women." Conventional women's magazines emphasized the female audience it was "serving" but defined that group as one united by its interest in home, beauty, relationships, and, most importantly, from a commercial standpoint, consumer habits. *Ms.* worked to define women as a group joined not only by consumer habits but also, and primarily, by a political consciousness and a female culture. Women had something in common with each other as a subordinated group fighting to free themselves from male domination, and as a group who shared specific ideals and ways of thinking and living. *Ms.* played a central role in helping to create and disseminate a feminist consciousness across the nation, as it rejected the way women traditionally had been constructed and spoken to in the mass media, and as it helped to solidify women's sense of themselves as a group who had collective political goals and social characteristics.[20]

Scholars and critics have frequently categorized or dismissed *Ms.* as espousing career feminism, egalitarianism, or liberal feminism.[21] These observations are valid to the extent that *Ms.* generally avoided, despite the forays into discussions about poverty, any critique of male domination that linked that form of oppression to that caused by our economic system. The way that *Ms.* discussed feminism cannot be so easily pigeonholed as "careerist" or "egalitarian," however. In the early years, the magazine promised that the new "survival skills" it offered would help to transform the world into one more humanist, one less defined by the deleterious effects of false distinctions of feminine and masculine. *Ms.* editors delineated a feminism that emphasized self-help and sisterhood. The focus on personal change differed from traditional women's magazines in that it was rooted in an understanding of sisterhood, of an underlying female culture and female cultural superiority that would help to revolutionize our society. This dual perspective on individual change and cultural sisterhood was a strategy that allowed the magazine to navigate among a wide range of readers' perspectives, extreme commercial demands, and the constraints imposed by staking out territory within the industry and genre of women's magazines.

Ironically, this strategy, well chosen for the reasons listed above, also limited the magazine's ability to be a mass media center for debate and dialogue among women. An emphasis on sisterhood and individual change both followed and helped to create the changes going on at large within the women's movement, as cultural and liberal feminism eclipsed the primacy of radical feminism within the women's movement. The blending of individualism and sisterhood, of a focus on personal change, yet a broad concern with women's issues, emerged from two sources: the imperative to be a magazine that blended the genre of the women's magazine with the new philosophy of feminism, and the perspectives of the editors who founded the magazine, particularly Gloria Steinem. *Ms.*'s editors rarely addressed or seemed to consider the contradiction between these two desires of individuality and sisterhood, however. As a media text *Ms.* borrowed from both the cultural and the egalitarian strands of feminism prevalent in the early 1970s, often replicating the same philosophical contradictions inherent in the movement at large. The editors promised readers the dreams of the women's movement — sisterhood, equality, democracy, and their own national resource in the form of *Ms.* magazine. The metamorphosis of the individual as well as the collective power of women united in sisterhood were at the root of these dreams.

Personal Transformation

From its origins, *Ms.* spoke in a language familiar to readers of traditional women's magazines, an intimate voice promising personal transformation. The "personal" — i.e., the person — served as the philosophical basis for the construction of feminism in *Ms.* as well as the basis for the relationship editors attempted to forge with readers. This underscoring of the person coincided with both the genre of which *Ms.* was a part — women's magazines — and the prominent slogan of the women's movement — "the personal is the political." While this slogan suggested multiple meanings, it clearly worked as a powerful metaphor for women beginning to see the political connotations of their own lives. For *Ms.*, the slogan worked to mesh the distinctions between the magazine as a commercial women's magazine and as a political resource, for the women's movement was, according to one interpretation of the slogan, about women's personal lives.

More than a superficial rhetorical move designed to allow *Ms.* to blend with the other women's magazines, the editors' focus on self-help and personal transformation was a fundamental way of understanding social change. According to *Ms.*, the goal of this self-help movement was the transformation of humanity. The early issues of *Ms.* described the women's movement as a humanizing force: phrases like "liberated female human being," "whole person," and "human liberation" emerged in editorial comments and advertising slogans to express the goals of the new social and political move-ment for women. This emphasis on the complete human being was by no means a new philosophy, having its roots in eighteenth-century Enlighten-ment thinking. European Enlightenment philosophers argued for the rights of man based on the "infinite perfectibility of each person," not on property, wealth, or status. Revolutionary philosophers in America drew from this new philosophy of individual rights in their justification for independence from England. In the last thirty years, historians and philosophers have ana-lyzed in detail how the original conception of "human" excluded women, blacks, Native Americans, and other non-European and nonwhite people from its very definition. Since the eighteenth century, however, women and other excluded groups have argued for equality based on the concept of indi-vidual rights. The philosophies of full democracy, freedom, and individual liberty have provided powerful sources for the justification of suffrage, edu-cation, property rights, and other claims for all oppressed groups.[22] Much of the editorial rhetoric within *Ms.* during the 1970s focused on the devel-opment of individual liberty for women. Articles emphasized the need for women to increase their self-esteem, to assert their needs and desires, and to gain knowledge and power in areas previously denied to them.

In a 1975 *Ms.* article, contributing editor Robin Morgan outlined how the humanizing "revolution of the individual" was to work. Her words articu-lated the philosophy often expressed less explicitly in many of the "Personal Reports," the editorial introductions to articles, and the columns them-selves. She wrote, "Our feminist revolution gains momentum from a 'ripple effect'—from each individual woman gaining self-respect and yes, gaining power, over her own body and soul first, then within her family, on her block, in her town . . . and so on out from the center. . . . This is a revolu-tion in consciousness, rising expectations, and the actions which reflect that organic process."[23] As Morgan explained it, the origins of change resided with the individual woman and her examination of her own personal experi-ences. That personal knowledge, and the increased self-esteem it produced, would transform our culture.

At the root of this process of cultural transformation was the act of indi-vidual consciousness-raising, a practice central to the second wave of femi-nism. Kathie Sarachild, an activist in the group New York Radical Women, coined the phrase "consciousness-raising" in the late 1960s to refer to the process in which women discussed the ways they saw themselves oppressed as women, and thus began to see the root causes for male supremacy.[24] The push for consciousness-raising emerged most forcefully from women like Sarachild, Shulamith Firestone, and others, radical feminists who had been activists in the Civil Rights movement and the New Left. Quickly, however, the process of consciousness-raising spread across the country, particularly after the widely publicized 1968 demonstration against the Miss America Contest. Formal and informal groups met in women's homes, child care groups, churches, and schools to discuss all that had previously been considered "private" or "petty": sexuality, language, housework, child rearing. Thousands and thousands of women found themselves drawn to these discussions where they could vent their feelings, voice their anger, and see the commonalities among themselves. The activity of oppressed people speaking to each other about their problems had a significant historical legacy prior to the women's liberation movement, both within the United States, particularly among civil rights workers, and across the world.[25] For women beginning to see their own oppression, the act of consciousness-raising had particular saliency, as all the activities traditionally *labeled* "female," and thus "private" and/or "unimportant," were given status as political and significant.

As consciousness-raising gained in popularity in the early 1970s, feminists debated its significance and, most centrally, its connection to political action. Those feminists who saw themselves tied to either civil rights or leftist organizations (the "politico" wing) and those whose activism sprung primarily from government channels (the "liberal" or "egalitarian" wing) both doubted the efficacy of consciousness-raising, arguing it promoted "navel gazing" over useful action. In contrast, the radical feminists who promoted consciousness-raising argued that its purpose was not "therapy," was not to "change women," but to change "the conditions women face [and] . . . male supremacy."[26] Consciousness-raising, therefore, was to provide the means for women to formulate political theories that emerged from the concrete experiences of their own lives, theories that would point to useful activism. Indeed, groups like Redstockings saw consciousness-raising as a dialectic process linking theory and action, a "method for arriving at the truth and a means for action and organizing."[27]

From its origins, *Ms.* editors described the magazine as a tool in readers' consciousness-raising, with articles, editorials, and the long section of readers' letters published in *Ms.* in the early 1970s all working to reframe and to redefine the reality traditionally presented to readers in women's magazines. In the premier issue of *Ms.*, Johnnie Tillmon, the first chairwoman of the National Welfare Rights Organization, wrote an article entitled "Welfare Is a Women's Issue." "No woman in this country can feel dignified, no woman can be liberated, until all women get off their knees," she wrote, adding that "the truth is that A.F.D.C. is like a super-sexist marriage. You trade in *a* man for *the* man. But you can't divorce him if he treats you bad." Pointedly, she asked readers to "stop for a minute and think what would happen to you and your kids if you suddenly had no husband and no savings." [28] Similar to many other pieces written for *Ms.*, particularly in its early years, Tillmon's article typified the consciousness-raising aspect of the magazine. Every issue, editors and writers pointed out, is a women's issue. Every problem, every situation can be viewed through a different lens, one that emphasizes the role that male domination and female subordination plays — either literally or metaphorically. From car mechanics to marriage, from finances to child rearing, every topic could be viewed anew once one had that "click of recognition" that male domination existed, that women could and should resist, that problems that previously had seemed invisible or simply "personal" were connected to broader social roots. Moreover, all women were linked by a common sisterhood, a shared culture and a shared fate, potential or actual.

During 1972 and 1973, *Ms.* published two lengthy articles on beginning and sustaining consciousness-raising groups, what the first article referred to as the "heart and soul of the Women's Movement." According to an interview between *Village Voice* writer Robin Reisig and Sarachild, *Ms.* approached Sarachild with the request to write a book on consciousness-raising for *Ms.* Sarachild reported being "surprised" that they asked her, considering that they had never asked her to be part of the original group that formed *Ms.*, and that she had publicly objected to the emphasis on personal therapy in the way that *Ms.* portrayed consciousness-raising and feminism. She eventually turned down the offer, arguing that *Ms.* was going to claim consciousness-raising as their own invention with the title "*Ms.* Guide to Consciousness-Raising." [29] Indeed, Sarachild's rejection of the *Ms.* offer exposes the divisions that were prevalent among feminists at this period, particularly between those who sought more emphasis on the "personal" and those who did not want to see consciousness-raising repackaged as personal therapy. It also points out, once again, the resentment many women felt that *Ms.* was beginning to "stand for" the women's movement.

While radical activists like Sarachild argued that the consciousness-raising groups should formulate useful theory and generate political action, the first *Ms.* guide to consciousness-raising emphasized the importance of personal guidance:

The rap group is a free place; a place to be honest. It is a group of supportive and nonjudging friends who are there to help when we come back battered or ridiculed from trying to change our worlds. It is some version of the often repeated statement, "You feel like that? My God, I thought only *I* felt like that." It is a place to discover and sustain each other and ourselves. Eventually, we find out not only who we are, but the political relationship of women, as a caste, to society as a whole. We learn or invent practical ways of changing our own lives, and the lives of women around us.[30]

The guide described "c-r" groups as places of friendship and support, where women identified their similarities to one another. Clearly, *Ms.* emphasized the collective nature of women's problems in its reference to "the political relationship of women, as a caste, to society as a whole." Importantly, however, whatever political theorizing and action this statement might have suggested was cut short with the final comment that rap groups were there to "invent practical ways of changing our own lives." According to *Ms.*, consciousness-raising alerted women to the political nature of their problems but provided them with primarily individual solutions.

The second major *Ms.* article on consciousness-raising provided an in-depth look at a group to which one of the editors, Letty Cottin Pogrebin, belonged. In her description of the group, Pogrebin mentioned nothing about political action or analysis; she focused on the personal transformations in the group, referring to it as "Feminists Anonymous": "We confess that we come together to *use* each other in many different ways. For emotional problem-solving, of course. But also for job leads, and professional ideas and inspiration and for the chance to vicariously live an alien lifestyle."[31] In Pogrebin's description, the person was both the root of change and the goal of change. Within Pogrebin's consciousness-raising group, the movement appeared to have lost some of its "ripple effect," remaining firmly rooted in the individual.

Of course, not all the rhetoric within *Ms.* suggested the women's movement should or could go no further than the individual. But even in articles focusing on the ramifications of feminism, the crux of the analysis rested on personal experience, which often manifested itself as a rejection of "theory" or any kind of overarching conceptualization of sexual politics. In the same article in which she discussed the "ripple effect," Robin Morgan explicitly turned to the personal; she said that she began to write her "personal retrospective" on the women's movement in "obscure, yea, unintelligible" theoretical language. "But the risk-taking, subjective voice of poetry is more honestly my style," she wrote, "and so, to look at the Women's Movement, I go to the mirror — and gaze at myself. Everywoman? [No, she answers.] I *do* still believe, though, that the personal is political . . . and that this insight into the necessary integration of exterior realities and interior imperatives is one of the themes of consciousness that makes the Women's Movement unique, less abstract, and more functionally *possible* than previous movements for social change." [32]

Shying away from abstraction of any sort, other authors focused their writings on the specific, the personal. In her article on motherhood, Pogrebin outlined the multitude of contradictory choices facing those around her, then returned to her own experiences: "If anything can be said at this time about being a mother and a committed feminist, it must be no more ambitious and no less honest than a personal commentary—even if it comes out disconnected, vulnerable, and frankly sentimental." [33] The editorial comment introducing the 1975 issue on men articulated a similar approach. "Instead of . . . a theoretical discussion of patriarchy," it read, "we've gathered diverse personal testimonies on sexual politics in everyday life." [34]

The "vulnerable and frankly sentimental" voice that Pogrebin described meshed well with the established personal voice of the mass media women's magazines. What is important to note is the way that this focus on consciousness-raising and the person translated into an anti-intellectual, antitheoretical perspective. To a certain extent, the antitheoretical, anti-intellectual perspective of the editor was an attempt to reach out to a broad audience. Indeed, much of the advice and explanation offered in the magazine was less a repudiation of theory than a distillation of it, an attempt to use the theory as it came "floating through the air," to speak to "individual" women in "personal" tones.[35] The emphasis on "personal words" and anecdotal evidence rather than theoretical statements signified more than editors' attempts to keep the magazine readable for a mass audience, however. It also represented a genuine skepticism of anything overly intellectual. Many of the writers chose to concentrate on the person so as not to construct totalizing doctrines about women and society, which they had found so reprehensible in the work of the primarily male New Left and of socialist feminists. As the 1972 *Ms.* "Guide to Consciousness-Raising" explained, "generalizing, theorizing, or talking in abstractions is bound to misrepresent or alienate some member of the group to whom those generalizations don't apply." [36] Any kind of overall theory of gender oppression, sexual identity formation, race relations, or class relations, therefore, was likely to find a skeptical audience at *Ms.*, not just because of editors' desire to connect with a mass readership, but also out of a strongly held conviction that these theories were distorted and falsified the diversity of women's lives. Editors argued that the focus on the personal allowed the writers (and readers) to remain grounded in that which they had experienced and understood themselves.

One of the few areas within *Ms.* where "theory" or more analytical approaches were not explicitly rejected was the "Forum" section, where well-known feminists and radical voices within the movement found space to voice their opinions. Writers like Jane Alpert, Jo Freeman, Kate Millett, Robin Morgan, and Charlotte Bunch published essays and carried on rather lengthy debates within these pages. JoAnne Edgar described the "Forum" section as "the place in the magazine where we publish theoretical and controversial articles, articles that push the boundaries of feminist thought and action."[37] The introduction to the first Forum in July 1973 did not explicitly state that the new section would be more theoretical and more controversial than the rest of the magazine, but its tone made it clear that this was to be a place where some difficult questions would be asked.

> Here and in other countries around the world, the Women's Movement has been growing in depth and strength. It is beginning to be recognized as part of the most fundamental revolution: the worldwide revolt against caste, against all economic and social systems that determine futures according to race or sex. But what tactics should be chosen? What coalitions formed? And what will be the economic implications of this fundamental change? What kind of social forms may evolve? This article begins a forum for such explorations — a series of essays and predictions and new thoughts.[38]

The "Forum" section provided a national, all-encompassing resource for the women's movement, because it could speak not only to those women who had no previous ties to the movement but also to those who had considerable experience as activists, writers, and organizers. By 1975, the Forum column was described as a "place for theory, controversy, and personal opinion; for dialogue inside the Women's Movement now, as well as futurist thought that extends the boundaries of feminism."[39] The antitheoretical stance inherent in much of the editorial perspective, however, worked against this promise; by the 1980s, for instance, the "Forum" section disappeared and was replaced by a "Personal Words" column.

Ms. took the personal voice of traditional women's magazines and transformed it into one that could speak to and thus empower women who, living within a patriarchal culture, had often believed themselves crazy, powerless, and incapable of action. The personal stories and self-help the magazine offered suggested more than an acquiescing to the structures that overpowered women in their daily lives; they offered numerous solutions and suggestions as to how to fight back. The discussions in many ways provided women with what Sara Evans and Harry Boyte have referred to as a "free space" in which to explore and analyze their own lives.[40] In addition, these analyses often did have a "ripple effect"; women recognized similarities with other women and joined together to work for change. *Ms.*'s "Gazette" section, for instance, was designed to be a vehicle for that change.

The *Ms.* focus on the individual had negative repercussions, however. By focusing on the individual, *Ms.* did support women's belief in their own agency, their own power to analyze and change their environment. At the same time, an exclusive concentration on the person led to a tendency to fail to look beyond one's own life, and ironically, since this was what it was supposed to avoid, to make assumptions about others' lives based on one's own experiences. This was particularly dangerous when writers in *Ms.* made assertions about others' lives based on their own experiences as relatively privileged, white, economically secure, heterosexual women. In addition, the emphasis on the personal lead to an inability to see the larger cultural and societal structures that do indeed shape one's personal experiences. In focusing on the personal stories of individual women, *Ms.* created its own model of normalcy, despite the desire for diversity. Finally, a feminism based on the personal dovetailed with a feminism constructed through a consumer ideology. That is, if the solution resided with the person, with personal growth and satisfaction, it was a short step to understanding feminism as a movement that involved problem-solving through the purchase of consumer goods. In a way, the editorial focus on individual change in *Ms.* unwittingly conspired with a commodification of feminism that was apparent in the magazine at its inception. The consequences and dilemmas created by a personalization of feminism created heated and often angry debates among readers, critics, and writers in *Ms.*

Sisterhood

An emphasis on personal growth also created a paradoxical combination with the editors' other primary focus on the sisterhood of feminism. In the early years of *Ms.*, editors encouraged readers to have faith in the new self-help skills and personal consciousness-raising that would aid in transforming the world into one more humanist, one less defined by the deleterious effects of false distinctions of feminine and masculine. While most articles, directed as they were to a female audience, focused on the way that women needed to change their lives, the columns on men emphasized the necessity for men to recognize the emotions and vulnerability within themselves. According to the *Ms.* philosophy, what thwarted the potential for a "perfect" humanity were rigid and artificial sex roles. Editors strongly refuted those who argued that the emphasis on the need to change female identity was simply a call to duplicate masculine identity. The purpose of the movement, editors argued, was to create a new, fully recognized, fully balanced human being; they rejected all assertions that the movement would "make women into men." In response to a reader's letter arguing that military women simply duplicated male roles and ideology, editors wrote, "We agree: the point is not to imitate men but to humanize both roles, male and female." [41]

In their rejection of the masculine sphere, however, editors simultaneously evoked a superior female culture. [42] "When women do have power," they wrote in the same response, "there is considerable evidence that their use of it reflects the less violent values of the women's culture." [43] What comes across clearly within this passage is a belief in something one can point to as "the women's culture." The feminist philosophy in *Ms.* combined an emphasis on the individual and full humanity with a belief in a self-evident women's culture, uniting all females. So *Ms.*'s focus on personal change was different from that in traditional women's magazines because it was rooted in an understanding of sisterhood, of underlying female culture and female superiority that would help to revolutionize our society.

These contradictory approaches to feminism—one asserting the fundamental sameness of women and men, the other asserting women's difference as superior—was by no means a new combination. Within the United States, the long battle for female suffrage in the nineteenth and early twentieth centuries joined claims for women's vote based on a concept of equal rights, the shared humanity of men and women, with claims for suffrage based on a belief in women's moral superiority: women should have the vote so that they could clean up politics, make the cities safe for other women and children, and provide a balance to the corrupt culture created by men. As Denise Riley argues in her pathbreaking work *"Am I That Name?": Feminism and the Category of "Women" in History*, this elision between arguments based on the essential sameness between men and women and arguments based on an intrinsic difference between men and women was not peculiar to the fight for suffrage: it has been fundamental to the construction of feminism since the Enlightenment. [44] As a media text, then, *Ms.* borrowed from both the cultural and the egalitarian strands of feminism that had a long history in the United States and were particularly prevalent in the early 1970s.

The concept of a superior female culture uniting all women dominated the editorial perspective since the publication of Gloria Steinem's piece "Sisterhood" in the first issue. Emphasizing the bonds and the sexual oppression that transcend differences of race, economics, religion, and all other social categories, this editorial set the tone for other editorial pieces that focused on both a unique female culture and a fundamental oppression that united all women. Steinem's article most explicitly constructed a women's culture that obscured all differences among women.[45] According to major editorials and cover stories in the 1970s, women were neither power hungry nor violent but thought like the "conservers of life."[46] If women took part in the oppression of other women, for instance, it was due to economic, physical, and psychic pressure from the men to whom they were connected. As Steinem wrote in the cover story on child pornography, "Yes, there have been some women who help produce such pornography, but their need seems to be money or the approval of men they're dependent on, not the personal need for intimate, obscene power that creates the pornography market in the first place." Or, perhaps women's oppression of other women was due to ignorance of the conditions of other women's lives; Steinem believed that education about the lives of poor women of color in the United States, for instance, was the solution to white, middle-class women's scorn or misuse of these women.[47] As Steinem noted in her essay "Sisterhood," patriarchal culture was to blame for the artificial distinctions among women. If one moved beyond the fissures caused by men, women could easily begin to see the commonalities among themselves.

A Diverse Sisterhood

The focus on sisterhood resulted in a widespread optimism about the ability of the women's movement, and *Ms.* in particular, to speak to all women, in both the United States and the world. The July 1972 issue of *Ms.* published a lengthy letter from a Chicana woman who found the magazine accessible and important to her. "Being a Chicana did not detract from my enjoyment of your magazine. We all stand on common ground, i.e. we are all women in a society where being female is being inferior."[48] Not only could the magazine, and the movement, bridge differences among women in the United States, it could reach women in all countries. Female culture and female oppression transcended even national boundaries. Introducing her piece on the 1975 International Year of Women, Steinem wrote, "There are many, many such recent proofs that the contagion of feminism is crossing boundaries of space and language; that women on every continent are beginning to question their status as, in Yoko Ono's famous phrase, 'the niggers of the world.' At its most global, there is a conviction that feminism is itself a natural and antinationalist force. At its most personal, there is an unexpected, exhilarating, and intimate sense of true connection with other women's lives—unknown women living many worlds away."[49] The concept of sisterhood provided both a powerful rationale for women of all races, classes, and nationalities to work together and an overwhelming confidence in women's ability to provide a unified vision of a transformed culture. The promise of sisterhood within *Ms.* made it a unique periodical among mass media women's magazines. Even the ad for *Ms.* in the preview issue explained that "*Ms.* is written for all women, everywhere, in every occupation and profession—women with deep, diverse ambitions, and those who have not yet had a chance to formulate ambition—women who are wives, mothers, and grandmothers, or none of these—women who want to be fully a female person and proud of it. In brief, women who want to humanize politics, business, education, the arts and sciences . . . in the home, the community, and the nation."[50]

Importantly, the promise of sisterhood and an "open forum" mandated the inclusion of articles by and about many different women. While *Ms.* had a relatively consistent feminist perspective emphasizing personal growth and sisterhood, evidenced in the "Personal Reports from *Ms.*," the cover stories, the essays written by the editors, and the articles by other writers showed more variation. Indeed, if anything characterized *Ms.* it was the juxtaposition of differing visions of womanhood and feminism. The July 1972 issue of *Ms.* included an ad for *Essence* magazine, the periodical directed to black women. It pictured a row of women's magazines, including *Vogue*, *Seventeen*, and *Cosmopolitan*, and in bold print the caption read, "Ever get the feeling when they're talking about 'women' they're not talking about you?" While the advertisement did not specifically critique *Ms.*, the question itself asked readers to challenge any notion of universal womanhood that did not explicitly include the needs, desires, experiences, and perceptions of black women. The critique of a "universal" womanhood and the refiguration of feminism took place in the articles as well. In June 1973, for instance, *Ms.* published an article entitled "Two American Welfare Mothers," and in May 1974 it published the National Black Feminist Organization's organizational philosophy. In July 1976, Susan Braudy published an article on women and children's experiences in an Indian Survival School. Articles about, and often by, women involved in Afro-American feminist organizations, Native American women, and women living on welfare provided a powerful counterpoint to the articles that assumed a more homogeneous, middle-class, white audience. *Ms.* also frequently published excerpts from the works of well-known minority feminists, usually African American. In the early 1970s, for example, *Ms.* began its long-standing tradition of publishing Alice Walker's essays; in June 1975, Angela Davis's essay on Joanne Little, the black female prisoner who had allegedly killed a white prison guard while defending herself against his sexual assault, was published in the "Forum" section; and in 1979, *Ms.* published Michele Wallace's "Black Macho and the Myth of the Superwoman."[51]

Throughout its history, *Ms.* worked to accommodate the diverse constituencies encompassed in a mass readership. But this goal of pluralism within the mass media set *Ms.* up for failure; it could never please everyone. Yet editors frequently referred to this ambition as one of their strengths as well as one of their weaknesses. Either by picketing the magazine's offices, or, more frequently, by writing lengthy letters to *Ms.*, readers let the editors know if they felt excluded. From their first "Personal Report," when they acknowledged that teenagers, older women, and blue-collar women were included in only a "marginal way," editors continued to promise readers more coverage and more sensitivity to difference.[52]

From its origins, *Ms.* included lesbians and lesbian rights in its representation of women and feminism. Ignoring the warnings of Elizabeth Harris, one of the founders of the magazine, Steinem and the others published an article by Del Martin and Phyllis Lyons in the July 1972 issue. In their rejection of the perspective that argued that lesbianism "divided" women and diverted attention from the "real" issues of feminism, editors anchored themselves to the position that the problem with lesbianism is the stigma attached to it and the way that patriarchy uses lesbianism to label and threaten. Not all early articles demonstrated this sensitivity, however, as was the case with Letty Pogrebin's piece "Down with Sexist Upbringing," in which she reminded readers that homosexuality resulted from family problems, not boys playing with dolls.[53] An otherwise powerful interview by Anne Koedt with a woman who had recently fallen in love with another woman, for instance, portrayed love between women as a natural extension of caring about women in the movement. This explicit statement about the normalcy of lesbianism, however, was weakened by a blurb about the two women that assured readers that both had previously had only heterosexual relationships. Throughout the 1970s, however, *Ms.* regularly published articles on lesbian issues, including Joan Larkin's "Coming Out: 'My Story Is Not about All Lesbians,' " Charlotte Bunch's "Forum: Learning from Lesbian Separatism," and Del Martin and Phyllis Lyons's "Lesbian Mothers," that indicated the magazine's commitment to inclusivity and rejection of antilesbian perspectives.[54]

Despite editorial promises and the mandate to include a diversity of articles, however, speaking to all women was an impossible mission. Many of the articles, even those that *Ms.* republished in its *First Ms. Reader*, a collection of early *Ms.* articles, could speak to only certain women, as was the case with Jane O'Reilly's piece "The Housewife's Moment of Truth." The scarcity of responses among women of color, lesbians, or working-class women suggests that they experienced a weak connection with O'Reilly's vision.[55] As bell hooks so clearly argued in *Feminist Theory: From Margin to Center*, the focus on sisterhood masked the complex reality of women's lives and ignored the intersections among race, class, and gender. "The idea of 'common oppression' was a false and corrupt platform disguising and mystifying the true nature of women's varied and complex social reality. Women are divided by sexist attitudes, racism, class privilege, and a host of other prejudices. . . . Divisions will not be eliminated by wishful thinking or romantic reverie about common oppression despite the value of highlighting experiences all women share."[56]

Among the constituencies that accused *Ms.* of misrepresentation and lack of coverage were full-time mothers and housewives. Throughout its history, *Ms.* grappled with the dilemma of what kind of coverage to give to housewives and how to reach this audience. Certainly, the questions raised by these debates about housewives belied any notion that *Ms.* would be able to encompass the experiences and points of view of all women. In 1975, a reader's criticism of *Ms.* and inquiry about doing a series on feminist women who choose to devote their lives to home and children generated a lively dialogue among editors. The reader pointed out that many women felt estranged from the movement, and from *Ms.* in particular, because they felt left out; and, more specifically, they felt their own decisions to take care of their own children were unfairly criticized by women who either hated their husbands or had selfishly chosen "careers," often further burdening "stay at home" mothers with the care of others' children. She argued that a series of articles on feminist full-time mothers, on fathers' roles in the family, and on choosing to go back to work would help to connect these disaffected readers to *Ms.* and to the movement in general.

None of the editors agreed that there should be an on-going series on housewives and feminism. Many, however, felt a responsibility for helping to assuage "the alienation of 'stay-at-home' women from the movement, as indicated in the [writer's] interviews here and by numerous letters and phone calls we receive." One of the editors pointed out that much of the hostility women felt toward the movement was generated not by feminists themselves but by "their image of the movement from the press." Editors pointed out that many of the writers, editors, and staff at *Ms.* were married, had children, and were housewives themselves when they "weren't working for pay." For example, Phyllis Langer, one of the staff members, combined work and child care; she had been bringing her daughter Alix to *Ms.* since infancy. Indeed, *Ms.* highlighted the family connections of their staff and published numerous articles on family, marriage, and feminism, beginning with O'Reilly's key "click" essay. In 1973, *Ms.* published an article entitled "Mothers are People," a "family album" of staff members with their mothers, children, and siblings.[57] Letty Cottin Pogrebin wrote regularly on raising children in a non-sexist way and was also a key instigator for the *Free to Be* children's recording and *Ms.*'s award-winning collection *Stories for Free Children*. What set these articles apart from the series that the critical reader proposed, of course, was they all questioned women's traditional relationship to home and children. Certainly they did not condone the abandonment of marriage and family (indeed, many criticized *Ms.* for focusing too much on motherhood and marriage), but they challenged what women's and men's roles within those institutions should be.

The request for a series on housewives and feminism prompted Pogrebin to write a lengthy memo detailing the fallacy of "equal coverage" within a feminist magazine. Referring to the reader who wanted more coverage of feminist housewives, she wrote, "She's bought the myth. Now she's feeling guilty. We do tend to dismiss homemakers with a 'that's their option' answer. But that's, I think, because it's too arduous to go into Engels with the casual questioner. I think we believe (most of us) that such an option is false; that it is an indulgence allowed to the few who can afford to choose it. So it's bullshit to evolve a series, column, or even one article that presents it through the eyes of the beleaguered Middle Class homemaker." She continued her comments, echoing the feelings of another editor who argued that if they did a housewife and feminism piece it needed "to be an in-depth piece, not another 'It's o.k. to stay at home' try."

The consensus among editors, according to the notes circulated among them, seemed to be a Forum dialogue among women on the issue of feminism and housewives. Even Pogrebin, who clearly felt "pro-housewife" material had no place in *Ms.*, agreed with this tactic. "To respond appropriately to all the letter writers and kitch critics and 'feeling-left-out-accusations,'" she wrote, "I think we should do a dialog in Forum. It would answer these accusations and facile complaints with some of the heavy, difficult, but crucial reasoning that women shouldn't be let off the hook from considering."[58]

Ms. editors met with a number of women who considered themselves housewives sympathetic with feminism but alienated from the movement. Despite the editors' determination to publish some "crucial reasoning," however, they decided to let one of the women "speak for herself." Indeed, in this case the editors' preference for "personal" coverage once again took precedence over any kind of theoretical discussion. The imperative to make *Ms.* a home to a plurality of views got in the way of the editors' original desire to confront conventional notions of motherhood and housewives and to articulate a feminism with boundaries more explicit than simply being "pro-woman." In May 1977, *Ms.* published a cover story on thirty-seven-year-old Jane Broderick, who described herself as "the mother of eight, a housewife, a feminist — and happy." The cover pictured a close-up shot of her lined, smiling face, with no makeup and a broken tooth. This unattractive portrait of a housewife was coupled with the equally unflattering pictures of her home and her decidedly atypical feminist beliefs and practices. Though Broderick described herself as liberated ("feeling that there is nothing you cannot do as well as or even better than a man"), as a practicing Catholic she didn't use birth control because of the Church's teachings and considered her husband the real "authority figure in the family."[59]

Significantly, the editors chose the hook of a personal story over any kind of theoretical debate among women on the issue of traditional marriages and feminism. Certainly Broderick's story is compelling and even rather voyeuristic, as we get to look inside her crowded house and hear her stories about laundry and exhaustion with the eighth pregnancy. By publishing the individual story, *Ms.* avoided making any direct criticisms of traditional housewives themselves. The strong words that Letty Cottin Pogrebin wrote about the "myth" of homemaking were never printed in *Ms.* By avoiding any "theoretical" perspective, *Ms.* never had to make a specific stand about housewives and feminism and could more easily dodge criticism. *Ms.* might take flack for printing Broderick's story, but readers could hardly criticize the magazine for Broderick's personal opinions.

In many ways, however, Broderick's story sinks itself. While editors may have been sincerely impressed with her articulateness and by her criticisms of the movement, she looked like a caricature of the downtrodden housewife within the pages of *Ms. Newsday* picked up on the Broderick story and uncovered that not only was Broderick against abortion, she also supported an anti-abortion amendment to the U.S. Constitution. At this point, *Ms.* did have to do some backtracking. Carbine wrote to *Newsday* that while Broderick's individual opinion regarding abortion in no way compromised her description of herself as a feminist (indeed, feminism was all about individual choice, Carbine reiterated), taking that choice away from other women was "essentially anti-feminist."[60] As with most controversial issues, however, editors let readers do most of the criticizing; angry readers questioned Broderick's stand on the Church, abortion, and fatherly authority. Other readers, who identified themselves as housewives and feminists, asked that Broderick not be used to represent their views and lifestyles. Interestingly editors created a debate and dialogue without explicitly taking part in it themselves. Indeed, by including Broderick's story, without commenting on it themselves, they could continue to cast a broad net of "sisterhood" without addressing the very real differences of perspective and purpose among women.

The magazine's focus on sisterhood mandated attention to the diversity of women, but, at the same time, it emphasized women's underlying commonality, both in a shared oppression and in a shared (and superior) female culture. Ironically, then, a philosophy of sisterhood required editorial attention to all women, and thus to differences among women, at the same time it assumed women's sameness. The editorial focus dealt with this contradiction in a number of ways. Sometimes the magazine suggested that all women's identities were equal and could easily coexist. For instance, in the "Where to Get Help" article, organizations for women on welfare stood side by side with organizations for academic women. Designed to publicize a broad spectrum of organizations for all U.S. women, the list was indicative of the way the magazine initially attempted to compile a liberal plurality of female identities and to gloss over differences among women in the name of sisterhood. As an example, Steinem told the story of a white housewife, a "dignified" woman, who began crying in a consciousness-raising session run by black domestic workers when she realized how she had been oppressed. The black woman sitting next to her comforted her, telling her, "If it's your own kitchen or somebody else's, you still don't get treated like people. Women's work just doesn't count."[61] While this meeting may indeed have been a productive one, for both breaking racist barriers and encouraging white women to support the domestics' cause, the story itself denies the differences in power, money, and status between the two women. Most importantly, it denies the fact that not all oppression is identical.[62] (That the black domestic worker comforts the white housewife is a telling example.) Ironically, *Ms.* editors referred to the differences among women as signs of women's fundamental sameness rather than the source of discord. In describing the creation of consciousness-raising groups, for instance, the editors wrote, "Groups that are not homogeneous take longer to break through differences of style, but they have the advantage of showing dramatically how women's problems tend to survive the boundaries of age, economic status, and ethnic background."[63]

The "sameness" of women also allowed *Ms.* to gloss over the contradictory positions of sisterhood and liberal individuality. Editorials construed all women to be fundamentally the same. The first consciousness-raising article, which emphasized shared feelings and perceptions ("You feel like that? My God, I thought only *I* felt like that."), reflected this stress on sameness. What is important to recognize, of course, is that the "*I*" speaking in this passage is one of the editors, who were predominantly white, middle-class, and extremely well educated. Most discussions of "just like me" assumed a universal "me" who was white, middle-class, educated, and heterosexual. That is, even though *Ms.* overtly emphasized a policy of inclusivity, it nevertheless constructed a "normal" woman, one from whom certain characteristics were excluded. Del Martin and Phyllis Lyons, two of the founders of the national lesbian organization called the Daughters of Bilitis, wrote regularly for *Ms.* about lesbian identities, political perspectives, and social concerns. But, as Martin and Lyons's writings make clear, these articles worked primarily to introduce "difference" and to educate the "mainstream" audience about women who were not like themselves. In their first piece, for instance, Martin and Lyons spent considerable time defining lesbianism: "A lesbian is a woman whose primary erotic, psychic, emotional, and social interest is in a member of her own sex, even though that interest may not be overtly expressed."[64] As Onka Dekkers argued in her *off our backs* editorial, these kind of articles could revolutionize a whole culture because they spoke about the forbidden and the silenced in open and clear terms. The power of "breaking silences," as both Tillie Olsen and Adrienne Rich have so eloquently argued, can never be underestimated.[65]

From a different perspective, however, it is also important to recognize that these articles rarely spoke directly to those women whose lives were under discussion. In articles like Jane O'Reilly's "Housewife's Moment of Truth," the reader is presumed to share traits and concerns with the author. There is tone of "Don't you hate it when. . . ?," a perspective that assumes that the reader will empathize, indeed will have had similar experiences. In contrast, articles about welfare mothers, lesbians, and African American feminists presumed much less similarity. Instead, they assumed the position of educator: "Lesbians don't all . . ." or "black feminists don't separate themselves from black people in general." The inferred reader hailed by most of the articles was white, middle-class, and heterosexual; the authors worked to explain differences among women to an audience who presumably would not have had the experiences of or identified themselves as lesbian, welfare recipient, black, and so on. Ironically, the articles excluded certain women even as they attempted to be inclusive. In this way, *Ms.* spoke about difference within a feminism that spoke primarily to white, middle-class, heterosexual women. "Difference" needed to be explained to the reader, as she herself stood as the model of normality. While these articles helped to explain a variety of experiences and perspectives to a wide range of readers, they also restricted *Ms.*'s ability to act as a forum for debate among feminists.

The emphasis on sisterhood worked as a double-edged sword, for it provided justification for gender consciousness among women as well as a shared opposition to patriarchal culture. Most practically, it justified the existence of a magazine designed to reach a large spectrum of women, to be an "open forum for all women." While this philosophy of sisterhood, with its assumption of universal womanhood, undercut the magazines's ability to deal adequately with the differences among and complexities within women, it also, ironically, provided readers the legitimation to argue that the magazine should speak to everyone. Readers, as we shall see in Chapter 4, claimed this offer of sisterhood and used it on their own behalf.

Voices Excluded

The dual emphasis in *Ms.* on sisterhood and liberal individuality, on the commonality among women and the ways that individual women could help themselves, in many ways mirrored the dominant feminist philosophies in U.S. culture in the early 1970s: liberal feminism, the ideology that emphasized individual rights, equality with men, the elimination of sex role socialization, and cultural feminism, the ideology that emphasized the oppression common to all women and a shared female culture. As Alice Echols explains in her fascinating study *Daring to Be Bad*, the heyday of radical feminist groups, whose ideology generally connected female oppression to racial and class oppression, had begun to decline by the early 1970s. During this same period, it became more difficult to distinguish between cultural and liberal feminisms, since activists began forming feminist businesses and institutions that combined a liberal perspective, which focused on self-help and working within the system, with a cultural perspective, which focused on a superior female space.

As an institution, *Ms.* both mirrored and led this eclipsing of radical feminism and merging of liberal and cultural feminism that was going on in the larger social context. *Ms.* worked to negotiate the contradictions that emerged from its dual emphasis on shared sisterhood and individualism by focusing on personal stories, letting readers speak, and making differences among women appear to be similarities. An overall framework of liberal pluralism, in which multiple and often contradictory positions were believed to be able to coexist, informed editors' understanding of how to articulate a popular feminism.

It is clear that from its early days *Ms.* jettisoned any articulation of socialist feminism, the ideology that links women's oppression to economic oppression. As *Ms.*'s early statement of feminist philosophy stated, "caste" was the enemy; class, which Steinem explained as being more "malleable," was not a focus of *Ms.*'s inquiry. The magazine's rejection of socialist feminism can be understood from two vantage points. First, many of the regular editors and contributors, in particular Robin Morgan, had been active in the very leftist movements that spawned radical feminism. In fighting the sexism of the leftist activists, however, many feminists rejected as well the premise that class had anything to do with women's oppression. Second, as a business endeavor, *Ms.* was firmly rooted in a capitalist system, both economically and in the belief systems of those who created the magazine. That is, the founders did not want to reject capitalism; they wanted to reform it enough to make a place for a feminist periodical. Thus, it is not surprising that *Ms.* focused on "caste" systems rather than the centrality of class in the interlocking oppressions facing women. While various articles certainly focused on women and poverty, and while socialist writers like Barbara Ehrenreich contributed regularly to the magazine, the overall viewpoint of the magazine maintained its distance from any overarching criticism of class structure.

In spite of *Ms.*'s avoidance of socialist feminism, one voice that did clearly articulate this perspective in the early 1970s was that of Ellen Willis, a founder of Redstockings and a contributing editor to *Ms.* Willis's piece "Economic Reality and the Limits of Feminism" argued that the optimism that originally characterized the movement based itself on a false sense of other women's lives and needs. "We were convinced that unlike the left,—a tiny, elite minority—we could create a mass movement. We would unite women —secretaries, waitresses, housewives, students, welfare mothers—*half the people*. It was a heady vision. We didn't realize that most of us had only a superficial understanding of how the experience of women who were poor or black — or, for that matter, rich — differed from ours." [66] Arguing that "the very circumstance that gives feminism its unique strength — that women's oppression transcends barriers of class and race — is also a limitation," Willis attacked any sense of sisterhood that overlooked the economic privileges that separate women. She pointed specifically to the consciousness-raising groups that focused on "individual liberation" but ignored political issues dividing women as a manifestation of a movement that had begun to protect its most privileged members and to avoid the problems and lives of those dealing with class and race oppression. While Willis never actually mentioned the description of Letty Cottin Pogrebin's consciousness-raising group that had appeared in an earlier issue of *Ms.*, her criticisms clearly applied to that group.

While Willis's criticism of *Ms.* in the Forum article was relatively indirect, Redstockings criticized *Ms.* explicitly. First printed in their publication *The Feminist Revolution* in 1975 and reprinted in full later that year in the periodical *off our backs*, Redstockings developed a wide-ranging critique of *Ms.*, focusing on everything from Gloria Steinem's politics to the ability of *Ms.* to reinforce the status quo. Their most damning attack linked Gloria Steinem to the Central Intelligence Agency (CIA) and suggested that *Ms.*, specifically the "Gazette" section, which collected news clips about women and feminist activities from around the country, and the letters section, to which readers sent long and personal stories, formed part of a larger conspiracy to gather information for the government. The basis of Redstockings's critique centered on an argument that the "powers to be" were using *Ms.* to replace the radical women's movement with an establishment women's movement. As evidence, they pointed to the infusion of money from corporations, the staff whom "no one" had heard of (meaning no one Redstockings had heard of, with the exception of Gloria Steinem, whom they did not respect), and the way *Ms.* presented itself as the originator of the movement. "One of the ways *Ms.* has carried out this policy of replacing the original radicals is by either ignoring or rewriting the history of the women's liberation movement. *Ms.* represents itself as the movement, as if nothing else had existed before it came along." The authors then quoted Gloria Steinem from an interview in the *New York Times*: "I think of us [*Ms.*] as a kind of connective tissue for women all across the country who felt isolated until we came along and let them know they were not alone." Their purpose in writing the exposé, Redstockings explained, was to reveal *Ms.*'s unsavory connections (to the CIA, for example) so that the real women's movement could continue to flourish. "Researching this article gave us a glimpse into the behind-the-scenes interest groups which have been responsible [for the establishment form of feminism in the shape of *Ms.*]. The interest groups must be brought into the full light of day if the authentic women's liberation movement is to emerge from its current eclipse." [67]

Redstockings presented their accusations as if Gloria Steinem, Patricia Carbine, Warner Communications, Clay Felker, and the CIA formed a unified front consciously attempting to usurp the already existing women's movement. Their critiques of *Ms.* appear less paranoid, however, when taken in the context of the often well-founded fear of infiltration by government agents within leftist organizations in the late 1960s and 1970s. In addition, Redstockings's accusations emerged at a moment of extreme disintegration of the radical women's liberation movement. They pinned onto *Ms.* their anger about the "mainstreaming" of feminism, a real change within the movement, in which feminist concerns moved into already established institutions, from schools, to corporations, to mass circulation women's magazines.[68] For Gloria Steinem and Patricia Carbine, the decision to create a mass media feminist magazine reflected a conscious belief that the movement needed to move in the direction of the major institutions of society. To Steinem and Carbine, a magazine like *Ms.* would help to create a more "authentic" movement. They argued that a more mainstream movement could speak to and include a broader range of women. To Redstockings activists, however, the mainstreaming of feminist concerns disguised and destroyed what they saw as the "authentic" movement, one separate from these mainstream institutions, which, they argued, discredited radical feminists and allowed corporations to translate a mass movement into a profit-making endeavor. Moreover, Redstockings's accusations reflected a widespread anger among many activists in the women's movement about the ability of the media to create the movement through its choice of who to highlight, who to ignore, and what questions to ask. *Ms.* illustrated both the power of corporations to profit from a movement and the power of the media to silence certain voices.

While the *off our backs* staff found no concrete evidence to link *Ms.* or Gloria Steinem to the CIA or some larger government conspiracy, Redstockings's criticism caused considerable damage to the magazine. Years earlier, in an exposé in *Ramparts*, Steinem had acknowledged that she had worked for the Independent Research Service, an international organization for youth that had been partially funded by the CIA. She denied any further involvement with or support by any governmental organization. Not until late in

1975 did Steinem reply directly to the accusations, writing a lengthy piece in *off our backs* that criticized the quality of the Redstockings's research, their personal attack on her, and their basically "pessimistic" outlook. Despite her defense, however, Redstockings's criticism and Steinem's slowness in replying to it caused great doubt about the integrity of the magazine among many women's groups and readers. One *Ms.* reader, who identified herself as a "moderate" and "sincere feminist," wrote: "I *want* to hear these charges dismissed. I want to believe that *Ms.* is sincere in its feminist beliefs and not a pawn of the corporate structure. But to hear it *you* must say it first — publicly. Otherwise, my conscience will not allow me to support you any longer in view of these most serious charges." [69] To compound many readers' suspicions, Ellen Willis resigned from the *Ms.* staff soon after *off our backs* published their accusations. Willis explained that she based her decision to leave less on her belief in Redstockings's accusations of *Ms.*'s CIA affiliation than on her anger that Steinem and the *Ms.* editors in general ignored and refused to consider seriously the criticisms of radical feminists. In addition, as a socialist feminist, she had little patience with a feminism based on personal transformation and a (false) sense of universal sisterhood, and she found *Ms.* too little willing to make room for her perspectives. [70]

Redstockings's accusations and Willis's experience at *Ms.* suggested that the creation of a popular feminism had its limitations. As we shall see in the next section, however, the commodified voice of feminism articulated in the advertising more obviously impeded *Ms.*'s potential to be a forum for discussion and debate than did its alleged CIA connections.

Selling Feminism

While the million-dollar funding from Warner assured editors they could run for a year even without strong responses from advertisers, the *Ms.* founders quickly had to forge strong ties with potential sponsors. After its first issue, for which all the advertisements were solicited by *New York* magazine staff members, *Ms.* developed a stringent advertising policy, one that was supposed to allow for the financial benefits of advertising but mitigate against the major problems the founders associated with advertising. They hoped not only to bring in enough business to support the magazine and to fund a foundation but also to transform the advertising industry itself, changing its practices of using sexist imagery and of hiring only male sales people. In a 1974 article, the *Ms.* advertising staff explained their goals: to create a "fair and aesthetic portion of advertisements to editorials" (more articles than ads); to choose advertising that "accurately reflects the way women spend our hard-won consumer dollars"; to accept only ads that treat "women as people"; and to train "advertising sales people who themselves would be agents of change."[71] Editors promised to reject ads that were either "downright insulting" or "harmful" (i.e., feminine hygiene deodorant). They also sought more advertising for "unfeminine" products like cars and stereos.[72]

Editors had an optimistic vision that the advertising industry could be transformed with some effort and education on the part of women in the publishing industry—that advertisers would agree to change campaigns offensive to women, that they would choose to buy space in women's magazines once they became aware that women too bought cars and plane tickets, and that they would willingly accept women into their all-male staffs once they realized *Ms.* had trained a competent group of saleswomen. In sum, editors believed the advertising industry could be reformed and would evolve as women made demands on it; unlike Ellen Willis and others like her who saw the economic structure as a primary cause of women's (and women's magazines') problems, the editors believed the commercial structure could work to their advantage with both minor and major adaptations.

Finding advertisers for *Ms.* constituted a real and ongoing challenge. In its early years, the *Ms.* sales staff faced the formidable task of convincing advertisers that *Ms.* was a desirable space, quieting advertisers' doubts that feminists bought personal products or that women made financial decisions to buy "hard goods." In later years, after wearing down these original doubts, *Ms.* had to compete with a whole new array of magazines, like *New Woman* and *Working Mother*, that provided advertisers access to monied and professional female readers without the "undesirable" political edge. As a result, the *Ms.* business staff created a discourse of sales, one that sold feminism and the "*Ms.* woman" to potential advertisers. In sharp contrast to its editorial purpose, which was to create a magazine far different from those "cash cows" that Gloria Steinem so scornfully spoke of in the 1980s, *Ms.* had to sell itself as a marketing opportunity to advertisers. Feminism had to be packaged as a commodity, and the diversity of *Ms.* readers had to be recontained as a portrait of "desirable consumers." Significantly, the two strands of feminism that most clearly informed the *Ms.* editorial philosophy sometimes dovetailed and sometimes contradicted the imperative to be a commercial vehicle as well as a political resource. The emphasis on the "person," on individual change and growth, on the humanizing aspect of feminism, meshed nicely with the push to attract advertisers. But the language the *Ms.* ad staff had to create to describe *Ms.* readers worked directly against the editorial desire to speak to the diversity of women, the sisterhood of feminism.

Throughout the 1970s, the *Ms.* ad staff consistently worked to find advertisements that mirrored the feminist philosophy of the editorials and articles. In explaining their advertising policies, editors acknowledged that because "advertising words and images are such a pervasive influence on our expectations and those of our children" they would solicit ads that "reflect the real balance of our lives." As the editors wrote, "We don't spend half our money on makeup, for instance, and the other half on food, as traditional women's magazine would make it appear. We also buy cars, books, airline tickets, . . . liquor, gasoline, insurance, and the many products that aren't usually directed to women at all."[73] Clearly, this advertising policy reflected the editors' focus on full humanity and individual liberty as a primary goal of the women's movement. The products a woman bought, and was expected to buy, constituted to a large degree who she was and how she perceived herself and others perceived her. Indeed, *Ms.* magazine was the first major women's magazine to advertise big-ticket, traditionally "male" products like cars, insurance, and credit cards. Not only did these ads have the significant advantage of requiring no complementary copy, they also identified the *Ms.* reader as a "full" human being, not limited to the home, to children, or to relationships with men.[74]

Ads in *Ms.*'s early years frequently urged women "into the mainstream," an aspect of a feminist philosophy sociologists Ferree and Hess have identified as "career feminism."[75] Some of the most prominent ads in *Ms.* during the 1970s urged women to move "into the mainstream," as the National Organization for Women's original statement of purpose read. For instance, NOW's Legal Defense and Education Fund pictured a boardroom with nine white male executives. Under the picture the copy read: "What's wrong with this picture? Somebody forgot to include the women. . . . Half the talent and brainpower of our country is missing . . . an important half—women."[76] Large companies also began to speak to *Ms.* readers as potential executives and well-to-do consumers. American Express, one of the first national corporations to move into this new market, advertised a credit application "for women only." The copy explained, "No discrimination intended against men—the application is the same for both men and women. However 5 times as many men have the Card and we'd like to start evening things up."[77] Throughout the 1970s, other advertisers—for charge accounts, executive clothing, and business correspondence courses—picked up on this trend of portraying the women's movement in terms of economic advancement.

In the 1970s, *Ms.* instituted a regular ad section, entitled "Human Development," that featured corporations like ITT and Merrill Lynch who wanted to hire more women onto their executive staffs.

As early as 1974, the editors of *Ms.* solicited ads for traditionally feminine products, legitimating this decision on the basis that the "full range" of women's lives would be represented. The founders thought that they would be able to transform the way that advertisers presented these products to women, but they found that the bulk of advertisers were not willing to change any ad campaign solely for *Ms.* The result, as Barbara Phillips pointed out in her 1978 study, was that ads for personal products in *Ms.* generally resembled those in magazines like *Family Circle*. Ads for products like shampoo, perfume, and lingerie failed to challenge traditional, normative notions of femininity. While *Ms.* did include more ads directed at single and working women than *Family Circle* did, both magazines' ads promoted fairly obvious and powerful messages about what was normal and desirable in a woman. Clearly, a desirable woman was white, thin, and attractive, according to these ads. It was "normal" to shave body hair, paint nails, obsessively worry about weight, and choose to be with men rather than with women.[78]

Moreover, even when *Ms.* did change its policy about ads for traditional women's products, this did not immediately bring forth the desired response from advertisers. Not only did advertisers expect supporting, complementary (also complimentary) copy, they also doubted that feminists actually concerned themselves with personal appearance, children, or housekeeping. As a result, the most prevalent ads found in *Ms.* were for cigarettes and alcohol, two products that most companies would advertise without complementary copy and with slogans the editors perceived as relatively innocuous. The staff did reject certain ad campaigns they saw as most offensive, however. One of the most lucrative accounts they refused was the Virginia Slims "You've Come a Long Way, Baby" campaign, after failing to convince the company to change the slogan to "You'll Go a Long Way." According to publisher Patricia Carbine, the choice to refuse Virginia Slims ads cost them significantly.[79]

Ms.'s attempt to shape advertising content and the advertising industry broke both symbolic and literal boundaries. To gain advertising money without providing supplementary, supporting articles was to gain significant editorial freedom. To pull in ads for stereotypically "masculine" products was to represent visually a different image of women as consumers. At the same time, however, the ads themselves necessarily reinforced a perception of women, specifically the *Ms.* readers, as consumers. Many ads constructed feminism as a key to rising in the business and professional world, or presented consumer products as the solution for women's problems. The "new woman" to whom *Ms.* referred so frequently was a new type of consumer, more educated, more monied, and more enabled to make product choices. Designed to sell a product to a consumer, the ads by their very definition ignored other issues significant to feminism. Not only did the ads present a specific, commodified version of feminism, they also defined "ideal readers" for *Ms.* In advertising "masculine," big-ticket items, *Ms.* had to prove to those companies that the magazine attracted readers with enough money to buy those products.

The *Ms.* sales staff was under constant pressure to convince advertisers that *Ms.* provided a good marketing atmosphere. Indeed, the language that the sales staff created to encourage advertisers was far different from that the editors used to speak to readers. Even as the editors insisted that there was no "*Ms.* woman" but rather a "diversity" of readers across the nation, the sales staff had to convince advertisers that reaching *the* "*Ms.* woman" through their magazine was an excellent "marketing opportunity." Demographic statistics on what *Ms.* readers bought (from how many toilet bowl cleaners to how many transatlantic airline tickets) culled from the Simmons Research Market Bureau and Target Research Index provided the basis for *Ms.* promotional material. Most significantly, the sales staff had to create promotional circulars that deflected the political import of the magazine, emphasizing instead how the "difference" of *Ms.* provided advertisers with visibility and access to a monied and educated audience.

Even as *Ms.* editorials talked about "sisterhood," the promotional material *Ms.* circulated to advertisers presented a much more narrow conception of the *Ms.* reader. An ad for *Ms.* magazine appearing in the *New York Times* in 1974 described the *Ms.* reader as being part of a high-income household, likely to hold a managerial or professional job, and young, between the ages of eighteen and thirty-four. In 1975, *Ms.* put out a forty-two page booklet for advertisers, entitled "The *Ms.* Most." Taking its statistics from the 1974 Target Group Index, this early promotional material demonstrates the key ways that *Ms.* worked to convince advertisers to buy space in the magazine. *Ms.* compared itself in this material to six other women's magazines, all with much larger circulation (735,000–7,500,000 as compared to *Ms.*'s 400,000). These included *Redbook, McCall's, Ladies' Home Journal, Cosmopolitan, Glamour,* and *Mademoiselle. Ms.* also compared itself in this booklet to three general newsmagazines, explaining: "for comparisons that are in some ways even more significant, we've added *Time, Newsweek,* and *Psychol-*

ogy Today."[80] This dual comparison clearly indicates that *Ms.* was working to position itself in advertisers' eyes as a crossover newsmagazine/women's magazine, a strategy that apparently did not work well, since the comparison was dropped from later promotional material.

Ms. also worked to downplay its smaller circulation by emphasizing its "quality demographics." "The findings: In the places where it counts the most, *Ms.* is the most," the headlines read. The booklet went on to give a "profile of the *Ms.* woman." It read: "Among the women in magazine audiences cited here, the *Ms.* reader ranks first in youth (18–34), in household income, professional/managerial status, education, and full-time employment. She is married (68.6 percent) and has multiple bank accounts, stock certificates, and credit cards. Among the audiences covered, she is the most likely to live in the central city and the suburbs, and in A & B counties. In sum, she is young, affluent, well-schooled, well-positioned, and in the center of things—the emerging 'new woman' of the American marketplace."[81] Clearly, "new woman," as defined for advertisers, meant nothing about being antipatriarchal or a creator of new social formations; it was about moving into spheres where she could become a superior consumer.

In addition, *Ms.* emphasized that being a "new woman" meant that the reader had the responsibility and privilege within her family of being the "decision maker" regarding consumer purchases. Advertisers long considered women the primary consumers for goods like groceries and personal products, but advertisers for cars, high-priced appliances, and financial services thought their money wasted in women's magazines, since men were expected to make decisions about these commodities. The ad staff drew extensively from the TGI data on "decision makers" to demonstrate that these companies could profitably spend their money in *Ms.* The TGI defined "decision makers" as "any person in a household who is involved in the buying decision on a major household purchase, such as a car or large appliance. This concept is significant because it isolates the buying habits of only those people who are really responsible for making decisions." "In the liquor industry," the booklet read, "it is often believed that when there is a man-of-the-household, he alone makes the decision on what type or what brand of alcoholic beverage the household will buy. Not true in the case of *Ms.* The *Ms.* woman leads all women magazine readers in making those decisions for herself and for others in the household, and then in making the actual purchase." The ad staff also worked assiduously to convince advertisers that *Ms.* readers made more than the superficial choices connected with the purchase of big-ticket items (like the color scheme of a new car). Indeed, *Ms.* worked to educate advertisers about *all* female consumers, writing that "the TGI data . . . demonstrates just how great a percentage of women (both in *Ms.* and most of the other magazines used for comparison) do consider themselves 'Decision Makers' in the selection of cars for the household. . . . What we hope that this demonstrates to the automotive industry is that women are important in new car selection — and that they influence much more than just the color of the upholstery and the choice of accessories." Part of the strategy for landing accounts with the automotive industry was this evidence that women made the decisions; part of it was also proving that the readers had enough money to buy the cars. The *Ms.* promotional material stressed the fact that readers generally were married, which indicated access to a male income and need to buy goods for a household, and had high household incomes. They also underscored the high personal income of the readers, and, importantly, that readers have "earned their own credit," with "71.9% having their own credit card."[82]

Ms. magazine was always notorious among advertisers for being a "cause" rather than a "marketing opportunity," attracting anticonsumer readers, politicos, and complainers. From its origins, *Ms.*'s promotional material attempted to turn this "activism" into a portrait of the involved citizen, a reader concerned about her world, participating in "schools, local government, charity, and politics," one who translates this work into "thoughtful" readership. Readers "spend an average of 2/6 days reading each issue of *Ms.*, which is more time than readers spend with other women's magazines (some of which are twice our size)."[83] On the one hand *Ms.* worked to take the genre of the women's magazine and transform it into a text relevant for feminist activism, while on the other, in the case of advertising, they did just the opposite, working to make feminist activism appear to just another kind of "concerned" activity in which monied consumers took part.

In spite of their efforts, by the mid-1970s, the founders' initial enthusiasm for the potential of advertising accounts to fund the movement in the form of the magazine fell drastically. But despite this change of heart, Steinem, Carbine, and others decided to move ahead with the decision to begin a foundation for women.

The Ms. Foundation for Women

Gloria Steinem and her cofounders had begun *Ms.* with the vision that profits made from the magazine would be returned to the movement through a foundation for women. They knew that such an organization was sorely needed; a study reported in *The Grantmanship Center News* found that from 1972 to 1974 less than one-fifth of 1 percent of foundation-giving was "designed to improve the status of women." Breaking even after only one year of publication, the magazine founders were optimistic that their magazine would soon make profits sufficient to launch a foundation. In the *First Ms. Reader*, editors wrote that they hoped to "give a healthy percentage of our profits back to the Women's Movement; to programs and projects that can help change women's lives."[84]

In late 1972, the founders decided to incorporate the new Ms. Foundation for Women, despite the lack of profits forthcoming from the magazine. Primarily this decision stemmed from the publication of Marlo Thomas's recording *Free to Be . . . You and Me* in 1972. Thomas worked with *Ms.* to put together an original collection of nonsexist children's songs and stories performed by well-known figures like Alan Alda, Carol Channing, and herself. In anticipation of the funding received from *Ms.*'s first recording and children's endeavor (portions of the royalties from *Free to Be* were to be donated to the women's movement), *Ms.* incorporated the new foundation. Four women signed on as the board members: editor Gloria Steinem and publisher Pat Carbine, Marlo Thomas, and editor Letty Cottin Pogrebin, who was beginning to specialize in children and family issues. Throughout 1973, the foundation did not publicize itself, as profits from the magazine were not forthcoming and the royalties from *Free to Be* had not yet materialized. Despite the lack of explicit publicity, however (other than the promises in the "Personal Reports" and the various interviews with *Ms.* staff), women's organizations began writing to *Ms.* for funding, often beginning their inquiry with a "plea for help." In responding to one of these requests, JoAnne Edgar wrote, "The Foundation was set up to distribute profits from the magazine to various projects within the Women's Movement which would otherwise have trouble getting money. However, the magazine itself has no profits to distribute — yet. We are just beginning to break even and it will be some time before profits actually start building up. . . . Hopefully, for all of us, that won't be too long, but at this point we can't really tell."[85]

Although Edgar and the entire *Ms.* staff were optimistic about *Ms.*'s profit-making potential, the magazine failed to ever make the money needed to support the foundation. Reflecting on those early days, Steinem wrote that in the beginning they were "still naive enough to believe that serious magazines made enough profits to give away."[86] This is not to say, however, that the magazine failed to support the foundation in any way; most obviously, it provided the name recognition of a feminist institution, particularly as most people did not distinguish between the magazine and the foundation. More specifically, the magazine in its early days did provide in-kind support to the foundation: office space, some staffing, postage, and xeroxing. By the middle of the decade, however, it became clear that the foundation would be on its own to raise funds.

In 1974 and 1975, the *Free to Be* project generated sufficient royalties to infuse the foundation with the cash needed to hire the first executive director, Brenda Brimmer, and associate director, Rochelle Korman, who later became the legal counsel for the foundation, and to begin giving out grant money.[87] Minutes from the early board meetings reveal the board members' optimism that the magazine would eventually make money and that the board's purpose was activist, not fund-raising, in nature. The function of the board, the minutes read, is "basically to give out money put into the foundation from profits of *Ms.* magazine. The money should be aimed at the most radical, but still sensible, projects—high risk projects that the regular foundations would never think of funding." Early documents also indicate the founders' original conception of the purpose of the foundation: "to support generally the Women's Movement; to improve the status, skills and condition and the rights of women, . . . including support by the way of grants . . . to female artists, authors, photographers, and business women of any nature; . . . to support studies; . . . to grant scholarships and fellowships to women; to generally encourage the development of women's talents and increase the opportunities open for the use of their talents in the arts, business, education, and government."[88] Significantly, the focus in this description was on helping women to advance in various fields, with less attention paid to the inherent question of whether their work was feminist in nature. Part of the women's movement agenda was, of course, to propel more women into writing, the arts, and business. This goal stemmed partly from the belief that women deserved opportunities in all these fields and partly from the commonly held opinion that women would necessarily bring a perspective different from men's into their respective fields. In its earliest stages, the founders imagined a foundation similar to the magazine, one focused on getting women into the "pipelines" of various fields, and one focusing on the arts and research.

By the time the foundation advertised itself as available to potential grantees, however, the original priority on the arts, educational research, and moving women into nontraditional fields had shifted dramatically. In setting the foundation policy, board members chose to focus on "survival issues," or, "action projects that provide services and/or education to women and children and which are involved in organizing women to work on their own behalf." Significantly, these "action projects," besides excluding arts and research projects, also emphasized the empowerment of women and prioritized those projects that worked to connect women across class, race, and age barriers. In explaining their focus on "survival issues," a term the foundation commonly used to describe its funding priorities, Brimmer explained that "maybe later on, when we have a nice endowment and a lot more money to spend, we will be able to put our money into the arts and into research, but right now we have to put it into such areas as health care, and battered women and employment projects."[89] The foundation appropriated the magazine's philosophical emphasis on self-help and sisterhood but defined these terms in somewhat different ways. That is, self-help meant those empowerment projects that focused on groups of women, not individual women. Sisterhood meant projects that would help to connect women across race, class, and age lines, not the inherent similarity of all women. The foundation gave out small grants, usually no larger than $10,000, to grassroots projects that would have difficulty finding funding elsewhere. The board gave priority to those projects that stressed "activist, public advocacy strategies," ones that could be modeled elsewhere in the country. These were one-time-only grants, usually seed money, given with the expectation that the project would find funding elsewhere after the grant ended. Publicity materials explained that the foundation wanted to "support changes in women's lives that are as practical, immediate and inclusive as possible." Specific examples of the kinds of projects funded in the 1970s include the Brooklyn Legal Services Corporation, for printing and distributing copies of "A Handbook for Beaten Women"; The Youth Project, which supported women migrant farm workers in Ohio and Indiana; and the Coalition for the Medical Rights of Women in San Francisco.[90]

Besides providing funding for grassroots activism, the foundation quickly became established as a clearinghouse of sorts for women's projects across the country. Providing technical assistance and linking relevant groups were only two aspects of how the foundation worked as more than a grant-giving institution. When the foundation rejected projects that were outside its focus on "survival issues" (i.e., proposals that focused on the arts or media; conferences and higher education; research; requests to support individuals' work), the foundation always sent information on soliciting funds elsewhere.[91] Frequently this included the Women's Action Alliance booklet "Getting Your Share," which was supported by a *Ms.* grant. Interestingly, much of the advice the staff and board members gave to potential grantees resembled the masking strategy used by the magazine in soliciting advertising: Focus on the least controversial aspect of the grant, emphasizing the "health" in women's health projects, for instance, rather than the feminist perspective. As Marjorie Fine Knowles, a Ms. Foundation board member wrote, "While it may be valid to view the grant-seeking process as an educational one for foundation executives as well as the applicant, it may be counterproductive if the goal is to get the money."[92] Even as the foundation and the magazine moved in different directions, they faced similar issues of political positioning and negotiating among competing demands.

Building an Organization

The philosophies of liberal and cultural feminism extended beyond the pages of the magazine to influence as well the way the magazine was run in the 1970s. On the one hand, Ms. emphasized the importance of staking out a position for women within the mainstream Madison Avenue publishing industry; on the other hand, Ms. wanted to run the magazine in a fashion informed by the egalitarianism and collective spirit of the new women's movement and, by extension, to transform the entire advertising and publishing industry. As Chapter 1 explained, ideals of collectivity informed the editorial side of the magazine more than the business side of the magazine. As the magazine moved into the 1970s, those ideals of collectivity and of individual advancement were both carried out and sorely tested.

From its origins, Ms. was primarily a white organization, speaking to and emerging from the white women's movement. Sisterhood was a predominant theme in the founders' vision of the magazine, but its limitations were clear once one began dealing with the real diversity of the magazine's staff. Correspondence between Margaret Sloan and the Ms. staff in the early 1970s, for instance, highlights some of the strain she felt as a black woman working for Ms. One of Sloan's responsibilities was to write up "news highlights" for Warner Communication's internal newsletter. When Carbine found that Sloan had missed a deadline, she wrote Sloan a terse memo: "Margaret, When I consider how little I've asked you to do for Ms., I find it maddening to have to read this. What happened???" Sloan took the opportunity to respond to the entire Ms. staff about the tensions she was feeling in the office.

I am having a lot of trouble finishing my article on black feminism. since this is a collective, i write to you all. my life feels that it must be written. white women make me feel guilty for not coming along sooner. page 5 my mother calls me to tell me how they are going to take her job away from her. . . . she filed a complaint against them 3 years ago because of their racism and they watch her like a hawk. told her to stop falling down on the job. . . . if anyone talks to me about all the money i make from speaking ill break their ass. movement lawyers ask for 500. gloria says they are struggling. they have an east side office with outdoor carpeting so your feet can feel good before going inside. i want to struggle like that. my child goes to a great, good expensive school i will turn tricks to keep her in if i must— come into the office and there is a note on my desk from pat asking why didnt i send that "ms news to warner" considering how little i ask you to do for ms i just dont understand, this is not a cry but a statement of where i am right now. the article wont be ready because i am not ready. you may be dealing with an irresponsible black woman but i want that right too i suppose. even if it does hurt us in the south.[93]

Sloan's passionate memo revealed significant frustration with the expectations that she live up to a certain standard of feminism, despair over the poverty and racism her mother was facing, and resentment toward well-to-do liberals. Mostly, her memo expressed a refusal to be pushed around and an overall sense of anger at her coworkers' inability to understand her life and the demands placed upon her as an African American woman. Sloan left *Ms.* by 1975.

The founders of *Ms.* wanted to create a more egalitarian process within a larger publishing industry that required clear lines of responsibility and accountability. The editors negotiated this tension by designating individual staff members to different areas, such as editing, research, and design, otherwise maintaining an alphabetical listing on all mastheads. Because everyone had their specific duties, the running of *Ms.* was much less chaotic than the outside world perceived, managing editor Suzanne Levine argues. But since the goal was to allow everyone access to decision making, the organization was much more dynamic and loose than many editors had previously experienced. The lack of titles, Levine explained, allowed the staff more fluidity in their jobs, but it also created a situation where the chain of command was often unclear. Editor Mary Thom explained that this posed a significant problem for training newcomers, who often did not know who to go to for help or for final "okays." Letty Cottin Pogrebin suggested that the antihierarchical goals were admirable, but they had to be tailored to reality, to ensure that qualified staff had responsibility for editing.[94]

Mary Peacock also suggested that the collective process of editing, in which any one writer might receive comments from and have to please a host of editors, made some writers furious. Jo Freeman, in particular, recalls that her articles were overedited and one was even lost among the piles on an editor's desk. Yet some of the editors suggest that "collective editing" never existed. According to both Edgar and Pogrebin, one editor would be in charge of an article, it would be circulated among other editors, and then returned to the first editor, who would combine the comments. My own examination of the editorial files indicates that most articles had on the first page the initials of three to five editors, among whom the article was apparently circulated. It was not clear whether the writer received the copy with the multiple comments or one that had been "cleaned up" by a primary editor. Edgar argued that *Ms.* was forced to do more editing than other magazines, for it published a range of writers instead of maintaining a "stable of writers" as many other publications did. (Indeed, the magazine published 530 writers in its first years.) She also suggested that many writers were sensitive to criticism of their *Ms.* articles because they were "writing from their heart." [95]

Because of both the small budget and the desire for an antihierarchical workplace, *Ms.* never hired a secretarial staff to help with the editorial work. Rather, *Ms.* hired high school and college interns. Those secretaries who did work at *Ms.* found other staff members felt uncomfortable about their pink-collar jobs. A letter from Gloria Steinem's secretary to the *Ms.* staff, written in the early 1970s, called for an end to the silence that surrounded her work. "There seems to be much embarrassment and confusion about what to call the work I do in this office—just where do I fit in? How to describe my 'department'? When staff people bring visitors around to show them the offices, I notice they come up the stairs explaining, 'This part is advertising, and this is circulation, and this is the business office, and . . . tell them what you do, Jolly.' I do secretarial work. In this case, I answer letters addressed to Gloria, either on my own or dictated by Gloria." With humor, Jolly Robinson asked the staff to acknowledge her work and its worth, writing, "Secretary is not a dirty word." [96]

Indeed, this issue of recognizing the hierarchy that did exist within the organization came up frequently in interviews with former staff members. Editors Harriet Lyons's and Mary Peacock's views of the collective process echoed those of Jo Freeman, who in "The Tyranny of Structurelessness" pointed to the way a collective-type organization could create its own, unacknowledged, power structures. "The idea [of structurelessness] becomes a smokescreen for the strong or the lucky to establish unquestioned hegemony over others. This hegemony can be so easily established because the idea of 'structurelessness' does not prevent the formation of informal structures, only formal ones. This structurelessness becomes a way of masking power, and within the Women's Movement is usually most strongly advocated by those who are the most powerful."[97] Interestingly, *Ms.* reprinted Freeman's article in the 1973 "Forum" section, but with no specific reference to the *Ms.* organization. However, interviews with the former editors, suggest that Freeman's warnings were indeed applicable to the *Ms.* organization. Lyons referred to the way those with the strongest personalities could run the organization: "Without a defined structure," she explained, "it becomes the power of personality. We often thought that those who could stay the latest would have the most to say." Mary Peacock was even less sanguine in her assessment of the collective process, remarking that "those with experience ruled." She recalled an instance where one of the less-experienced staff members complained that if it truly was a collective, her suggestions should not go unheeded while the more established staff's comments always merited consideration.[98]

Former editor Mary Peacock argued that by the second half of the 1970s a definite split between "women's movement people" and "women's magazine people" had emerged. Identifying herself as a "women's magazine" person, Peacock said she wanted *Ms.* to be the best popular women's magazine on the newsstand, "not an academic journal in a plain brown wrapper." Leaving in 1977, Peacock pointed to what she saw as too much political policing, too much emphasis on deciding someone's feminist credentials, and too much stress placed on presenting women in a positive light. Lyons, in addition to wanting *Ms.* to pay her more money, became tired of the collective process and wanted her name on the masthead as assistant managing editor. Others, however, like contributing editor Ellen Willis, felt *Ms.* too closely identified with the mainstream women's magazine industry, not with the women's movement.[99]

For others, the ideal of sisterhood fell short when it came to issues of money. Summing up her decision to leave *Ms.* for the *Daily News* in 1980, editor Harriet Lyons explained that "you worked at *Ms.* for love, and after a while, love didn't pay the bills." For Lyons, the economic budget-cutting that took place after the move to nonprofit status made it impossible for her to stay at *Ms.*: "I wasn't making ends meet. I was sole support of what was becoming a teenage daughter. Everyone was tightening their belt, taking vows of poverty. I didn't have other sources of income as some of my colleagues did — either by being married, or being productive through book contracts." Arguing that *Ms.* "didn't do enough to marshall its own resources to take care of its own," Lyons said she left *Ms.* a bitter woman, with two weeks severance pay to show for her eight years of work.[100]

Indeed, *Ms.* paid writers and editors far less than they would have received at other women's magazines. The standard fee for a full-length article in the late 1970s ranged from $500 to $750 at *Ms.*; magazines like *Good Housekeeping*, *Ladies' Home Journal*, *Family Circle*, and *McCall's* paid $2,000–$2,500 for the same length article. As a result, many good new writers, after establishing themselves at *Ms.*, moved on to other magazines; this was particularly true after the more mainstream women's magazines began to accept more articles written from a feminist perspective. For those editors and writers who had previously worked for radical periodicals, the money that *Ms.* offered seem relatively good. Jo Freeman, for instance, remembers that she felt she was being paid "quite well" for her articles. *Ms.* was never able to pay editors as much as they could make at other women's magazines, either. In 1978, for instance, the average editorial salary at *Ms.* was $17,166; at other women's magazines the comparable position earned $25,000.[101] Throughout the *Ms.* editorial files there are notices that the magazine would not be able to offer pay increases but would discuss loans with individual staff members.[102] This meant that those who had inherited money, were married, or who published independently of *Ms.* were more likely to be able to stay with *Ms.* Others felt they needed to try to make more money elsewhere.

Many of the editors, however, considered *Ms.* to be an ideal workplace, one where they could combine their journalistic skills with their commitment to the women's movement. Letty Cottin Pogrebin and JoAnne Edgar stayed at the magazine until 1989; Suzanne Levine also stayed at the magazine for nearly two decades, leaving in 1988. Mary Thom stayed with *Ms.* even when it was sold to Lang. Contributing editors like Marcia Gillespie and Lindsy Van Gelder continued their relationship with *Ms.* for an equally long time. (Gillespie is now the editor of the new, noncommercial *Ms.*) Even Peacock, who clearly perceived the organizational goals as utopian and unrealistic, stressed that others on the staff felt the "social experiment" was equally significant to the final product, even if the process in action worked less well than originally anticipated. While the attempts at collectivity could mask the real "bosses" and complicate the editorial process, they could also allow for more fluidity, more shared responsibility, and more input from the entire staff. Women writers and editors learned skills and gained positions of responsibility, volunteers could provide the ideas for a new cover story, and no one was allowed to hide behind positions of prestige or power.

JoAnne Edgar explained that there was much more "loyalty to *Ms.* than editors usually show to other magazines." If anything, she said, editors "stayed longer than we should have," because they found their work and their colleagues "stimulating and interesting." [103]

The sales and business staff experienced more turnover than the editorial staff. The sales staff had an extremely difficult job at *Ms.*, one that the editors recognized and respected. Suzanne Levine remembers sales people returning to the office "battered down"; JoAnne Edgar even recalls one instance when a sales person was literally spit on when making her presentation. Throughout the history of *Ms.*, the sales staff was paid considerably more than the editorial staff; initially all the founders agreed to this, since the sales staff needed expense budgets and a more professional wardrobe than the editorial staff. At least one editor felt, in retrospect, that *Ms.* always paid the sales staff too much, the editorial staff too little; or, after some thought, she suggested that *Ms.* should have paid everyone more. [104]

Although the sales staff earned more than the editorial staff, it still was not enough to keep them at *Ms.* For Carbine, hiring a female business and ad staff was an excellent way to get women into what she termed the "pipeline" that led to the role of publisher. She explained that it was "part of the game plan, for *Ms.* to serve as a launching pad . . . [so the sales reps could] take on roles on leadership in publishing." As a result, however, there was a constant turnover of sales staff, as other, larger, publishing corporations hired away *Ms.* employees. Other organizations knew that if a sales person could bring in advertising for *Ms.*, they could do a fine job anywhere. Carbine explained that if *Ms.* had more money to offer raises, if they had been larger and able to allow for more responsibility, they may have been able to retain the sales staff. Instead, employees like Kathi Doolan and Cathleen Black moved to lucrative and more powerful positions at the *New York Post*, *USA Today*, and *Connoisseur*, leaving Carbine to the continual training of a sales staff. [105]

In her essay on feminist media, Marilyn Crafton Smith points out that many radical feminist publishers feared that their writers would use the feminist publications as stepping stones to mainstream publishers, so much so that they included clauses in writer's contracts that forbade them from republishing their work with nonfeminist publishers. [106] Publisher Patricia Carbine thought about this issue completely differently, encouraging her staff to use *Ms.* as a vehicle through which to move "into the mainstream." While this was part of Carbine's plan, for *Ms.* to act as a sort of "training ground" for the publishing industry at large, the constant turnover made *Ms.* more difficult to run and symbolically made *Ms.* seem to be the "kid sister" of "real" publications. But at the same time, Carbine—and *Ms.* magazine—helped to change dramatically the gendered face of the publishing world. Popular feminism was helping to create a new kind of workforce for the publishing industry.

For *Ms.* magazine, the 1970s were characterized by a number of internal struggles as the founders and staff worked to articulate a popular, diverse feminism, to respond to the demands of advertisers, to begin a foundation, and to negotiate the realities of running a feminist business. The 1980s, as we shall see in the next chapter, were characterized more by struggles with external forces, as *Ms.* labored to adapt to and survive within a changing political and economic climate. The challenges to creating a popular feminism in the 1980s proved extreme.

CHAPTER 3

This Side of Combat Boots

Ms. in the 1980s

I n 1981, Lindsy Văn Gelder, a participant in the *Ladies' Home Journal* 1970 sit-down strike and a regular writer for *Ms.*, submitted a piece on traveling to Europe with another woman.[1] Her piece recounted the various forms of offensive behavior that they had received from their male hosts, from pinching to lewd stares and unwelcome advances. Bitingly and sarcastically, Van Gelder told readers how the strategies she had learned to fend off New York harassers were sorely limited by her high school French. Van Gelder ended her essay with the kicker, "As for me, I've decided not to let my misadventures abroad stifle my thirst for international culture. I've signed up for *jujitsu*."

Van Gelder's article generated a lively set of responses from the editors, most of whom objected to the tone, a sense of rage they argued was out-of-date and reminiscent of early 1970s activism. They asked her to cut many of her most explicit remarks, explaining that "it's very important that tone stay on this side of combat boots." After much correspondence, Van Gelder's article was finally accepted, with many of the most "angry" comments deleted and the first ending eliminated.[2]

As this "combat boots" anecdote indicates, *Ms.* editors were very sensitive to the tone and image the magazine presented to the world. *Ms.* sought to be a moderating voice, one that translated feminism to a mass audience and brought a mass audience to the feminist movement. *Ms.* pushed at the boundaries of "respectability" and "normality" that the mainstream women's magazines upheld, but it also hesitated to push too far outside those borders, fearing it would lose its mass appeal. This was particularly true as *Ms.* entered the more conservative 1980s. Working in a climate hostile to feminism and confronting serious economic problems, the editors found they had to walk an increasingly narrower tightrope, answering to the demands of advertisers less willing to see *Ms.* as an opportune marketing outlet and the expectations of readers who continued to want to see *Ms.* as their feminist resource.

The 1980s

By the late 1970s and into the 1980s, feminist activists had to exert increasing effort simply to maintain what they had won earlier in the decade. The threats facing the women's movement caused many feminists to reassess the confidence they had felt in the early 1970s. By the late 1970s, *Ms.* editor Harriet Lyons said she felt like they had "hit a wall"; the great wave of feminism had been threatened, if not replaced, by the rising tide of conservatism.[3] The loss of enthusiasm stemmed not only from direct threats to feminism but also from the increasing invisibility of the movement, as activists moved into existing organizations like schools, corporations, churches, and the military to enact changes. Political scientist Mary Fainsod Katzenstein refers to this transformation of the women's movement from outward agitation and street politics to a more internal dynamic as the "unobtrusive mobilization of the 1980s." By no means did the feminist movement die in the 1980s, but it changed shape, and importantly, lost its prominence in the mainstream mass media, causing many to perceive the decade as "post-feminist." At the same time, however, women activists continued to make inroads on a patriarchal, economic system that oppressed them; a primary example of this relatively invisible activism was the battle to adopt comparable worth legislation.[4]

Activists' loss of confidence, expressed most aptly by Lyons's statement that they had "hit a wall," did not result only from the invisibility of the movement, however. Women faced specific political and economic threats, causing many to rethink their initial belief in the inevitable progress of the movement. Significantly, the same issues around women's personal lives that had been politicized by the women's movement—the family, child raising, reproductive rights—were taken up by a conservative constituency, who vehemently opposed both the Equal Rights Amendment and abortion. By the late 1970s, even optimistic feminists became convinced that the ERA would not pass by its initial deadline, although the 1978 rally to extend the deadline brought renewed energy to the movement. By 1982, the constitutional amendment that had begun in the early 1970s with bipartisan political support and widespread public backing had been defeated by an extremely well organized, vocal, and politically savvy minority of conservative groups.[5]

The 1970s and 1980s saw the slow erosion of abortion rights as well, beginning with the Hyde Amendment in 1976. Prohibiting the use of public funds to pay for abortions, the Hyde Amendment in practice eliminated poor women's reproductive choices, making abortion an option available only to women economically able to afford one. Throughout the 1980s, groups like the National Right to Life Committee (NLRC), which had over 11 million members by 1980, staged rallies, picketed abortion clinics, and, through extremely well-organized economic and political campaigns, forced out of office prochoice politicians.[6] They targeted corporations as well, threatening extensive boycotts if companies dared to either advertise in periodicals or on television shows presenting a prochoice perspective, or donate to groups like Planned Parenthood. Their political and economic strength overshadowed the fact that throughout the 1980s a majority of Americans continued to support a woman's right to choose, particularly in the case of rape or incest.[7]

Historians and social critics have dubbed the culture and politics of the 1980s as Reaganism, the era of an extreme conservative backlash to the progressive advances won in the 1960s and 1970s. The growth of conservative think tanks, the well-funded institutions that lobbied the government and instituted public campaigns to discredit and to eliminate these progressive gains, fueled the momentum of the backlash. What was particularly troublesome about these campaigns was the way the mass media generally jumped on the conservative bandwagon, without investigating the charges fully.[8] Groups with parallel causes to those of *Ms.* found themselves increasingly under attack. Karen Nussbaum, the executive director of Working Women: The National Association of Office Workers (no relation to the magazine), for instance, wrote to *Ms.* in 1981 to warn them of the Heritage Foundation's critique of the National Endowment for the Humanities (NEH) for funding "political projects" such as Working Women's curricular endeavors. The *New York Times* supported the Heritage Foundation's attack, arguing that the NEH should stop funding "artistic circuses" and refocus on "humanistic endeavors." While Working Women's funding did not suffer that year, Nussbaum accurately forecast the problems facing progressive causes when she wrote, "They are creating a climate that makes it far less likely that organizations like Working Women will receive government funding in the future."[9]

The 1980s brought economic threats to U.S. women as well. While more women worked outside the home for wages in the 1970s and 1980s, the rate of poverty among women also increased, a phenomenon that became known as the "feminization of poverty." This stemmed in part from liberalized, "no-fault" divorce laws, which allowed women greater freedom to leave abusive or unhappy marriages but also plunged more women and children into poverty, as the new laws required less financial support from ex-husbands. Becoming a single, female, head of household nearly guaranteed poverty. Not only did child care responsibilities prevent women from gaining stable and lucrative employment, but the structure of the economy segregated women into low-paying, "no-future" jobs. An economic study completed in Los Angeles County revealed that one year after divorce "women's 'economic well-being' (income minus expenses) dropped 73%, while that of men gained by 42%." This differential did not improve significantly unless the woman remarried and regained access to a male income.[10] In addition, the recession in 1982–83 and President Reagan's fiscal policies encouraging de-industrialization eliminated whole tiers of better-paying jobs that may have been opened to women by the late 1970s. Above all, the slashing of social services and welfare programs like Aid to Families with Dependent Children and Women, Infants, Children forced thousands of women and their children into destitution.[11]

Exhibiting her characteristic optimism and energy, Steinem refused to be beaten down by the conservative climate of the 1980s. In a 1987 interview in the *Boston Herald*, Steinem was quoted as saying, "I think actually that Reagan helped us speed it [the liberation movement's momentum] up. I'm not saying it was worth the price, but I think his presence made it clear that this was not going to happen by itself. That we're going to have to work hard."[12] The transformations that *Ms.* magazine had to undergo in this decade, however, belied the optimism that Steinem expressed at the end of the decade. While the founders of *Ms.* had created the magazine during the crest of the movement, they had to maintain it through a period much less conducive to the goals of the women's movement. During the late 1970s and into the 1980s, problems with advertisers, increasing postal and printing costs, a conservative climate, and the complexities and contradictions inherent in the movement itself placed *Ms.* in an increasingly embattled position.

Gloria Steinem and her cofounders had begun *Ms.* with the vision that profits made from the magazine would be returned to the movement through the Ms. Foundation for Women. In the early years of the magazine, this had seemed possible; in 1974, for instance, the magazine had actually posted a profit, and the spin-offs from *Ms.*—like the Wonder Woman book and the *Free to Be* series—had been immensely successful. By the latter half of the 1970s, however, the conflicting demands of a feminist resource and a business enterprise made it clear that *Ms.* could not be both successfully. In a 1979 editorial, Steinem recalled their early vision with some cynicism. The

Ms. Foundation for Women, she wrote, was "given seed money from *Ms.* Magazine and its staff members, partly to create a way of giving eventual publishing profits back to the Women's Movement. . . . That was in 1972 when the magazine began, and we were still naive enough to believe that serious magazines [in contrast to light-hearted, traditional women's magazines] made enough profits to give away."[13] By the late 1970s, it became clear that not only would the magazine never realize profits but it also faced serious financial difficulties that threatened its very survival. The July 1978 "Personal Report from *Ms.*," entitled "Reader Alert!," gave readers a sense of the financial and social predicament *Ms.* faced. Focusing on the good news of increased readership and low yearly subscription costs, the editorial then emphasized the rising postage and production costs as well as increased censorship that threatened to put *Ms.* out of business. The editorial stressed the magazine's "unique connection with its readers," whom it asked to help out by fighting censorship and buying subscriptions. The reader activity that this report encouraged, however, was far from enough to compensate for the serious financial difficulties *Ms.* faced in the late 1970s. Production and postage costs had increased dramatically in the years since the magazine began publication, by 123.5 percent and 400 percent respectively.[14] And, while the 1978 report thanked advertisers for their support, as a women's magazine that refused to provide complementary copy, *Ms.* never pulled in the numbers of advertising dollars to make a profit. According to a study commissioned by the magazine, by 1979 the magazine was losing money at the rate of $500,000 a year. There had been a particularly dismal loss of $978,000 in 1978.[15] Clearly, as it would many feminist institutions and organizations in the 1980s, the new decade would challenge the very survival of *Ms.*

Charting the Future of *Ms.*

As a crossover magazine, a periodical that attempted to carve out a feminist space within a patriarchal, capitalist context, *Ms.* necessarily was a contradictory text that evoked equally contradictory responses. As *Ms.* moved into the 1980s, that mixture of responses continued. A *Christian Science Monitor* article on the tenth anniversary of *Ms.* described the wide range of responses this institution had come to evoke. It reported that while some still referred to the magazine as the "torchbearer" of the women's movement, others perceived it as a magazine that had lost its radical edge, transformed into a magazine representing commercial feminism. Martha Thurber, the editor of Boston's feminist periodical *Sojourner*, commented that "the fact that [*Ms.*] was established at all was very important at the time, but it has come to represent middle-of-the-road feminism." Others saw it as the last vestige of an old-fashioned movement. Claire Gruppo, the managing editor of *Savvy*, a magazine for "executive women," remarked, "We don't feel we have to fight the battles women were fighting 10 years ago, that *Ms.* thinks we're still fighting."[16]

Clearly, Gruppo's remark about the necessity of *Ms.* ignored the economic and political realities facing women in the 1980s. Her belief in the outdated nature of the women's movement, however, spoke to the new conservative era beginning in the late 1970s and 1980s, when the rhetoric dominating national political campaigns emphasized "feeling good" about America and believing that all one needed to improve one's lot in life was a bit of optimism and a lot of energy. Ironically, Gruppo spoke from a position that the women's movement, and *Ms.* in particular, had helped to create—the growing genre of magazines for the "new woman," including *Savvy*, *Working Woman*, and *Working Mother*. But while these magazines emerged in a space created by the women's movement, they also created a different version of the backlash facing women, for they helped to construct the growing mystique of the superwoman, the woman who could excel as wife, mother, and executive simultaneously, with a little help from consumer goods. In addition, these magazines ignored any connections between women's lives and the oppression created by racism, poverty, and ageism, refusing the responsibility of sisterhood that *Ms.* promised to fulfill. As soon as these new career-woman magazines emerged on the market, *Ms.* worked to distinguish itself from them. Steinem, for instance, commented, "They're doing superwoman, saying, 'Yes, you can be a lawyer or an engineer, *and* provide three perfect children, a perfect marriage, and gourmet meals.' It makes you tired to read it."[17]

The *Sojourner* editor's remark about *Ms.*, however, suggested that—in the eyes of many critics—*Ms.* had already become a *Savvy*-type periodical by the late 1970s. Numerous readers and feminist critics shared Thurber's disenchantment, arguing that while initially pathbreaking, the magazine had become dull, mainstream, and commercial. Of course, this perception ignored the fact that *Ms.*, from its origins, had been firmly enmeshed in a commercial context as a self-help, women's mass media periodical. Moreover, Thurber's changed impressions of *Ms.* probably spoke more to the novelty of this feminist periodical when it first appeared on news stands in 1972; by 1981 *Ms.* appeared commonplace.

While *Ms.* had begun as a revolutionary new forum in 1972, by the 1980s it was perceived as an institution within the feminist movement. Less visible to the public eye, however, was the fact that it was under constant pressure simply to survive. In 1978, *Ms.* commissioned Patricof Associates, Inc., a consulting firm, to assess its current and future financial viability as it approached funding sources for substantial loans. Patricof based its study on interpretations of comparisons with the Magazine Publishers' Association (MPA) figures and a survey of about five former readers of *Ms.*[18] The Patricof Report raised a number of fascinating points. Above all, it highlighted the different understandings of what a magazine should be and how it should function. According to the consultants, *Ms.* came along at an opportune moment, cashing in on a new social phenomenon, feminism. The cultural milieu had changed, they argued, the fad of feminism was over, and now *Ms.* should transform itself to fit into the new marketing scene. Certainly, the late 1970s did differ culturally and economically from the early 1970s. The purpose of *Ms.*, however, had never been to act as a simple reflection of culture, but to change that culture. Feminism was more than a passing fad, editors argued, but a transformative perspective that would entail significant battles.

Those who conducted the study certainly understood the magazine's history as a feminist magazine. "*Ms.* came along at the right moment in history. It gave a voice to the women's movement. It touched subjects that other women's magazines wouldn't dare. It challenged the advertising community and forced them to treat women as serious consumers of products that were traditionally sold to a male audience," the report read.[19] However, the consultants primarily understood that history in terms of marketability, not political significance. Indeed, the report is very revealing of the way the magazine industry viewed *Ms.*; it concurred with Claire Gruppo, the editor of *Savvy*, that the magazine had become passé, a harbinger of radical ideas that should be relegated to the past. *Ms.*, they concluded, had not kept up with the times:

> The title "MS." seems synonymous for the aggressive, tough, political, liberated woman. Unfair as that may be, the magazine is generally perceived in that manner — by potential readers and advertisers alike. Unfortunately for Ms., there has been a distinct change in the attitudes of many women (or for that matter, the nation as a whole) since the early 70's. They are no longer as "issue" oriented as they were. They've achieved success, and now want to enjoy it. Thus, many women have abandoned or are reluctant to start reading Ms. It's not as relevant as it once was. Likewise, advertisers of traditional women's products believe the editorial atmosphere of Ms. is not conducive to selling their products. While these stereotypes are wrong, it will be up to Ms. to change the attitudes of potential readers and

advertisers, a difficult and long-term repositioning problem. Ms. retained as readers the active women's rights advocates. But it has been difficult to attract, and subsequently hold, the more moderate women, who want to hear about politics and women's rights, but also about beauty care, raising a family, personal finance, and careers.

Referring to readers who had quit subscribing to Ms., the report concluded, "It no longer filled a need for these people. They outgrew it."[20]

The Patricof Report challenged the increased readership figures Ms. provided to advertisers, arguing that much of the increase from 400 to 500 thousand was "forced" rather than "voluntary"; readers had been "bought" through subscription services, such as Publishers' Clearinghouse. They pointed to decreased newsstand sales and the increased competition from other women's magazines to support their argument. "It appears that once the 'women's movement' picked up steam, the other women's magazines started to editorialize and develop articles on subjects that were strictly Ms.'s domain. Thus, if a woman wanted to read a story on politics, she no longer was restricted to just Ms. She could read Cosmopolitan and pick up, along with the political article, another piece of advice on skin or health care, etc. In short, other women's publications, and sometimes even men's, started to steal much of Ms.'s editorial 'thunder.'" Not only did traditional, more established magazines pick up on some of the feminist issues Ms. carried (Redbook, Patricof argued, was the closest competitor, as it was the women's magazine most often read by Ms. readers), but a host of new women's magazines (Working Woman, New Dawn, Cosmopolitan Forum, Women at Work, and New Woman) were launched, carving into Ms.'s readership and advertising pool.[21]

The Patricof Report compared Ms. solely with other women's magazines, despite the fact that few readers of Ms. necessarily read them. Indeed, as a crossover commercial/political magazine, Ms. could as easily be compared with general interest news magazines like Time or Newsweek or alternative periodicals like Mother Jones or Psychology Today. In marketing terms, however, women's magazines were the sole relevant comparison group, since this was the group with which Ms. competed on the newsstand and in advertising circles. Significantly, Patricof portrayed typical readers as having "grown up" from Ms., turning now to a more "balanced" life, one in which "issues" interested them less and family and cosmetics more. In the eyes of marketing experts, their consumptive and lifestyle habits equaled who these readers were and what they necessarily "wanted" in a magazine.

In describing the way other magazines seemed to be stealing *Ms.*'s "thunder" without appearing so "tough, aggressive, political," the Patricof Report pointed to a range of editorial problems. The magazine, they asserted, "often conveys too negative a tone. . . . The editors argue that no other magazine dares to report the bad news, an accurate enough point in view of the relentlessly cheerful, upbeat, even dishonest quality found in many other women's magazines. But it may be that readers prefer that tone to the down feeling emanating from some issues of *Ms.*" They pointed to an editorial "bias toward politicized, feminist issues" that may "account for the neglect of more natural, practical topics like jobs." The report continued, "Moreover, Pat Carbine admits that the editors, all strong feminists, frequently hesitate to edit or cut the articles of committed feminist writers, even though their professional judgement would dictate a shorter or more modulated piece. They are, as she put it, vulnerable to 'emotional blackmail' of the 'how can you of all magazines do this to me' variety. Needless to say, this clearly reflects a conflict between whether Ms. is primarily a profit-making venture or a social cause."[22] According to the Patricof consultants, to be a social cause meant that one dwelled on the "negative," ignored the "natural," and pandered to the demands of unreasonable feminists. Clearly, for the Patricof consultants, *Ms.* had to jettison its political strivings in order to see itself as a "profit-making venture."

Indeed, the Patricof consultants considered unreasonable the editors' hesitancy to change its policies. The issue, they argued, was whether the magazine could continue to attract traditionally men's products if it turned to women's products, not whether the magazine could continue to act as a feminist resource if it made the changes necessary to attract this new category of advertisers. In describing the history of *Ms.*'s relationship to advertisers, the report read, "Like many things in Ms.'s past, advertising sales have been difficult, primarily because of the controversial nature of the magazine itself. It was and still is the women's rights magazine and many advertisers were very reluctant to place a schedule with them. An interesting historical comparison would be Playboy. There was a period of many, many years when companies like General Motors forbade their advertising departments and agencies to advertise their products in this publication." They pointed to *Ms.*'s advertising successes while underscoring its need to attract a new market:

Ms. has made significant inroads with advertisers of traditional men's products — cars, cigarettes, liquor, etc., but the magazine is almost completely void of advertisers of traditional women's products—apparel, toiletries, cosmetics, shoes, etc. They enjoy support from the former because of the high demographic profile of the Ms. reader and a concerted sales effort in that market. Their lack of advertising from the latter stems from a number of factors. Ms. has a high cost per thousand readers when compared to other women's magazines, and relatively low circulation. But perhaps more important, these advertisers do not feel the editorial environment of Ms. Magazine is conducive to selling their products.[23]

As an answer to the problems *Ms.* faced, Patricof encouraged the magazine to take a number of steps, many of which were designed to make *Ms.* a more "reliable commodity" for readers and advertisers alike. They urged *Ms.* to pay more for a stock of freelance writers (*Ms.* had published too many writers in the past, creating a product no one could count on from month to month, they argued), rethink the editorial staffing, and publish more "well-known" writers. Also, the report urged *Ms.* to "develop a more balanced editorial mix between 'issue oriented' articles, service features, and profiles." These changes, they argued, could turn around the financial future of the magazine: "We believe . . . that with changes in editorial policy . . . a significant increase in advertising sales could be generated without losing any significant amount of the business it now has in the non-traditional market." Managing editor Suzanne Levine's insistence that the magazine not publish beauty service articles, ones found in other women's magazines and that beauty product advertisers required in order to place an ad, struck them as utterly nonsensical. "We question this logic in a time when other magazines are aggressively moving into Ms.'s turf of the independent woman."[24]

The Patricof Report clearly indicates that editors resisted the consultants' suggestions. Part of the magazine's purpose, the editors' believed, was to report "bad news," not just ridiculous, upbeat drivel. Another part of the magazine's purpose was to raise the standards of women's magazines, not to be blackmailed by advertisers to include "complementary copy." At the same time, however, editors recognized that the consultants had pointed to some unhappy truths about the marketing context in which *Ms.* existed. They could not simply dismiss the report. Editor Letty Cottin Pogrebin responded to the report with a mix of "fascination, anger, panic and action." She felt dismayed at the "facile" tone of the report and some blatant errors in it, but she felt the overall analysis was accurate and necessary. She suggested twelve possible stories, from "getting organized" to "male celebrity confessors" and noted:

There is not a political, theoretical, analytical or vaguely serious article suggestion in the lot. I'm ready to assume Patricof is right about one thing, the balance of personal and political. I'm willing to see us jazz up our tone with the kind of articles people seem to get hooked by: the trivia, the personalities and the self-help stuff is worth developing in a Ms.-manner if it helps us attract readers, advertisers and a long life. I'm convinced that we can find an honest, peppy, feminist approach to these concerns, and that we can publish a more popularized product without ceasing to publish the substantive, important articles that make Ms. different from — and better than — anyone else. But I think we have to face up to this diagnosis, and all agree that we can publish froth without allowing it to be dross — and that there is nothing impure or dishonest about trying to survive by way of this compromise.

Summing up her analysis of the magazine's future, Pogrebin called it, "Compromises En Route to the Revolution."[25] To survive in a competitive marketplace Ms. had to reach enough readers to convince advertisers to buy space in the magazine. Moreover, the point of Ms. had never been to reach out solely to those who already considered themselves feminist activists; editors wanted to reach as many readers as possible, not just to hook advertisers but also to help create a mass media meeting ground for women. In addition, some of the compromises that Pogrebin spoke of were compatible with the overall direction the magazine had taken in the past, highlighting the personal and rejecting anything that smacked too much of "theory." Indeed, if moving away from extensive coverage of "issues" meant avoiding what the editors called "theory," then Ms. could easily follow Patricof's suggestions. For Ms., the revolution of feminism was just as much about personal change as it was about political analysis, and its strength were the moments when it could connect the two. Patricof's report urged Ms. to highlight not just "personal" stories but ones that would speak to and attract readers with "quality demographics," and to reject those stories that were too "issue" oriented or that reinforced Ms.'s "aggressive" reputation. These were substantive changes that would indeed undermine Ms.'s attempt to be a mass media forum for feminist change. Ironically, however, even as Ms. moved toward this "personal" focus in the late 1980s, other structural changes it underwent, for example, changing from a for-profit to a nonprofit magazine, pulled it in the direction of the "issue" coverage.

Ms. Becomes Nonprofit

By 1979, it became clear that the magazine's best bet for survival was for it to be acquired by the Ms. Foundation, so that it could function under the tax laws and regulations of a not-for-profit entity. In August of 1979, the IRS approved the tax-exempt status of the Ms. Foundation for Education and Communication (MFEC), which would function as a subsidiary of the parent Ms. Foundation for Women, much as the Free to Be Foundation did. Soon after the approval by the IRS, the MFEC moved to acquire the magazine, with the majority of the stock donated by Warner Communications, Gloria Steinem, and Patricia Carbine.[26] As an asset owned by the Ms. Foundation for Education and Communication, Ms. magazine could function as a tax-exempt organization under the 501(c)(3) code of the IRS. This meant not only that any profits from Ms. would be tax-exempt (excluding profits from selling advertising in the magazine) but also that Ms. could solicit donations more readily—from both foundations and individuals—because donors would more likely give money to organizations they saw as charitable and/or educational, and because those donations would be tax-deductible. Equally significant at the time the decision was made to go nonprofit was that the move would save the magazine hundreds of thousands of dollars in postage expenses. An unsuccessful Ms. proposal to the Ford Foundation for additional funding makes this impetus abundantly clear: "Such status would provide mailing privileges to the magazine which would produce savings in excess of $500,000 in the first year and substantially greater amounts in subsequent years. In the face of this Postal Rate reality, the reasons for seeking non-profit status are overwhelming and preclude our pursuing private venture capital."[27]

In introducing the "new Ms." to readers, Steinem stressed the way the nonprofit status would allow the magazine to act more forcefully as a feminist vehicle for change. Steinem primarily stressed that the acquisition of Ms. by the MFEC provided legal acknowledgment of what readers already realized: that Ms. acted to educate, not to make profits. "Most of all," Steinem asserted, "this new status is a recognition of the true educational value in both past efforts and future plans. It confirms once again that Ms. is the exception among women's magazines." She then listed the changes that readers could expect to see in the Ms. of the 1980s, attributing these to the "aid and encouragement of our new status." While perhaps noteworthy changes (i.e., publishing an in-depth, original investigative piece in each issue, adding more short, useful articles, and adding new departments such as "Working," "Parenting," and "Good Health"), these were not, despite Steinem's explanation, inherently related to the switch to nonprofit status, nor clearly connected to a feminist perspective. Indeed, shorter articles and new departments like "Working" and "Parenting" could be seen as changes stemming from the kinds of suggestions the Patricof Report had made regarding redesigning the magazine to make it more marketable. Other changes, however, related directly to the new emphasis on *Ms.* as an educational magazine, a focus that needed to be highlighted in order to maintain the magazine's, and thus MFEC's, status as a "corporation organized and operated exclusively for . . . educational purposes." These included distributing more reader questionnaires to guide the magazine and to "add to the public sources of research by and about women"; publishing reference lists for additional reading; providing free subscriptions and reprints to schools, institutions, conferences, and individuals who couldn't afford them; granting internships to high school and college students; and creating a "direct exchange between *Ms.* and high schools, colleges, graduate schools, and job training programs and the like, to report their activities and to become more useful as a current supplement." The new, explicitly educational focus also prompted *Ms.* to create an advisory board of scholars, headed by Catharine Stimpson, noted feminist scholar and the founder of the academic feminist journal *Signs*, to report on academic feminist developments on a regular basis.[28]

The one explicit restriction that the new nonprofit status placed on *Ms.* was in its political coverage. In the 1970s, *Ms.* did endorse specific campaigns and candidates; as a nonprofit, however, *Ms.* could no longer "carry on propaganda or otherwise attempt to influence legislation . . . or participate in, or intervene in any political campaign on behalf of any candidate for public office."[29] Steinem explained to readers this change and the magazine's willingness to accommodate it:

> A restriction of this new status is, of course, that *Ms.* cannot support declared candidates for electoral office. We weighed this fact carefully — not without regret — but from the point of view of the Women's Movement as a whole, we realized that there are now many organizations and groups devoted to direct activism or endorsement and candidate-rating in political campaigns (the National Women's Political Caucus, the Women's Campaign Fund, and others, both national and local) that were not yet a force in 1972 when *Ms.* initiated critiques of candidates on issues concerning

women. Moreover, our long lead-time and limited space has always confined us to a few major or symbolic campaigns.[30]

This new "non-political" status meant that direct and explicit involvement in electoral politics was out of the picture. But as a nonprofit, feminist magazine, *Ms.* could also now more easily ask for money in the name of feminist organizing. A direct mailing letter in 1980 asked readers to send money to MFEC as a step toward countering the huge financial resources of ultra right-wing religious organizing like Jerry Falwell's Moral Majority, the Christian Broadcast Network, the Praise the Lord Club, and the 700 Club. "We need to organize. We need to depend less on the mass media. We must develop our own," Steinem's direct mail campaign letter read.[31] For *Ms.*, intervention in politics had always suggested a stage larger than electoral politics. Politics, for *Ms.*, meant the daily world of power struggles as women worked to transform the economy, the family, schools, the church, and other institutions that made up the fabric of twentieth-century America. Engagement in the power struggles related to the feminist movement would certainly affect how readers would choose politicians and vote on issues, but as part of an overall shift in perspective rather than as part of a specific campaign for an individual running for office. Steinem explained to readers the ways that *Ms.* would continue its political coverage in the broadest sense of the term:

> The new *Ms.* will keep its readers informed on issues of special concern to women and children. . . and will conduct its own study and research on them, whether or not they are the subject of current legislation or campaign debates. Part of our increased public distribution will be to legislators and other elected and appointed officials who need such research and perspective, and who too rarely have access to it. And, of course, we will also continue to report on politics at the more anthropological depth — as well as the more intimate, daily level — of the ways in which the power structures of sex and race affect our lives; ways that go far beyond the superficial scope of the electoral system.[32]

In introducing the *Ms.* of the 1980s, Steinem promised a media forum that would be "our own," a renewed focus on research related to women and children and to analyses of the ways that race and gender shape our lives. Noticeably, as in earlier editorial descriptions of the magazine's focus, class analysis remained absent. Also absent from this editorial were any renewed promises to speak to the full diversity of women. While this may have been simply an oversight (indeed, the Ms. Foundation for Women was increasingly focused on issues of serving a diverse constituency), the editorial thrust of the magazine and its continued reliance on advertising made it difficult, if not impossible, for it to promise to serve a true diversity of women. Indeed, the limitation on explicitly "political" coverage constrained *Ms.* from becoming feminism's own "mass media" in its second decade far less than did its continued emphasis on the centrality of the "person" in social change and its need to offer readers to advertisers as a lucrative commodity.

Textual Transformations in the Nonprofit Period

From the late 1970s, and into the 1980s, *Ms.* continued to be a primary circulator of feminist authors and discussions, printing articles by authors as diverse as Audre Lorde, Catharine Stimpson, and Alice Walker, as well as a host of previously unpublished authors. In addition, it provided a forum for the analysis of the growth of the New Right, the loss of the ERA, the feminization of poverty, and a range of other issues and changes facing women in the 1980s. The 1980s, however, did see a transformation in *Ms.*, most markedly in the way the magazine packaged itself, sold itself to readers and advertisers, and presented the ideology and issues of feminism. In a 1981 interview, Gloria Steinem remarked, "In the beginning, we had articles proving women were discriminated against. Today it's more our task to report on how the problem's being addressed." [33] By the 1980s, *Ms.* had moved from an emphasis on consciousness-raising, explicating and analyzing the roots of female oppression, to a greater focus on self-help, on practical suggestions for women to use in their own lives. This by no means constituted a complete shift, however. The December 1982 issue on women and power, for instance, included the survey, "What's Your Power Quotient?," which asked readers to rate their own personal, professional, and domestic power. In contrast to this rather "fluffy" self-help article, the cover story included extensive commentary from feminist anthropologists, sociologists, and psychologists analyzing in great detail the basis for gendered differences in how people use and assume power. As in other mainstream women's magazines, this article relied on sanctioned authorities to speak to the readers, but in this case they were feminist scholars who rarely found their ideas in widespread circulation.

While *Ms.* did not shy away from feminist discussions and authors in the 1980s, it did redirect the packaging of those discussions. *Ms.* became less explicitly a magazine for the women's movement and more a magazine for women. In the same 1981 interview from which Steinem was quoted, editor

Suzanne Levine commented, "Nobody says 'women's libber' today. People do say 'abortion' and 'ERA'—all the time."[34] Both Steinem's and Levine's comments point to a shift from direct discussions about feminism or the women's movement to discussions about issues related to women. In the context of the conservative 1980s, this refocusing enabled Ms. to mask its oppositional perspectives so that it could fit on the newsstands with other women's magazines and continue to solicit advertisements from companies who were skittish about buying space in a "political" magazine. Thus, an increasingly mass media "look"—including more white space, shorter articles, sensational, "catchy" titles, and an increased reliance on the images of "successful" women—coexisted with reviews of feminist films and books, feminist analyses of contemporary issues, and the continued outpourings from readers. Ms. maintained a space for feminism within a public, commercial realm but, in transforming its shape, allowed the commodified vision of feminism to take center stage.

The threat of boycotts from advertisers, censorship from librarians and newsstand operators, and the necessity to attract a mass readership shaped Ms. into a magazine that looked more and more like other mainstream women's magazines. In contrast to the explicit covers of the 1970s, picturing sexual harassment, violence against women, and child pornography, the 1980s covers shifted away from controversy, although they continued to play with the symbols of commercial magazines and to articulate concepts that spoke to the changing conditions of women's lives, such as the February 1985 "blended family" issue. Throughout the 1980s, covers increasingly deflected attention from the feminist analyses contained within the pages of the magazine and focused more on self-help and enthusiastic headlines about the possibilities in women's lives. In September 1977, Ms. had published an issue on women and body image; the cover pictured a slim white woman's torso, with the words "Why Women Hate Their Bodies" tattooed on her back. Some readers objected to this cover as a "cheap method of selling magazines," but editors responded that they had attempted to make a statement about the ways all women, even those with the most culturally perfect bodies, experienced self-hate about their bodies.[35] By the 1980s, this focus on the politics of health and the politics of body image had evolved into a yearly issue entitled "The Beauty of Health." The covers on these issues displayed models and famous women in the bloom of health; they were no longer making a complex statement about women's relationship to their bodies. The May 1984 cover provides a revealing contrast to the 1977 cover, as it too pictured the back of a white woman's torso. This time, though, no tattooed words forced the reader to question this representation of women; rather, the woman was pictured in the shower, with soap sensuously dripping down her naked back. In addition, the title itself, "The Beauty of Health," redirected attention from any "feminist" articles contained in the issue and provided a perfect set-up for advertisers to sell their products.

Throughout the 1980s, the editors of *Ms.* increasingly turned to the image of the successful woman to construct a crossover magazine, one that spoke "feminism" and "women's magazine" simultaneously. As with any mass media periodical, the covers of *Ms.* worked to sell the magazine and to convince advertisers that this was a comfortable and attractive space in which to sell their products to readers. *Ms.* clearly attempted to sell to both audiences by choosing images that focused on "positive" representations of women and that deflected attention away from controversial feminist issues. Women like Cory Aquino, Loretta Swit, Whoopie Goldberg, Geraldine Ferraro, and Bette Midler found their faces on the covers of *Ms.* in the 1980s. As these examples illustrate, many of the cover women held significant positions in the public world, although they were not always as famous as Bette Midler or Cory Aquino. Models expressing enthusiasm, health, joy, and power were other positive images featured on covers. Visually, these were the covers that blended best with the other women's magazines—the women looked cheerful, well groomed, and confident. They did not shock, nor did the photographs themselves challenge or question patriarchal norms. Importantly, these covers meshed the demands of advertisers, who required an atmosphere devoid of controversy or negative images for their sales pitches, and the philosophy of the magazine, which highlighted the power of individual transformation and growth through feminism. By the late 1970s, many editors were criticizing the magazine for focusing too much on the victimization of women; the positive images of women presented in the 1980s steered *Ms.* away from any "negative" portrayals of women.[36]

The significance of these public images of women who identified themselves as feminists cannot be underestimated. In the 1970s, *Ms.* played an important role by placing these images of feminists into public consciousness. In the 1980s, *Ms.* continued to play a crucial role by keeping these images in circulation, despite the other media's assertion that we had entered a "post-feminist" age. In particular, issues like the January 1980 "80 Women to Watch in the 80s," and the yearly "*Ms.* Women of the Year" issues provided readers with information and perspectives about women, their lives, and their work, to which they likely may have had no other access. Of equal consequence, these covers featured women who were not simply "successful" because they had made money or risen to heights in major corporations; rather, they made a name for themselves as feminist activists, writers, artists, and politicians.

This reliance on "positive" images of women to negotiate the terrain between traditional women's magazine and feminist periodicals also limited how *Ms.* constructed feminism. Particularly in its early years, while *Ms.* espoused a theory of sisterhood, the focus on successful and positive images solidified *Ms.*'s construction of feminism as a liberal, individualistic philosophy. These "positive" images of women worked less to create a vision of a changed world, transformed by feminism, and more to compose a montage of the women who had somehow broken into the higher echelons of our patriarchal culture. Film critic E. Ann Kaplan, discussing the common distinction made between "positive" and "negative" images of women, argues that "positive" images of women simply create a different standard by which to judge women; a positive image is of a woman who seems to be "autonomous, self-fulfilling, self-assertive, socially and financially 'successful.'"[37] Kaplan asserts that these positive images in many ways reinforced the competition, individualism, and valorization of the masculine world that help to naturalize patriarchal capitalism.

Equally problematic, by placing emphasis on individuals, *Ms.* implied that the women's movement consisted only of specific leaders rather than a broad-based constituency. In its 1982 tenth anniversary issue, *Ms.* attempted to illustrate the diversity of the women's movement through a fold-out cover picturing women of color, working-class women, old women, women with children, and professional women. But the main cover, all that would be seen on a newsstand, showed a close-up shot of Gloria Steinem. The words above her read, "Our 10th Anniversary," but the photograph of Steinem obscured the involvement of other women at *Ms.* and in the movement. She became both the spokesperson for the movement, and the movement itself.[38]

While many in the feminist movement criticized Steinem's apparent arrogance in "selling herself" as the women's movement, *Ms.*'s use of Steinem is better understood as one of the magazine's most valuable marketing tools. One editor responding to the internally commissioned Patricof Report on the state of the magazine spoke to this understanding:

> The point is one we all know and don't say out loud. Gloria is our prime asset and we don't 'use' her. Let's get down to desperation and see what sort of *personal* exploitation you could tolerate, Gloria, without compromising yourself totally. Let's talk about a logical use of Gloria on the cover, and story ideas that recognize what every other publication in this coun-

try knows and can't do anything about: people want to know everything they can about you. Could you sit still for any of the following story ideas that would carry a cover: a) Gloria Steinem on "Why I Never Married" b) Gloria Steinem on "The Children in My Life" c) How To Use Pull (to help yourself and other women) by GS d) Surviving on Junk Food and Other Nourishment: Gloria Steinem's Idiosyncratic diet for all formerly fat feminists.[39]

While *Ms.* never published any of this editor's suggestions, the magazine continued to rely on Steinem as the major "draw" in insert offers, in fund-raising tours for the foundation, and in key headers on the cover. While this marketing ploy was designed to pull in more readers, attract advertisers, and keep the magazine afloat, the editorial effect was still, despite the lack of intention, to individualize the movement and to further the movement through the star system.

Mixing the Popular and Scholarly

At the same time that *Ms.* moved toward a deflection of explicit feminist perspectives, it also, as a result of its new status as an "educational and charitable" organization, renewed its focus on the "educational" quality of the magazine. While an increased emphasis on educational articles did not necessarily mean articles that were overtly confrontational or "angry" (indeed, scholars are generally known for their modulated tone even while writing passionate arguments), it did mean stories that were inherently "issue" oriented, researched, and perhaps theoretical. It also meant articles that were sometimes more radical than those published by regular *Ms.* writers, as activists who had previously written and worked outside of the academy moved into universities and colleges in the late 1970s and 1980s. Indeed, much of the most pathbreaking feminist work done in this period happened within the walls of the academy, where feminists found an uneasy but relatively safe site to explore the boundaries of feminist thinking.[40]

Within the pages of *Ms.*, this feminist academic work could be popularized and offered to a mass readership, an important goal of both the *Ms.* editors and the academics themselves, who wanted their work to have relevance outside the ivory tower. Indeed, *Ms.*'s attempt to work with academics was a powerful challenge to the socially constructed divisions between those who do "mind work" and those who consider themselves activists or even everyday people. The January 1984 issue provides a fine example of the way *Ms.*

worked to blend the scholarly and the popular. The cover story featured the feminist psychologist Carol Gilligan as the "*Ms.* Woman of the Year," a tradition begun in the early 1980s. Featuring a close-up shot of Gilligan, dressed conservatively in sweater, pearls, and subtle makeup, the cover merged the traditional women's magazine's practice of focusing on "successful" women with the newsmagazine's (like *Time*) custom of honoring certain "men of the year." At the same time, the headlines on this cover all clearly identified the magazine as part of the genre of the women's magazine. Speaking directly to the reader, they employed the language of self-help so common to mass media women's magazines. Across the top of the cover, printed in black print on a yellow strip, the text proclaimed, "HEALTH REPORT: SHOULD YOU USE THE CONTRACEPTIVE SPONGE?" Less sensational but no less directive were the words "HOW TO GET TO THE YEAR 2000" positioned under the headline announcing Gilligan as the *Ms.* Woman of the Year. In smaller print under that headline the text read, "Including: 10 Things NOT to Worry About in 1984" and "Bonus: A New Essay by Alice Walker." The rhetorical style of these headlines, the use of bold print, and phrases like "Bonus" clearly made this magazine appear at first glance a "lookalike" to any number of other women's magazines, ranging from *Self* to *McCall's*. Yet even this cover, the primary location of *Ms.*'s attempt to mask its feminist perspective, plays with the symbols of the traditional women's magazines. The "cover woman" is not a glamorous model but a psychologist. Moreover, she is a feminist psychologist who challenged the prevailing theories concerning female and male development and ethics, a perspective that resonated well with the overall emphasis on cultural feminism that *Ms.* highlighted in the 1970s. The author with whom the cover "teases" us is not a writer of titillating romances or stories of success in the business world but an African American writer connecting questions of race, gender, and the natural environment in her essay, "When a Tree Falls."

Even the rather vague and innocuous "How to Get to the Year 2000" becomes more complex when we look to the table of contents to find out what the title refers to. Many of the articles listed seem to fulfill *Ms.*'s original promise to "push the philosophical boundaries that brave and radical feminists are trying to explore." Besides an article exploring Carol Gilligan's new theories, and Alice Walker's article on racism and the environment, three articles focused on issues related to race and gender. One article featured Maxine Waters, the African American legislator from California; another explored high school programs designed for teenage mothers, predominantly African American and poor; and the third, an essay by Minnie Bruce Pratt, examined racism and anti-Semitism from an autobiographical perspective. This issue also contained an article by the feminist architect Dolores Hayden, who presented her plans for more equitable and livable housing arrangements.

The issue included short pieces, preceding and following these major articles, on women entrepreneurs, changes in competitive figure skating, raising a feminist daughter, and using computers for personal financial management. These minor articles mirrored the style found in other mass media women's magazines — the use of short, one- to two-page articles that allow readers to flip quickly through a magazine. The advertisements interspersed among the articles displayed both traditionally "masculine" products — cars, stereos, and liquor — as well as traditionally "feminine" products — shoes, makeup, feminine protection. *Ms.* had indeed created a "full woman" in these ads, although we might, of course, argue with its assumption that human identity is linked to consumer products. Finally, and perhaps most compellingly, while *Ms.* masked its feminist orientation on the front cover — and on the back cover, which advertised Myer's Rum Cream — the Back Page article featured an essay by seven feminist writers, activists, and scholars, including Nancy Chodorow and Lillian Rubin, on the future of feminism in the United States. In effect, this article, placed in an unconcealed position on the back page, "sealed" the magazine as an oppositional, feminist magazine. While the cover may have deflected the issue of politics, the back page made it explicit.

The *Ms.* academic-popular alliance proved to be an uncomfortable one. While *Ms.* needed to publish more "fluff" to keep the tone upbeat and light, it was also dealing with its own more fundamental questions about how to translate academic work into a popular context. In 1980, *Ms.* hired as a consultant Catharine Stimpson, the founder of *Signs*, to help form a scholarly board of advisers. The board of advisers met twice yearly to report on relevant and recent work in their fields, particularly that which would speak to a broad audience, to advise editors, and to provide a base for research ideas. Stimpson also kept in touch regularly with the editorial staff, in particular Martha Nelson and Ruth Sullivan, to brainstorm about article ideas and to follow up on the work submitted by academics. Not surprisingly, Stimpson took some criticism for her close ties with *Ms.* She wrote in one memo, "I have been picking up flak lately from academic women . . . about the magazine. 'It's like buying *Redbook*,' a famous feminist critic said last week. I am convinced that this has less to do with the comparative absence of serious materials from the academic world than with the heavy presence of such materials as how to sleep with your husband in socks."[41] Indeed, responses from academics to *Ms.*, while ranging widely, did not necessarily want *Ms.* to become another academic journal. What they wanted, in general, was less of the "fluff" and more of the impassioned articles that they found inspiring for themselves and for their students. One scholar, a sociologist, responding to a questionnaire *Ms.* sent to women's studies scholars, articulated this desire particularly well: "I wish you would put out a series of Ms. readers. This is your forte. . . . I need Ms. for the really great consciousness-raising articles it can put out. When you get all serious and sobersides and social sciency, you get dull."[42]

Ms. saw as part of its mission in the 1980s the translation of more academic work into a language meaningful for a mass readership. In general, however, women's studies scholars did not find a ready home in *Ms.*, despite *Ms.*'s new status as an educational magazine. Many scholars submitted their pieces with a note explaining that they were willing to edit their piece for a "more general audience." They clearly wanted to reach a broader audience, and they saw *Ms.* as a likely vehicle in which to do that. Similarly, editors felt a commitment to publishing the work of scholars and translating it for a more broad readership. In 1980, for instance, Susan Sands, a popular writer who had become a practicing clinical psychologist, submitted a scholarly article on women, men, and nurturance. She focused in particular on how women are expected to nurture and are punished if they don't. In her cover letter, Sands offered to "loosen up the style a bit"; indeed, the fact that she had previously worked as a popular writer may have been part of the editor's decision to work with Sands' piece. Clearly, editors had complex feelings about scholarly pieces, as demonstrated by this thoughtful note by Letty Cottin Pogrebin: "This paper has something to say that we can use and I think it tests our determination to transform it and other scholarly stuff into popular journalism. . . . What's 'old hat' to us re Horney-Dinnerstein themes still lacks an easy handle for the average reader. Needs both myth *and* anecdote to gain contemporary force." Mary Thom wrote to Sands, asking if she would be interested in "focus[ing] anecdotally on the situations we find ourselves in. . . . If you could direct the piece towards women (and men, of course) who will recognize these patterns in their lives instead of towards new directions in therapy, I think we'll have a terrific piece." When Sands sent in her revised copy, she wrote, "I probably didn't add as many anecdotes as you'd like, because I'm afraid I'm more interested in the ideas than the anecdotes."[43] This exchange exemplifies editors' commitment to publishing the work of scholars as well as their equally strong demand for "anecdotes," compelling stories and details that would connect with readers' personal lives. Even though she agreed to add more anecdotal material to her piece, Sands had difficulty, for she valued the "ideas," the theories behind the anecdotes, more than the compelling individual stories.

Not all scholars' work found the friendly reception that Sands's did, however. Many academics voiced anger at *Ms.* for rejecting their work, expressing dismay, as many readers did, that *Ms.*, of all places, should treat them poorly. "I wrote a long piece for you," one scholar wrote, ". . . which was briefly rejected in a form note. . . . I felt somewhat insulted. I am sure your approach has changed since then."[44] According to editors' notes on the submitted pieces, scholars' articles were too long and full of jargon, and they lacked compelling details. "Timeliness" was the most significant problem that scholars faced in getting their work published in *Ms.* This was particularly true after the rush of submissions in the early 1970s. In 1986, for instance, a recent graduate from the master's program at the Columbia School of Journalism submitted her master's thesis on women in their twenties who, despite nearly two decades of intense feminist activism, continued to make choices to trim their career aspirations in order to meet a husband and to accommodate his needs. Her work included interviews with women and commentary by psychologists and sociologists. JoAnne Edgar's comments, both in the margins of the paper and in the formal letter of rejection, focused not on the quality of the writer's work but on the "old-hat" quality of the research. "Although the young women cited in your piece are themselves in a new position in history, the restraints and conflict are much the same as before," Edgar explained, adding that much of what the writer said *Ms.* had been saying since 1972. She added that the writer needed to provide a new perspective, and some forecasts (Will these women drop out? Will they have careers?) to make it publishable. A year earlier, poet and scholar Marjorie Agosin submitted an essay about the mothers of the Plaza de Mayo, the Argentinian women who in the late 1970s began to protest the fate of the "disappeared ones." Agosin felt that *Ms.* would be a good place in which to publicize the plight of these women. Edgar's rejection letter to Agosin highlights the "present" orientation of the magazine. "We've covered the basic story in the past," Edgar wrote, "and since most of your article concentrates on the origin and original purpose of the group it seems too repetitive. For us to even consider it, it would need to be grounded in the present. . . . For us, as a monthly magazine, an article needs to be short, specific and up-to-date."[45]

In July 1980, *Ms.* published as its cover story an essay by feminist scholar Charlotte Bunch on leadership and power. The revisions that Bunch's piece underwent to "eliminate the problems of length and readability" illuminate typical writing style differences between academics and journalists. Steinem wrote to Bunch that the problems came from her background as a teacher, where ideas have to be repeated often, and from her "fear of making a declarative, unqualified sentence." She pointed out her "habit of summarizing the paragraph before in the lead sentence of the next paragraph, putting summaries at the end of each paragraph, and sometimes in the middle as well, and summarizing quotes before making them, thus telescoping the joke, as Henry Youngman would say." "The thinking is very valuable and helpful. Let it shine crisp and clear," Steinem concluded.[46] Sending the revised copy back to Bunch, editor JoAnne Edgar wrote, "We like the leadership piece so well that we're making it our cover for July," and she summarized the editorial changes: "It's been cut substantially, as you knew we were going to have to do, but I think the cutting highlighted your main points. Mainly, we cut out the repetition and let your specific statements stand for some of your more abstract statements. At this point, all it needs, in our opinion, is a few more examples to concretize some of your analysis; we marked in the margins the places where we thought this was needed."[47]

On one level, the revisions *Ms.* editors required of scholars' writings indicate a simple desire to make the prose "crisp and clear," to remove unnecessary wordiness and vagueness that can plague any writing, and to make accessible the often obscure language of academics. On another level, the revisions and rejections of scholars' submissions illustrate the very different discourses of scholars and journalists. History, a key element of much women's studies scholarship, has little place in a monthly magazine. While *Ms.* published a regular column called "Lost Women," which highlighted the stories of historical women, the magazine's overall editorial approach could not be too historical for threat of it becoming "repetitive." Academics pride themselves on providing in-depth evidence and demonstrating the validity of certain interpretations of that data. To journalists this might look like rehashing material that everyone "already knew." Academics shy away from making projections or speculations that stray too far from the study at hand; journalists, wanting to hook readers with news of future trends and wanting to convey a confident tone, see this hesitancy as "fear of making a declarative . . . sentence." Academics are responsible for shaping the data into generalizable wholes; anecdotes might provide some interesting "hooks" into the article but they don't constitute evidence. *Ms.* editors were looking for compelling stories, complete with detailed anecdotes and personal stories, ones that could powerfully connect with readers. This emphasis on the person as the vehicle for social change stemmed from both editors' own feminist philosophy and the exigencies of marketing to an increasingly competitive market in the 1980s. Considering these significantly different approaches to writing, it is surprising that as many scholars did write for *Ms.* as did. Clearly this is evidence of both scholars' desire to see their work reach a popular audience and editors' desire to serve as "translator."

Internal editorial memos, however, suggest that some of the problems the magazine had in working with scholarly submissions had less to do with the issue of translation than with editors' boredom with the new feminist activism and with the magazine's struggle to be both a popular "rag" of the newsstands and an educational magazine. One of the editors assigned to work with the board of scholars voiced her frustration with the magazine in a biting (and private) memo to another editor:

> The problem is in doing nothing well—or very little well. It is certainly not trendy (Marlo Thomas is not a new face or a very hot one) and it is certainly not intellectually inviting or challenging. Personally, I feel at a loss because most of the editors at Ms. aren't really very interested in what feminists are doing. That may be harsh, but many beats aren't covered. For instance, . . . there is a huge performance festival of women's artists taking place at the Franklin Furnace. Video, performance, installations, etc. Women from LA and London coming to NY for this special month of performances. Does anyone at Ms. know about this? Does anyone care? I have a feeling that the whole thing is much too avant garde for Ms., but it pisses me off, because it happens to be what feminist artists are doing. . . .
>
> When I was feeling especially bad about not being able to do more, I stood in the mailroom and looked at all the boxes, I realized that almost everyone else at that place was working to put out the magazine they'd always put out, and that it was small wonder Ms. wasn't changing much. . . .
>
> On a more practical level, I understand that part of the problem is that everyone is overworked, the workplace stinks and morale is low. This leaves very little energy and time for speculation, brain-storming and cultivating new people and ideas.[48]

This memo points to a high level of editorial burnout as well as a resistance to the newest developments in feminist cultural life. As *Ms.* moved into the 1980s, the level of resistance to new work within scholarship rose even higher, as studies in postmodern theory and discourse challenged notions of the "unified woman," on which rested the very basis of feminist thinking in *Ms.* Viewing this new scholarship as inherently nonpolitical and as the product of "career feminists," Steinem spoke critically of academic feminists in an interview with Cynthia Gorney: "Nobody cares about them. That's careerism. These poor women in academia have to talk this silly language that nobody can understand in order to be accepted, they think. If I read the word 'problematize' one more time I'm going to vomit. . . . But I recognize the fact that we have this ridiculous system of tenure, that the whole thrust of academia is one that values education, in my opinion, in inverse ratio to its usefulness."[49] But even as the editors dealt with their own internal exhaustion, their dilemmas as to the direction of the magazine, and their profound skepticism of new work in feminist scholarship, they faced another more fundamental definer of their project: the advertisers.

Advertising

Despite *Ms.*'s move to a nonprofit status in 1979, the magazine continued to solicit advertising in order to support its mass circulation. Anticipating readers' questions, the editorial introducing the new organizational structure explained the decision to maintain advertising:

> As for advertising, *Ms.*, like other nonprofit magazines, will continue to carry it. Earnings from ad revenues are taxable as unrelated business income, and without them the economic burden on the reader and on tax-exempt contributions would be too great. Besides, one of the accomplishments of *Ms.* has been improving the image of women in advertising, and diversifying the kinds of products that are considered appropriate for women. Since so much of the country's information and expectations come from advertising, we will continue to care about it and to take it very seriously indeed.[50]

Published editorials in *Ms.* muted any discussion of the inherent tension between the commercial context in which *Ms.* was situated and the feminist resource that it promised to be. Rather, the editorials pointed to the newly conservative atmosphere, the "anti-woman backlash," that could be seen most visibly in increased efforts to ban *Ms.* from newsstands and schools. "Each month we face a new and perilous balance," a 1978 editorial explained, in underscored type, "between the support of change (as expressed by our readers and advertisers) and the opposition to that change (as expressed by a hostile anti-woman backlash)."[51]

Ms. legitimated its decision to maintain advertising on two fronts. First, advertisements reduced the cost of subscriptions, thus subsidizing, in effect, the feminist movement through its most well known publication, *Ms.* Second, part of the magazine's goal had been to transform the advertising industry by improving the way women were represented in mass media and by encouraging advertisers to sell the full range of consumer products to women. The desire to maintain ties with advertisers was portrayed not just as a necessary but abhorrent "pact with the devil" in order to reach more readers but also a legitimate endeavor on its own to transform the advertising industry. It is important to remember that *Ms.* was never anticapitalist.

The 1980s posed difficult challenges to *Ms.*, particularly financially, as the magazine found it had to rely increasingly on advertising revenue despite the switch to nonprofit status. The "Ninth Birthday Personal Report (and Urgent Alert)," published in July 1981, explained that their most pressing concern was an unprecedented rise in postal rates. While *Ms.* had turned to nonprofit status in order to be eligible for the lower postal rates offered to magazines operated by nonprofit organizations, by 1981 the Reagan administration began to slash the postal breaks given to nonprofit and educational organizations, a policy that worked against any media without strong commercial backing. The staff explained that the cost of mailing each copy of the magazine would rise by 100 percent; in one year this would mean a jump from $700,000 to $1.4 million in expenses, including the cost of "billings and other necessary mailings." The staff asked each reader to send in a check for $2–$25, reminding them that this contribution was tax-deductible, that readers were still paying far less than the "real" cost of the magazine because of advertisers' dollars, and finally, that this kind of burden-sharing during crises was the organizational strategy needed to see *Ms.*, and the entire women's movement, through the Reagan backlash.[52]

What *Ms.* really depended on in the 1980s was the support of advertisers to see them through these financial crises. In an increasingly competitive market, however, advertising accounts were more difficult to land. The Patricof Report indicated that while the professional women's market was growing substantially, *Ms.* need to work harder to capture more of it.[53] But what the Patricof Report emphasized and the *Ms.* staff clearly already knew, is that *Ms.* could never compete with its sister magazines on the grounds of quantity of readers; it needed to convince advertisers that the *quality* of readers was superior to that of the readers of other women's magazines. And, as *Ms.* worked to increase readership in order to maintain the minimum number of readers needed to capture advertisers' interest, it needed to ensure that those were the "right" readers. That is, *Ms.* could provide free and gift subscriptions to women in prisons and battered women's shelters to augment its circulation, certainly part of the feminist goal of the magazine, but that would not speak to advertisers' desire for an additional 200,000 "quality" readers.

As the editors and advertising staff prepared to launch the new *Ms.* of the 1980s, it needed first and foremost to fight its "aggressive" image, to persuade advertisers that *Ms.* provided a good marketing context. One suggestion by editors was a high-quality promotional item designed to fight that 1970s image. We should "develop an item," the memo outlining the proposal read, "a piece of merchandise, that is uniquely ours . . . and produce it only for VIP's. . . . It should be our high-toned friend-maker, the gift we give to those tough to sell (on any score) and it should work subliminally to persuade the recipient that *Ms.* isn't blue jeans and combat boots and that *Ms.* readers are *worth a lot.*"[54] *Ms.* worked hard to fight the reputation of its radical roots and to sell its readers to advertisers. One 1985 promotional brochure spoke explicitly about the *Ms.* reader as trendsetter: "*Ms.* is the magazine of record for women, reporting *on* the women and *to* the women in the forefront of change. Our readers are the leaders who are making a world of difference. They're the innovators, the opinion makers, they create the trends. They're among the best educated, highest paid, most activist women anywhere. As a magazine, our goal is to inspire, to nourish every aspect of their lives."[55] Another promotional brochure from the same year announced, "Where *Ms.* Readers Lead, Others Follow!" The material argued that women leaders and trendsetters read *Ms.* precisely because it was a magazine different from other women's magazines. "*Ms.* is distinct from the service magazines written for women who work at home: we include investigative, political, and social reporting. *Ms.* is equally distinct from service magazines written for women who work outside the home: we include fiction, poetry, arts coverage, and children's stories. Both groups of magazines tell women how to 'play the game' — *Ms.* shows women how to change the *rules* of the game." Citing statistics that showed how involved readers were in civic and cultural life, i.e., writing to politicians, raising funds for various causes, and volunteering for environmental causes, the material went on to translate this activism into consumer terms. Drawing statistics from the 1984 and 1985 Simmons Research Market Bureau (SRMB), the promotional material pointed out that *Ms.* readers had the highest education of the readers of any other women's magazine, as well as those of *Esquire, Time,* or *Newsweek,* that 36 percent of readers held management positions, and that 33 percent were those "sophisticated professionals that SMRB ranks as Class I and II in social position." They owned more imported cars, shopped at gourmet and health food stores, and enjoyed culture and the arts. Moreover, more than 80 percent lived in "A or B" counties. All of these facts, the material argued, translated into "an involved, committed, and visible readership."[56] That last line, of course, could as easily be translated into an "affluent, consumer-oriented readership."

At times, of course, the articles in *Ms.* did not necessarily appear to be directed to those "sophisticated professionals" that advertisers wanted to engage. In these cases, *Ms.* often attempted to educate advertisers about the worthiness of a different audience, just as it had worked to educate advertisers about women consumers in the 1970s. For example, one advertising promotion for the November 1985 issue "Doing What You Love and Getting Paid for It!," rather than concealing the non-white-collar emphasis of the issue (i.e., nonquality demographic emphasis), made a case for blue-collar workers as readers. "After all," the form letter from Gloria Steinem read, "women with technical, scientific or blue-collar jobs actually make *more* than women with more traditional jobs in offices — *and advertisers have been missing this vast and growing market. The new truth is variety.*"[57]

In general, however, *Ms.* marketing made few references to variety and blue-collar workers, emphasizing instead a readership with an "extraordinary" demographic profile. And, while *Ms.* initially balked at the Patricof suggestion to make the editorial content more supportive of advertisers, as we chart the direction of the magazine in the 1980s we can see increasing acquiescence to the demands for "editorial support." Although *Ms.* never published cooking recipes or makeup "how-tos," we can see increased concessions to advertisers in the special theme issues as well as in various pockets of complementary copy. These theme issues were particularly important to the sales staff, as indicated by one memo written by a *Ms.* saleswoman who lamented the lack of "something unique, more tangible and appropriate to help sell the March issue."[58] Special theme issues included January's "Women of the Year," April's "Travel," May's "Beauty of Health," September's "Men's Issue," and October's "Campus Times." *Ms.* also created special subthemes for its catalog section, including "Home Style" and "Holiday" to attract advertisers.

While the theme issues billed themselves to readers as places to catch up on the latest news regarding the topic at hand, advertising circulars emphasized the hospitable atmosphere advertisers would find in these issues. The circulars announcing a special issue on campus life, for instance, told advertisers they would have double exposure to the "loyal *Ms.* reader and the affluent college market."[59] In selling the special issue on travel for April 1985, the promotional material reminded advertisers that women make up 55 percent of pleasure/personal air travel and 27 percent of business air travel. This growing market was one they should target, *Ms.* asserted, and the "Ms. Travel Advertorial," with its articles on "great adventures and unusual getaways, fitness vacations and quiet retreats, trips of a lifetime and weekend escapes and places to go when you've been everywhere. . . . will be," the material read, "a spirited, sparkling guide to the whole world of travel today, a bona fide service for our readers, and a big bonanza for you."[60] *Ms.* similarly persuaded computer corporations to buy space in the magazine, promising them a range of articles that focused on personal computers and related paraphernalia: "Computer Fitness — A Diskography" (July 1984), "The Electronic Campus" (October 1984), "For Kids: Sensational Software for Computerniks" (December 1984), and "Help for Technophobes: Think of Your Computer as Just Another Appliance" (January 1985). While these articles certainly provided valuable information to readers, they also served as mini-catalogs, listing brand names of specific products and prices. Moreover, these articles created a more attractive place for computer companies to advertise. In 1984 and 1985 WordStar and IBM bought multipage spreads. *Ms.* provided services to other kinds of companies as well, publishing catalogs with editorial copy, such as the June 1984 "*Ms.* Sun Sampler," which provided a coupon to order "this summer's hottest products." The regular May "Beauty of Health" issues promoted related products through their two- to five-page advertising supplements (May 1984, May 1985, May 1986). Certainly we can see in these sections and theme issues clear attempts to market to affluent readers, and in the "advertorials" attempts to provide complementary copy.

That *Ms.* published this complementary copy does not necessarily suggest it was moving away from the preferences of its readers. Feminists do buy sun products and computers, and they do travel. Moreover, recent research in cultural studies suggests that women buy popular magazines for a multitude of reasons, for practical information as well as for the pleasure of looking and of fantasizing about alternative lives.[61] And if *Ms.* could provide those fantasies and the practical information at the same time it articulated a feminist vision, then that made the magazine potentially able to reach out to yet more women. But from its origins, *Ms.* had wanted to avoid turning the *Ms.* reader into another statistic, a commodity to be sold to advertisers. Indeed, even in its title, *Ms.*, the magazine taunted advertisers with the specter of "unknown women," a diverse group of women who came together to read the magazine not because of shared tastes or the accident of demographic similarities (all mothers, or all working outside the home, or all 18–35), but because they shared a political perspective that transformed the way they perceived the world. As *Ms.* moved through the 1980s, however, it more explicitly packaged the *Ms.* reader, and the magazine itself, as a profitable commodity in which advertisers should invest.

Also making it difficult for the magazine to live up to its initial goal of being a feminist resource were the "supportive editorial" articles that often overshadowed the other, more political articles in the magazine. Indeed, it is this kind of contradictory content that Catharine Stimpson spoke of when she referred to a colleague who was bothered less by the absence of scholarly articles than she was by the endless drivel on "how to sleep with your husbands in socks." The light, complementary articles and the advertisements often overshadowed the more political or challenging articles published. Ostensibly, "theme" issues are supposed to attract the "right" consumers and provide a supportive atmosphere for ad copy. In *Ms.*, however, ads and articles frequently contradicted rather than supported each other. For instance, the October 1983 issue featured "FOOD: Secret Pleasures, Hidden Dangers." The cover story focused on an analysis of anorexia and other eating disorders from the standpoint that they primarily related to the societal imperative for women to be thin. Four of the ads, however, featured diet aids and foods, products that the article implicitly criticized. Another article in this issue asked who profited from the new industry for treating premenstrual syndrome; nevertheless, the issue also carried ads for Aqua-Ban and Pamprin, two products that treat this malady. Incongruities like these, necessary for the dual purpose of maintaining a feminist perspective and attracting advertising, pleased neither the advertisers nor the readers.

Throughout the 1980s, in spite of the range of problems that stemmed from publishing a feminist magazine in a commercial context—including the difficulty of attracting advertisements, the incongruity of those ads within *Ms.* once the accounts had been won, and, perhaps most seriously, the larger and more complicated issue of how that struggle to attract advertisers shaped the magazine itself—editors continued to focus on the possibilities and the successes they had in transforming the "image of women in advertising." In December 1980, *Ms.* began publishing a section entitled "One Step Forward," to which readers sent examples of "pictures, advertisements, and news items that prove change possible."[62] Like the "No Comment" section, which had been published from the early days of the magazine, "One Step Forward" published mostly examples of advertisements. Unlike "No Comment," however, to which readers sent examples of offensive ads, "One Step Forward" was designed to be a "happy corner," designed to "keep optimism alive" with its "positive images of grown-ups and children." "One Step Forward" themes included the September 1981 issue's women friends, the February 1982 issue's nurturing fathers, the May 1983 issue's women in sports, the June 1984 issue's women blue-collar workers, and the August 1984 issue's men showing affection to each other.[63] Certainly this section spoke to readers who wanted to have affirmation of the gains the women's movement had made. But the "One Step Forward" section also fit neatly with the imperative for the new *Ms.* to appear less "negative." *Advertising Age* and the "Media Industry Newsletter," two of the major publications of the advertising industry, certainly took note of this section, applauding it for being an "antidote to 'No Comment.'"[64] But the "One Step Forward" section also articulated a rather naive viewpoint regarding the way that advertising worked culturally. In the February 1982 column "Selling of the Nurturing Father," for instance, the editorial introduction read, "When love between men and children finds its expression in 'selling' images for national brands, we can be sure it's a growing fact of life."[65] The fact that advertising often celebrates the very forms of cultural life that capitalism and the marketplace have helped to destroy, including father/child nurturance, certainly is not taken into consideration here.[66] Moreover, mass communication's reliance on advertising, and thus on corporations, never merited discussion; instead, most editors accepted the advertising as an inevitable part of the package and worked to change corporations' unfair treatment toward women's magazines and the portrayal of women within the advertisements themselves. Importantly, however, the difficulties *Ms.* faced in attracting advertisers' dollars, or in changing advertising images, did not surface publicly in a significant way until the sale of *Ms.* in 1987.

Despite the optimistic tone put forth by *Ms.* in its "One Step Forward" column, by the latter half of the 1980s the magazine was facing steep competition from its sister publications for readership and for advertising dollars. The Patricof Report's prognosis for the 1980s had come true; the professional women's market had certainly grown, and *Ms.* had certainly worked to gain its share, but other magazines, both the already established women's magazines and the newcomers, especially *New Woman* and *Self*, had picked up this marketing niche more successfully. These other magazines provided advertisers with a readership that exhibited all the "quality demographics" of *Ms.* readers, but without the complicating political tenor or angry readers. *Ms.* worked to compensate for advertisers' lingering doubts about *Ms.* in its own promotional material, portraying the *Ms.* reader as the ideal consumer. As a consequence, *Ms.* had to speak primarily to this "professional woman" in its editorials and articles, thus constricting any broad conception of "sister-hood." As the readers became consumers rather than women, the magazine became a "marketing opportunity" rather than a cause.[67]

Ms. as an Institution

As a magazine owned by the Ms. Foundation for Education and Communication (MFEC), *Ms.* was a nonprofit organization, related to but not, of course, the same entity as the Ms. Foundation for Women (MFW). As the editors and staff at the magazine and each foundation continually pointed out, however, most people made no distinctions among the MFW, *Ms.* magazine, and the MFEC. As Marie Wilson wrote in an internal memo in the 1980s, "It is my observation that the majority of persons who are involved with us do not make distinctions between us. At fund-raisers, in the world at large, in the foundation community this is the case even when we go to great lengths to explain. More often, there are questions about the failure of one or both organizations to practically use the relationship synergistically."[68]

While the three entities grew out of the same endeavor, to publish a magazine that would both "speak to all women" and make money for the movement, they were actually separate organizations, with distinct, though sometimes overlapping, purposes and corporate members. (A number of key figures — in particular Gloria Steinem, Patricia Carbine, and Letty Cottin Pogrebin — overlapped in the three areas.) However, the two foundations and the magazine, though distinct entities, supported and influenced each other, if only because most of the public saw them as one body, and the image and reputation of one aspect of the foundational trio could clearly influence another.

When the MFW acquired the magazine through the Ms. Foundation for Education and Communication in the late 1970s, Steinem spoke of the way that the magazine would help to spread the word of the foundation's work. She explained that the MFW had been "looking for ways to let a wider public know about its giving service. . . . If *Ms.* Magazine could be acquired by the foundation as a nonprofit subsidiary," she continued, "and thus become even more of the publication that the foundation so obviously needed, then the foundation's work of aiding women's projects and survival issues could be expanded."[69] Indeed, the magazine did infrequently publish articles on the foundation, such as Rosemary Bray's 1986 article "Ms. Foundation: Dollars to the Grassroots," which distinguished between the Ms. Foundation for Education and Communication and the Ms. Foundation and explained that the MFW served to "empower women of diverse backgrounds and circumstances" and to fund projects that dealt with "survival issues" such as discrimination, violence, reproductive rights, economic and social empowerment, and nonsexist, multiracial education.[70] Part of the ostensible reason for the acquisition of the magazine was for the two entities to help each other through a synergy of efforts. Nevertheless, while the two entities faced similar problems in the 1980s, with funding efforts, fighting a conservative climate, and adapting to a changing feminist environment, the decisions each made to deal with the issues took them in different directions. Moreover, the magazine worked less synergistically with the foundation and worked more to create an image that the foundation had to fight. Certainly the magazine did nothing to counter the foundation's "white and middle-class" image or to encourage potential donors to get past the impression that the foundation was richly endowed.[71] Indeed, a letter from board member Jean Bolen to Maya Angelou, asking her to speak at a benefit, pointed out that "the majority of our grantees are also minority women — which belies the Ms. image that we're concerned with the interests of white, middle-class, urban women." Of course, it was true that the magazine, as a commercial product, was, of necessity, concerned with those white, middle-class, urban women. But that image necessarily worked against the desire of the institution as a whole to be a real feminist resource for change.[72]

Like the magazine, the Ms. Foundation had to confront the problems generated by an increasingly conservative climate in the 1980s. Despite the educational efforts by the foundation and by the movement in general, philanthropic donations for programs geared toward women and girls continued to be extremely low, as they were when the foundation began in the early 1970s. In 1984, for instance, donations from private and corporate foundations designated for programs for women and girls totaled less than 4 percent of $4.36 billion given, and activist groups received a very small percentage of that funding. That certainly was up from the 1.7 percent women's groups received in 1979, but it still was a far cry from any kind of parity.[73] In addition, like the magazine that had to compete with newer women's magazines, the foundation found itself competing for those few available dollars with an increased number of women's funds. In 1980, there were four women's funds; in 1986, that number had grown to twenty-eight. On the one hand, this was the very success that the Ms. Foundation had hoped to generate; the increased number of funds was, as Judy Austermiller, founding member of the National Network of Women's Funds, explained, a "reflection of women's decision to take control of resources that in the past [women] either had no control over or let others control."[74] In a climate where few philanthropic dollars went to women's projects, however, this overall success for feminism meant increased competition for the Ms. Foundation.

As the Ms. Foundation faced this increased competition, the board members and staff debated the direction of their fund-raising and their grant making. Like the magazine staff agonizing over the appropriateness of certain ads, the MFW board also grappled with the politics of the origins of their funds. This struggle was revealed most strikingly in the foundation's 1982 decision to return all contributions, approximately $10,000, that the Playboy Foundation had given to the Ms. Foundation since 1978. While initially willing to take the money because it would be used to help women, the board reversed its decision once *Playboy* began to publicize the donations to the foundation to argue that *Playboy* was good or, at least, harmless to women. Understandably, the Ms. Foundation, charged with the empowerment of women in all aspects of their lives, did not want to be used as the public relations tool to strengthen *Playboy*'s image.[75]

Questions of what a feminist agenda constituted in the changed environment of the 1980s also concerned the MFW board. From its origins, the foundation wanted to give funding priority to "survival issues" that they perceived to be on the "cutting edge" of change. In 1981, they were able to articulate clearly the boundary of that cutting edge, emphasizing that it did not mean "general social issues": "As supportive as we may be of the general social issues, *our* target should be feminist issues."[76] Just a year later, however, minutes from the board meetings highlighted the change of thinking demanded in the conservative and economically troubled 1980s: "Is it realistic to think we will find 'radical/innovative projects' in these times of 'survival' politics?"[77] As another memo pointed out, not only did the foundation need to recognize the pressure feminist organizations faced in the 1980s, but it also needed to reconsider the politics of its own funding priorities, particularly around issues of diversity: "We are also beginning to get inquiries and proposals from women of color groups who are developing their own perspectives, agendas and strategies and not necessarily using the words or strategies of the 'white' women's movement. In determining if a project fits our criteria, one of the recurring questions is 'How is this feminist?' If the words and strategies change, what do we measure it against?"[78]

The foundation's policy statement in the 1980s emphasized the funding priority given to projects that dealt with "survival issues," particularly those projects that encouraged women to work with each other across lines of race and income, and to the "support [of] newly emerging feminist issues as women organizing define them." What this exactly meant in practice, however, was something the board frequently debated. Jean Hardisty, one of the board members of the MFW, spoke eloquently of what it meant to support projects from a true diversity of women. She pointed out "the ways in which the projects initiated by women of color often differ in style and content from those initiated by white women who are feminists. These differences may reflect cultural differences, economic differences, differences in historical experience, and differences in access to resources. They are seen, however, as *political* differences, and as a result, the work of women of color often is labeled as 'not feminist.'" Hardisty continued, focusing on what this meant for the foundation:

> We must let the organizing that is being done by third world women, women with limited resources, and isolated women tell *us* what the new feminist issues are, and fund what is emerging, not hold out for what is no longer there to fund. We may mourn that a peculiar sort of spirit, zeal, courage and daring characteristic of early feminist organizing seems rare in our current proposals, just as we rebel against the conservative drift of the country and the reactionary nature of the Administration's policies. What we must not allow ourselves to do is to fail to see a new sort of spirit, zeal, courage, and daring in what is emerging, especially when it differs from what we participated in and even led in other times.[79]

As the Ms. Foundation moved through the 1980s, it was dealing with a transformation of the meaning of feminism, stemming from both a realization of the "treacherous times" the decade posed for feminist organizing and, most importantly, a recognition of the ways that placing too narrow a definition on "feminist organizing" closed off the work of a wide range of women. Interestingly, even as the magazine moved to a more narrow definition of "women" in the 1980s, with its increased focus on the professional working woman, the foundation broadened its definition of women and of feminism.

As the MFW worked to distance itself from the image generated by the magazine, however, the legal connections between the two made it evident that they were tightly bound together. This fact was made particularly clear when the foundation considered changing its board membership requirements. In this case, MFW's impetus to provide leadership meaningful for a diverse constituency actually worked against its goals to maintain the magazine as a feminist institution. In 1982, memos from MFW's lawyer to board members describe this dilemma. Rochelle Korman, the attorney for the foundation, wrote:

The problem created by the Foundation's unchanging Board (and which problem will be perpetuated if the membership remains intact) is that people do not see the Foundation as acting in a manner which is truly accountable to the larger community. Rather, the Foundation is all too often perceived as the private preserve of a handful of well-known women. This perception creates a credibility problem for staff in fund-raising and grant making, because of the appearance that the feminist principle of sharing power is not respected by an organization which considers itself to be a leader in the feminist and philanthropic communities. Therefore, staff are placed in the awkward position of challenging patriarchal structures and requiring grantees to conform, or attempt to conform, with feminist principles, and at the same time, having to defend or explain the Ms. Foundation structure.[80]

While the board concurred in the importance of a regular rotation of members in order to ensure fresh and diverse perspectives, they soon discovered a snag that complicated their best intentions. Any changes to the MFW would potentially affect the MFEC, its subsidiary organization over which it had legal control. And, since the MFEC owned *Ms.* magazine, then any changes to the MFW could potentially reshape the magazine. It worked this way: The MFW was run by two control groups: the board, made up of directors, and the corporation, made up of four permanent members: Gloria Steinem, Patricia Carbine, Letty Cottin Pogrebin, and Marlo Thomas. Primary responsibility for the corporation is actually vested in the board, but, as a part of New York State law, the corporation also has a "self-perpetuating body" of members who have certain powers of oversight over the organization. If the MFW eliminated those core members and moved entirely to a rotating board, then a group of directors who didn't share the board's vision of *Ms.* as a feminist magazine could actually take over the magazine. Korman explained the problem this way:

If MFW eliminates its membership and vests total control of the organization in the Board of Directors, then MFEC's Board will be elected by the MFW Board. And, once the rotation of current directors is completed, or nearly so, a 'bunch of strangers' could take over *Ms.* magazine or threaten to intervene in its operations. Therefore, I cannot imagine Pat, Gloria, or Letty agreeing to the elimination of the current MFW membership once they are informed of the ramifications for the Magazine. And, I believe their feelings and fears would be quite justifiable.[81]

The debate concluded with all the board settling on a regular rotation of the board directors. Most responsibilities would be vested directly with the board, with the exception of a limited few. The MFW would retain its four permanent members, Steinem, Carbine, Pogrebin, and Thomas, in order to avoid "the possibility of losing MFW's feminist philosophy and purpose, and the ability to have input on the selection of new board members to assure the above."

Debates over the direction of the Ms. Foundation for Women, its funding, and its grant-making goals illuminate the connections—in both structure and image—among the Ms. Foundation for Women, the Ms. Foundation for Education and Communication, and *Ms.* magazine, despite the desire of all three entities to keep the boundaries clear. By the second half of the 1980s, however, the magazine faced such financial difficulties that the foundation eventually needed to divest itself of *Ms.*, if the magazine were to survive. The process of selling *Ms.* was a complicated one, and, significantly, neither readers nor advertisers "divested" the magazine of its connection with the Ms. Foundation once the sale had taken place. Indeed, just as advertisers' demands on the magazine proved to be stronger than the founders originally expected, so too were the relationships that readers forged with the magazine more powerful than anyone could have anticipated. And it is to the readers' voices that we now turn.

Gloria Steinem speaking at a National Press Club News Conference,
December 20, 1977, assessing President Carter's first year in office, as the
image of the president, "pregnant," looks on.
(United Press International, Sophia Smith Collection, Smith College)

The first Ms. staff, 1973, including (standing, from left) Patricia Carbine (third), Mary Thom (fourth), Gloria Steinem (seventh), Letty Cottin Pogrebin (eighth), Suzanne Levine (seventeenth), and (sitting, from left) Margaret Sloan (first), Cathleen Black (second), Mary Peacock (third), and Harriet Lyons (seventh). (Mary Ellen Mark)

The preview issue of Ms. *hit the newsstands in January 1972.*
Dated Spring 1972 so that it could sit on the stands in case the public was
*not interested, it sold out in just eight days. (*Ms. *magazine © 1972)*

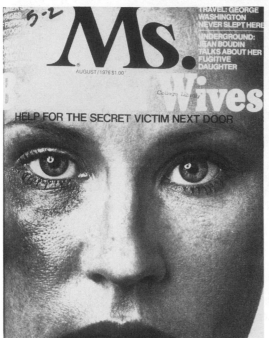
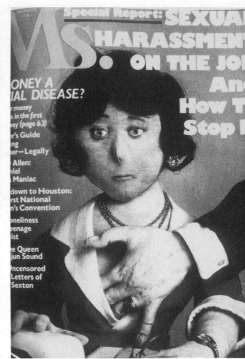

*In the 1970s, editors published covers like these that simultaneously
broke silences and raised some readers' accusations of sensationalism.
(Ms. magazine © 1976 [left], © 1977 [right])*

Covers of "plain" women, like this November 1980 cover of USSR exiles,
heightened advertisers' fears that feminists rarely bought makeup or fashionable
clothing. (Ms. magazine © 1980)

143

Throughout the 1980s, Ms. worked to translate feminist scholarship into popular terms, such as in this 1984 cover story on the feminist psychologist Carol Gilligan. (Ms. magazine © 1984)

144

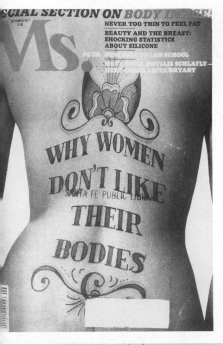

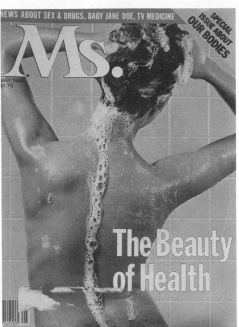

In 1977, Ms. *challenged
readers with the headline
"Why Women Don't Like
Their Bodies." By 1984, the
yearly health issue had been
transformed into a beauty
issue, which was much easier
for the marketing staff to sell
to advertisers with flyers such
as "Healthy, Wealthy and
Wise," which promised
advertisers an "environment
tailor-made for them."
(Ms.* magazine © 1977, 1984,
*Sophia Smith Collection,
Smith College)*

The tenth anniversary issue attempted to represent the diversity of women who made up the women's movement. On the newsstand, however, all that potential readers would see would be the face of the known leader of the movement, Gloria Steinem. (Ms. *magazine* © 1982)

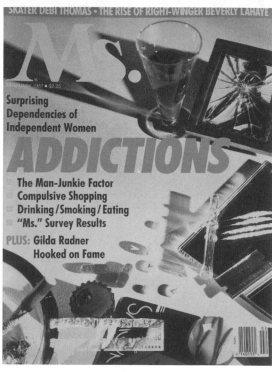

The February 1987 issue on addictions did not include the cigarette or alcohol advertising that Ms. relied on heavily. (Ms. *magazine* © 1987)

The Ms. *staff compiled and published regularly the
"No Comment" section, to which readers sent copies
of ads they found offensive. By the late 1970s, Ms. began
publishing "One Step Forward," applauding the efforts
of advertisers they considered progressive.
(Ms.* magazine © 1981)

The fifteenth anniversary issue (above) commemorated the range of feminist issues the magazine had covered. The next month, editors introduced the transition covers (opp. page) designed to deflect attention away from these feminist roots and attract a new investor. (Ms. magazine © 1987)

Ms.

...TEMBER 1987 · $1.95

FOR A...

NEW, NEW, NEW...
creative gossip, movie
tip sheet, personal
style, great ideas

GLORIA
STEINEM
ANSWERS
TO THE
ETHICS
CRISIS

HOW TO STOP
BORK AND SAVE THE
SUPREME COURT

THE WOMAN WHO IS
PROSECUTING
JENNIFER LEVIN'S
KILLER

TV
COMEDY:
IT'S TRACEY
ULLMAN
TIME!

149

In 1990, Ms. published its first noncommercial issue. The cover proclaimed its freedom from advertisers. (Ms. magazine © 1990)

CHAPTER 4

Readers Writing *Ms.*

Writing on everything from spiral notebook paper to business letterhead and flowered stationery, the women who wrote to *Ms.* were generous with their praise, their criticisms, their love, and their demands. They forged strong yet volatile ties with this mass media text that promised to serve the women's movement. The passion behind readers' letters belies the notion that they were part of a "passive culture," as some critics of *Ms.*, such as Adrienne Rich, have argued.[1] Indeed, the relationship readers created with the magazine must be of central concern to anyone interested in understanding how this magazine worked as a resource within the second wave of feminism. The history of *Ms.* is not simply the story of editors' and advertisers' roles, nor the analysis of the magazine alone; it also includes the way readers used, understood, and shaped the magazine. They played a central role in the cultural contestation over *Ms.* magazine, and over the word "feminism" that it articulated.

From its origins, women across the United States identified with *Ms.* and insisted it live up to its promise to be a resource for the women's movement.[2] When it fell short of their demands, they felt betrayed, angry, and disappointed, and they used the skills they had at least partially learned through *Ms.* to criticize and resist what they found offensive. The language of the women's movement and the marketing promises of *Ms.* provided ample ammunition for making strong claims. One reader, for instance, concluded her angry letter with the sarcastic comment, "I don't *believe* you, *Ms.* Magazine. In sisterhood??????"[3] Drawing from the language of the early women's movement, and mocking the closing of Gloria Steinem's renewal letters, this reader used *Ms.*'s promise of sisterhood to articulate her disappointment.

In preparation for writing this chapter I read thousands of letters readers wrote to *Ms.*, including all the ones published in the magazine from 1972–89 and a significant portion of the unpublished letters written to *Ms.* from 1972–80, which are collected at the Schlesinger Library. As *Ms.* received on average 200 letters per month, a much larger number than periodicals with comparative, or even much bigger, circulations received, the choices a researcher must make in culling through the collection are significant.[4] The Schlesinger Library chose to retain the general categories of letters into which the editors of *Ms.* had already organized the letters prior to their donation. As I was most interested in the relationship that readers forged with the magazine, I focused my research on the two categories with the most letters: "Personal" and "Praise, Criticism, Suggestions." The other categories were primarily focused on specific issues—the ERA, abortion, housewives, and so on. "Personal" was, as indicated by the title, the general category into which letters of a personal nature, in which readers wrote to *Ms.* with stories of their own experiences, "clicks," and problems, were placed. "Praise, Criticism, and Suggestions" included all the letters in which readers applauded *Ms.*, scolded it, berated the advertising, or discussed certain articles or the overall strategies the magazine was using. Generally, letters that focused on more than one issue—talking about the covers as well as specific issues on which the magazine was reporting—seemed to end up in "Praise, Criticism, and Suggestions"; letters that focused solely on one topic—abortion, family violence, academic tenure—ended up with their own folders.

Mine was not an exclusive focus, however; the letters were so fascinating that I often found myself spending hours reading letters from women speaking about miscarriages, their experiences reading Ayn Rand, contraception, or the ERA. My focus was, by necessity, on the letters that illuminated readers' relationship with the magazine. In analyzing the letters, I paid attention to which letters the editors chose to publish; generally, if the magazine received a large number of letters on one topic, they chose to publish a representative one or two. They also sometimes published a collection of letters on a certain topic, such as "Women and Money" (June 1973) or "Unforgettable Letters from Battered Wives" (December 1976). But researchers must be wary of extrapolating the numbers of letters written on any topic as a measure of what readers thought. Indeed, the letters must only be taken as indicative of what those readers motivated enough to write thought about the magazine. For this reason, I emphasized less the number of letters written on specific subjects than the general themes around which readers articulated their relationship to the magazine, their ideas as to the role the magazine should play, and what meaning the magazine—and feminism—held in their lives.

Current work within cultural studies suggests a useful way of exploring what role *Ms.* had in readers' lives. Cultural studies explore how subordinated groups resist and negotiate power relations, particularly through social practices connected with popular culture and mass communications. During the last ten years in the United States, we have seen pathbreaking work done by feminist scholars who blend textual, institutional, and audience analyses of popular culture texts like romance novels, television programming, film, and music videos, focusing on the complex ways these texts work to shape female subjectivity, desire, and power.[5] Cultural studies scholars emphasize the polysemous quality of texts, the gaps, fissures, and multilayered nature of commercial media, that allows for multiple and often contradictory readings by audiences. Drawing on the theories of literary scholar M. M. Bakhtin and cultural analyst Stuart Hall, these critics point to the ongoing dialogic process of communication. That is, they see communication as an active process, requiring the decoding of meaning by the receiver as well as the encoding of meaning by the producer.[6] Placing the emphasis on dialogue allows cultural critics to see how commercial media texts construct meanings, both dominant and oppositional, and to see how consumers engage with the texts, often resisting their overt messages and using the texts in ways unintended by the producers.

In this chapter, I emphasize the process of decoding over the process of encoding, the act of consumption over the act of production. Through their letters, *Ms.* readers figuratively wrote the magazine for themselves, infusing it with meanings and purposes they thought appropriate. In writing the magazine, they also worked to "right" it, to bring it back to its original promise to be a resource of and for women. Finally, in writing to the magazine they also literally wrote it, as their published letters and "No Comment" ads worked to subvert various other narratives within the text. In highlighting readers' relationship to *Ms.*, however, I do not want to suggest that this text can be reduced solely to what readers thought of it. Readers' decodings of *Ms.* were neither infinitely multiple nor simply idiosyncratic but were produced within a distinct historical context and in tension with specific signifiers inscribed within the text. Nor did readers have the authority of editors or the monetary power of advertisers to shape the representations of feminism in *Ms.* Despite these limitations, readers claimed this text as their own, from its origins in 1972 to its final sale in 1989.

Indeed, my research suggests that readers developed two distinct yet intertwined relationships with *Ms.* — one, a relationship of reciprocity and identification; the other, a relationship of resistance and contestation. *Ms.* magazine resonated with many readers' personal identities and changing feminist consciousnesses; their letters reveal a dialogue of mutuality, of identification, even of love. As a multilayered, commercial text, however, *Ms.* contained competing narratives of feminism that often offended readers, who in turn wrote angry, critical letters to the editors, creating their own counterdiscourse of feminism. Bakhtin's notion of a dialogic of communication provides a useful model for understanding both the relationship of identification and the more adversarial relationship readers had with *Ms.*[7] Significantly, these relationships of identification and of opposition reinforced each other; the strong identification many readers felt with the magazine gave them the legitimacy to claim it as their own and to protest dominant commercial and ideological practices within the magazine.

Speaking to Readers

In exploring the relationship readers developed with *Ms.*, it is important to recognize the ways editors attempted to shape reader interactions with *Ms.* Gloria Steinem and Patricia Carbine's attempt to create a "new kind of women's magazine" organization also paralleled the editors' attempt to develop a reader-centered text. Carbine envisioned an organization structured as a circle, the magazine at the center, with everyone involved having equal access to that magazine. Readers of *Ms.* quickly established themselves as part of that circular organization. Above all, the editors of *Ms.* magazine made a conscious attempt to speak to readers in a voice both personal and intimate. Within a women's magazine, anything but a personal voice would have been incongruous, but the apparent honesty and familiarity with which editors addressed readers was more extensive than in other magazines.

While I speak here of editors, since the relationship with readers was indeed a collective concern, the primary voice that readers "heard" was Gloria Steinem's, who signed many of the editorials and solicitation requests simply, "Gloria."[8] Other than the extensive letters from readers section, the principal area in which editors developed this relationship with readers was in the annual and sometimes biannual "Personal Report from *Ms.*" Significantly, editors chose the title of "Personal Report" rather than "Corporate Statement," or something similar, further reinforcing a sense of connection with readers. In the first "Personal Report from *Ms.*," published in the July 1972 issue, Steinem discussed the origins of the magazine, from the desires of writers to work for a magazine in which they believed, to the economic arrangements with Warner Communications. She also introduced the nontraditional, nonhierarchical editorial structure of the magazine, describing it not as a result of some new feminist philosophy but as a system that emerged from "gut experience": "As women, we had been on the bottom of hierarchies far too long. We knew how wasteful they really were." She reported as well the backgrounds of the *Ms.* staff, portraying them as a group similar to the readers of this magazine, despite her disclosure that most had been educated at private Eastern colleges. "All together, we're not a bad composite of the changing American woman," she wrote.[9] This was a magazine that could speak to readers because, according to the "Personal Report," those who wrote it resembled those who read it.

The "Personal Reports" in the next few years followed this basic format of the first report, although generally in abbreviated length. The report discussed the economic status of the magazine, the newest endeavors of the Ms. Foundation, and the growth in subscriptions as well as increasing costs of postage and paper. They also included a chatty and personal account of some member or members of the *Ms.* staff, as in the June 1974 "Personal Report," which described the "littlest Ms.," Alix Langer, who came to work daily with her mother. Other pieces supplemented this sense of "getting to know" the *Ms.* staff; the May 1973 issue, for instance, included "Mothers Are People — A *Ms.* Family Album," a pictorial montage of *Ms.* staff as mothers and daughters.[10]

If the "Personal Reports" presented the *Ms.* staff as a family, the readers were the most important members. From the beginning, editorial pieces gave prime position to readers, as the conclusion of the first "Personal Report" attests: "Most of all, we are joyfully discovering ourselves, and a world set free from old patterns, old thoughts. We hope *Ms.* will help you — and us — to explore this new world. There are few guidelines in history, or our own past. We must learn from each other. So keep writing. *Ms.* belongs to us all." *Ms.* editors and staff presented the new movement as a mission on which they were embarking with readers, a hopeful journey with readers acting as the most significant pathbreakers. The "Personal Reports" downplayed the role of editors and celebrated the success of *Ms.* and of the movement, attributing it primarily to reader activism. "More out of instinct than skill," the first report read, "the women of *Ms.* had tapped an emerging and deep cultural change that was happening to us, and happening to our sisters."[11] A year later the report was even more explicitly about the importance of readers. "It's clear to us . . . that this success [of the magazine] is due less to those of us on the staff than it is to you, the readers." The report also linked readers' responses to women in need to the great improvements in women's lives: "Whatever degree is possible for the individual reader, you respond to courage and talent and need in a very personal, tangible way. And that *has* made a difference."[12]

In its "Personal Reports," renewal requests, and editorial comments, *Ms.* explicitly promised to listen to readers. Editors assured readers that they did not simply toss uncommissioned manuscripts into the wastebasket, despite the overwhelming number the office received each day: "We *do* read every one that's sent in, and have published some unsolicited articles and stories during the last year."[13] In addition, they pledged to publish an extensive number of readers' letters each month, both as evidence of their responsiveness to readers and as a way for readers to communicate with each other. Indeed, *Ms.* did publish many more letters than its sister, mainstream publications. In July 1973, for instance, *Ms.* published five pages of letters, in contrast to *McCall's*, which published one page, *Good Housekeeping*, which published one page, and *Vogue*, which published no letters. The lengthy letters section, which allowed readers access to the magazine, set a pattern that *Ms.* followed in all subsequent issues. "After all," editors wrote, "using only women who happen to be writers is itself a kind of discrimination, and misrepresents the lives that women lead."[14] Certain cover stories and "Forum" pieces elicited extensive responses from readers, at which time *Ms.* often published an extra section of letters, such as the collection of letters about wife battering, in addition to the regular letters section.[15] In addition, *Ms.* published special supplementary letters sections, printed as if on the writer's own stationery, thus reinforcing the sense of personal connection both between the editors and the readers, and among readers.[16]

Particularly in its early years, the magazine attempted to solicit responses from readers even in rejections. In an early 1970s renewal notice, Steinem wrote a letter to readers, asking them to resubscribe. If they chose not to, she requested them to write with their comments, criticisms, and praise, directly on the back of the sheet if they wanted.[17] The message of this request was clear; propriety and formality of response was insignificant—what was important to the editors was *hearing* the readers' voices. In response, editors would speak to readers, through the format of the "Personal Report." By June 1974, they committed themselves to the regular reports: "We've developed at least one bona fide tradition: the occasional letter from us to you known as 'A Personal Report.' . . . We have to admit that we may *need* the Personal Report to keep this dialogue up to date."[18] Through the use of editors' first names and the publication of chatty stories and pictures of the *Ms.* workplace, the extensive letters sections, and the regular "Personal Reports from *Ms.*," the magazine made a deliberate attempt to forge a comfortable, intimate relationship with readers. Moreover, this was to be a relationship based on mutual respect and honesty: *Ms.* was to be forthright about the economic and philosophical basis of the magazine, while readers were to trust in their goodwill and be open about their concerns, criticisms, and praise.

Of course, the relationship between editors and readers was more complex than this. Despite the informality suggested by the use of first names, letters from readers, and "Personal Reports," readers and editors were not in a position of mutual equality; the editors clearly had more power to construct the shape of feminism within *Ms.* and to direct its future as a resource within the women's movement. Moreover, the honesty with which editors spoke to readers was often more apparent than real; I am not suggesting that editors purposefully lied to readers, but the economic basis and editorial organization of *Ms.* were much more complex that their explanations allowed. For instance, the Wonder Woman book and the *Free to Be* recording emerged not simply from reader excitement, as the "Personal Reports" suggested, but as a result of an intricate merging of commercial and political interests. The use of a personal voice and the solicitation of readers' responses were marketing techniques used to secure consumer loyalty. Indeed, critics like the group Redstockings saw the editors' strategies as evidence of the way they tricked women who believed in a movement, using women's hope as a way of bettering the magazine's commercial prospects.

These criticisms are, of course, part of a broader criticism of all commercial mass media, which argues that the promises of consumer culture simply lure consumers into desiring consumer products and into offering their money to various corporations. Frankfurt School Marxist theorists T. W. Adorno and Max Horkheimer have argued that consumer culture manipulates its users by exposing the problems of contemporary culture then radically closing down further analysis of the issue by offering consumer goods as a solution. This is the perspective T. J. Jackson Lears takes in his work *No Place of Grace*, in which he points to the way corporations channeled desires for authentic social relationships in turn-of-the-century U.S. culture into a consumer orientation. Stuart Ewen, in *Captains of Consciousness: Advertising and the Social Roots of the Consumer Culture*, takes a similar angle in his analysis of advertising executives' ability to manage consumer desires for profit. Indeed, from this perspective the extensive promises editors made to readers can be seen as what cultural critic Frederic Jameson calls "a complex strategy of rhetorical persuasion in which substantial incentives are offered for ideological adherence." [19]

The history of *Ms.*, however, suggests something more complex than a simple (mis)use of readers by editors. While the construction of a "personal relationship" with readers was certainly a marketing technique, interviews with the editors and publisher demonstrate that the editors also believed in the importance of their magazine to the movement and to the women who read it. In conversation after conversation with editors, I heard that the delivery of letter bags was the highlight of each day. Even after the novelty of this immense outpouring from readers wore off, the editors instituted a policy that insured that the concerns of readers were addressed. One staff person was assigned to read the letters, prepare a monthly report, and choose the ones for publication. In the early years of the magazine, the reports, which tallied and categorized the topics of each letter, illuminate the editors' surprise and joy at readers' vehement connection with the magazine. In describing the fifty-three Christmas cards sent to the magazine, for instance, editor Ingeborg Day wrote, "These are not cards by advertisers or people who either have had business with us of some sort, or who know staff members personally. This count includes only cards sent by 'just' readers. (Who ever heard of sending Christmas cards to a MAGAZINE?)"[20] Perhaps even more significantly, in these early years, an editor personally responded to every letter; the backlog, as indicated by these early letters reports, was enormous. Later in the 1970s, the letters' reports tallied the total volume of mail but categorized only those letters dealing with specific articles or advertising campaigns. Personal letters were not categorized, and form letters, for the most part, replaced the individual notes from editors.[21] While only one staff member was designated as official "letter reader," everyone received a copy of the readers' report, and one or two other editors would read the suggested letters for publication. While the monthly report sometimes failed to get written because of editorial pressure (it came out as often as possible, Patricia Carbine reported), its existence signified a serious attempt to understand the needs and concerns of readers.[22]

From the readers' perspective, the sincerity of editors' attention was in some ways less relevant than the outlet the magazine provided for reader expression. The large letters section gave readers more room, figuratively and literally, to air their concerns and ideas; the "No Comment" and classified sections likewise gave them space to use the magazine. In addition, the policy of speaking honestly to readers and taking their concerns seriously gave readers the legitimacy to claim the magazine as their own and to expect editors to pay attention to their interests and their identities. The text of *Ms.* itself offered readers promises that they then used for their own purposes. As Frederic Jameson argues in his work "Reification and Utopia in

Mass Media," all mass media must offer consumers some shred of utopian possibilities in order to gain their loyalty: "The works of mass culture, even if their function lies in the legitimation of the existing order—or some worse one—cannot do their job without deflecting in the latter's service the deepest and most fundamental hopes and fantasies of the collectivity, to which they can therefore, no matter in how distorted a fashion, be found to have given voice." [23] Readers attached themselves to the promises *Ms.* had voiced and insisted, quite passionately, that *Ms.* fulfill their expectations. As one angry reader wrote to *Ms.*, "You're not listening!" [24] She obviously did not perceive the editorial stance of *Ms.* as an empty assurance but expected the magazine to be responsive to her needs.

Friendship, Consciousness-Raising, and Community

Women often wrote to *Ms.* as if they were writing to a sister, a friend, a lover, a helpmate. As one reader in 1975 expressed it, "Writing to *Ms.* seems more like sending a message to a comrade or a love rather than a magazine." [25] Of course, this personification of a magazine was often problematic, since a magazine is not a person, but a business, a text, and a conglomeration of publishers, editors, writers, and advertisers. Some readers seemed to deal with this confusion by addressing their letters to "the editors," to "sisters," or to "readers." Yet often their language became more slippery, and *Ms.* was transformed into a person who could hear them. They imagined a supportive, attentive audience who would understand their stories. For example, toward the end of a seven-page, handwritten letter about body image one woman wrote, "I never intended for this to be such a long sob story. I guess I have the feeling that it's being read. I can picture somebody, reading it and nodding or frowning or reacting to my 'story' in some way." Many readers envisioned a listener with unlimited time, patience, and understanding. As one woman began her eight-page letter, written in minuscule cursive handwriting, "Thought you'd be interested in hearing a good story about discrimination against sex [*sic*]. It's a long one and happening to me. So, grab a cup of coffee and get ready." [26] Of course, readers did not always receive the sympathetic ear they imagined. For instance, the editor of the letter that instructed the reader to "grab a cup of coffee" had written "oh shit" in the margin of the letter. Importantly, however, the letter writers perceived *Ms.* as an audience for stories and feelings that generally would remain unspoken or that would be recorded only in a private journal.

Historians and sociologists have discussed at some length the importance of consciousness-raising groups, particularly in the early years of the women's movement. These groups provided women an opportunity to share stories that illuminated gendered power relations in their own lives, to lend support to others who were beginning to see themselves as women and as victims of a patriarchal system, and, sometimes, to encourage women to act to fight that oppression through political as well as personal means. Generally, these consciousness-raising groups were small and informal, and they emerged from political or community groups or friendship networks already established. According to historian Jo Freeman, by the end of 1970, women not connected to newly emerging groups were seeking them on their own, as indicated by the three letters a week on average the White House was receiving from women inquiring about women's liberation or consciousness-raising groups they could join.[27] Many women throughout the United States were either unaware of or did not have access to these groups. Indeed, the demand for women's groups and consciousness-raising sessions far outreached the resources available through newly founded women's organizations.[28]

Within this context, *Ms.* became a kind of mass media consciousness-raising forum. The letters section served as a place for women to share and to validate their changed perceptions of the world. In 1972, for example, a woman wrote a long letter recounting her experiences as a large-breasted woman. As if she were speaking to a roomful of sympathetic listeners, she described the mocking she received as a teenager, the ogling eyes of men, the disgust she felt at her body, and her envy of other women's bodies. She concluded by sharing her newly found feminist self-image: "I wish no longer to be a victim for insane people who generate these 'norms.' The media's message of body beautiful must be rejected, and the individual's right to her own body restored." The letters editor wrote this writer back, confirming her newly found perspective: "It's great to get a letter like yours: a woman who's had a very real problem and through hard work—raising one's consciousness is hard work—has licked her problem. You sound as if you're happy with yourself now, exactly the way you are. I could go on, describing my own story which is similar to yours, but I won't. You've said it all and as well as it can be said. Good luck! And our very best wishes."[29] While it is probable that letter writers valued the personal response from editors, they did not necessarily expect such a reply. As one letter from Michigan put it in 1973, after writing a long letter of her marriage and impending divorce, "I love you even if you could care less."[30]

Sometimes letter writers used their personal stories to warn other readers about specific injustices or problems. In 1974, a writer from Massachusetts cautioned other readers about the risk of pregnancy with the Dalkon Shield. "I want you to call attention to this issue so women with Dalkon shields will consider trying some alternative birth control device and avert the trauma I went through," she wrote. She explained her own sense of urgency in writing the letter: "You may well wonder how a woman who had an abortion this very day, who needed 10 milligrams of Valium just to be able to relax enough to lie still, could summon the energy to write this letter. My energy comes from pain—not the physical pain of abortion, but the mental pain of knowing that women's bodies have been messed with by the drug industry for too long and it's high time we started fighting back, not as individuals, but en masse as women. In love and sisterhood, . . ."[31] Indeed, this letter writer turned to *Ms.* as a feminist community, a national forum for consciousness-raising and activism. Other writers turned to *Ms.* less to alert other readers to the physical dangers of sexism than to validate their own sense of "reality." One woman in 1975, for instance, wrote a detailed, angry analysis of the portrayal of women in the movie *The Towering Inferno.* Her friends with whom she saw the movie told her she was making too much of it. She concluded her letter asking, "Did anyone see this movie the way I did?"[32] This woman sought the confirmation from the *Ms.* "community" that indeed her vision of this movie was on target. Like countless other women who wrote to *Ms.*, this reader assumed the *Ms.* community would share her perception of sexism.

Letters published in *Ms.* in later years expressed less emotional relief and focused more on debates about everything from sexual practices, to child raising, to television viewing. Yet as late as 1986, one reader wrote a letter about her husband's refusal to let her travel to see Halley's Comet.[33] A few months later, *Ms.* published a forum of letters from readers responding to her, speaking of their "pain of recognition" and their anger at her husband and giving her suggestions, ranging from urging her to take the trip regardless of his "approval," to stressing her need for financial and emotional independence.[34] Certainly the consciousness-raising function of the *Ms.* letter forum continued to serve many women, particularly those intellectually and emotionally isolated by geography or by familial circumstances.

Readers often concluded their stories by writing "click," a word taken from the "click of recognition," when it became all too clear that one was oppressed as a woman, that Jane O'Reilly spoke of in her early *Ms.* article "The Housewife's Moment of Truth."[35] Readers picked up on this language immediately, sending in letters by the thousands that concluded with a "click," or, by the 1980s, a "clunk," suggesting the disappointment and frustration of enduring sexism within the United States. In 1973, for example, a reader from

Kentucky wrote about the qualifications to become an ROTC Angel, the girls auxiliary organization to the Air Force Junior ROTC Program in her high school. "When I inquired as to what this [new organization] meant, I was told that it did not mean that girls would participate in the class activities. What it did mean was that the girls would march with the boys in parades to add color to the group. Qualifications for girls to join this ROTC Angel Flight included among other thinks, looks. CLICK!!!"[36] In 1975, a woman from New York City wrote to describe the physical problems she had developed due to both the IUD and the pill. When she decided to end her contraceptive dilemma by opting for a tubal ligation, her husband had to sign a permission slip. "Click, click," she concluded her letter.[37] When describing how she was "affirmed by the women in control" at the ERA rally in San Francisco, a woman in 1986 explained that she wanted to "share my 'click' experience because it has been those letters that have made me look a little more closely at my own day-to-day life and its hidden prejudices and discrimination."[38] In some cases the term "click," and the change in perception to which it referred, became a signifier of a changed identity, a new feminist persona. In a special collection of letters from younger feminists in 1974, a tradition that *Ms.* often repeated in subsequent years, Kristine Kazie from Massachusetts wrote, "I am an 18-year-old college student and about a year a half ago I *became* a feminist—I mean, experienced the click and everything."[39] The "click" and "clunk" terms clearly resonated with the feelings of a broad readership who used the words to articulate their changed perceptions and identities. This shared vocabulary became a shorthand way of documenting the concerns of feminists without having to go into the long, tedious, and frustrating explanations that would have been needed for a nonfeminist audience.

These letters suggest a strong need and desire on the part of readers to connect with a community outside of their own. Readers wrote detailed accounts of their daily encounters with sexism, their depression, their anger, and their joy at finding a magazine that spoke to their own perceptions and experiences. Of course, this identification with *Ms.* was limited to those who felt an essential sameness between themselves and the text. In other words, the "click of recognition" could be shared only between women whose experiences were similar enough for them to understand each other. While something like "The Housewife's Moment of Truth" clearly spoke to the lives of white, middle-class, and straight women, letters from readers demonstrate that lesbians, women of color, and working-class women rarely connected in the same way to O'Reilly's story.

For those women who did connect with *Ms.*, however, the experience was a powerful one. Many readers, particularly in the 1970s, wrote to tell *Ms.* how they felt "less alone" because of the magazine. In the mid-1970s one woman wrote a painful account of her marriage. She began her letter, "I've been feeling more and more depressed since I got married three years ago and hadn't known why until your magazine 'came out.'" She then recounted the ways in which her husband called her names and silenced her. She concluded, "Although I can't say that your magazine will definitely save me from insanity, it's nice to know that other women are in the same boat with me."[40] In 1975, a woman from Virginia wrote to "*Ms.* — all of you!," saying, "Every month, just as I begin to feel a wee bit too isolated in my feminism, too defensive, too angry, too vulnerable to the firm, calm-eyed 'realities' pushed on me by employer and co-workers — the new *Ms.* arrives to bolster me with the assurance of sisterhood and of purpose."[41] Another woman was even more blunt in her assessment of the magazine's importance: "Thank you for giving my life back to me."[42] This grasping for connection from a media text, or with a media community, speaks to both the literal isolation of many of these women — within nuclear families and circumscribed communities — and the power of patriarchy to naturalize its own ideology and practices, to force women to think there is something wrong with themselves and not with the culture. Particularly in the early years of the magazine, when few alternative mass culture forms of feminism were available, this yearning for a community was quite powerful. As the letter from the woman who wanted to see Halley's Comet indicates, however, for some women, this need for *Ms.* to serve as their feminist community did not die after the 1970s.

For most women, reading *Ms.* provided a relatively unthreatening way to connect with a national community of feminists, although some readers wrote that they literally read the magazine hiding in a closet. And although corresponding with the magazine provided another connection with that community, some readers felt that writing to the magazine was also risky. Letter writers frequently closed their letters with "not for publication" and "withhold my name for obvious reasons," indicating their expectation that the editors would understand the jeopardy a published, clearly feminist, letter in *Ms.* would cause for them. An elementary school teacher from Michigan, sending in letters from her students who loved the "Stories for Free Children," requested that their letters be printed, but with this caveat: "I would appreciate it if you wouldn't use their last names in the magazine! They are too young to understand what they are really doing in such a letter."[43] The risk in this teacher having her students write such letters, of course, was the political act of connecting with a feminist magazine, and, by extension, the feminist movement. And, one might add, these students were too young to understand the threat that such publication would pose for a teacher found to be "inculcating" her children with such readings.

Some readers looked to *Ms.* less as a sister sharing in a mutual process of consciousness-raising and more as a parental figure able to solve their problems for them. In 1974, a reader wrote to the magazine about the inequities in veterans' benefits: a widow lost her benefits if she remarried, whereas a widower maintained his benefits even if he remarried. She concluded, "I thought if I wrote to you you might be able to do something about this." [44] In this case, as in others where readers asked *Ms.* to intervene with their credit ratings, divorce issues, or medical problems, *Ms.* represented an institution far larger than either the magazine or the Ms. Foundation for Women; it became THE feminist movement, which promised to tackle any issue of sexism in the country.

Anger, Opposition, and a Counterdiscourse of Feminism

If these letters reveal a relationship of mutual identification, of love and respect, they also reveal one of anger and opposition. Through their demands, their criticisms, and their suggestions, readers developed a discourse of resistance and contestation, a counterdiscourse of feminism. Readers took very seriously the magazine's promise to be an "open forum for all women," to be a magazine that was a "real service to women." When that promise was broken, readers expressed their feelings with words like "shocked," "disappointed," and "dismayed." One Minnesota reader, canceling her subscription to the magazine in 1978 because of some offensive advertising, characterized her relationship with the magazine this way: "We've had a long love affair, *Ms.*, and it breaks my heart to leave you—but is betrayal with vaginal sprays coming next issue?" [45] Describing her relationship with *Ms.* as one of love, then betrayal, this woman revealed the high level of trust she invested in *Ms.* Indeed, this letter indicates that it was the relationship of identification, the strong connection this woman felt toward *Ms.* magazine as a vehicle of the women's movement, that inevitably led her to feel deceived when it didn't live up to her expectations. Many women felt so committed to the magazine that they refused to cancel their subscriptions, even when they felt betrayed and disappointed. "I am *not* going to ask you to stop my subscription, or refund my money, because I made a commitment to the magazine for two years, and I will live up to it. Are you going to live up to yours?" one reader from Pennsylvania asked in 1977.[46] Readers *expected Ms.* to be responsive to their demands.

Of course, *Ms.* was not the only mass media text that has successfully sought and built readers' identification and trust. All commercial media attempt to solicit consumers' attention and loyalty. As Frederic Jameson points out, even the most debased form of mass media must speak to consumers' fears and desires, or it will be unable to "capture" and retain an audience. Thus, there is a constant negotiation between pleasing an audience and serving advertisers, between speaking to the concerns of those who use mass media and constructing narratives and visuals that accommodate the dominant ideologies and perspectives of those in power.[47] *Ms.* magazine was the product of this same sort of negotiating process, and its contradictory text was the result.

Many of readers' most angry letters focused on *Ms.*'s inability to be an "open forum for all women." Part of *Ms.*'s failure to live up to this promise stemmed from the editors' original conception of who "all women" were. *Ms.* promoted a vision of feminism that assumed that female oppression transcended all other social categories, a vision originating with Gloria Steinem's keynote editorial, "Sisterhood," in the first issue. While this focus on sisterhood and common bonds of womanhood provided the basis for a feminist perspective, it also ignored the intersections between race, class, and gender and obscured the fact that for many women issues like the "housewife blues" and "natural childbirth" were not among their priorities.

However illusory the belief in the common experiences of all women was, though, it also encouraged *Ms.* editors and readers to continue their faith in a magazine that promised to be relevant and accessible to a number of different groups of women. Readers expected *Ms.* to move beyond a white, heterosexual, middle-class focus. As one reader in 1977 reacted to the "Mom Goes to Law School" article, "Such sagas of middle-class success and women bolstered by supportive husbands and sufficient cash belong to the domain of traditional women's magazines."[48] This kind of comparison of *Ms.* to other women's or mainstream magazines played an important role for readers who pushed *Ms.* to be more inclusive. "Please print more articles like Alice Walker's trip to Cuba, news of international events, problems of poor women as well as the middle and upper classes, and especially your muckraking, progressive articles such as the one on breast enlargement operations. . . . I am sending you my check in good faith hoping that your magazine will not become just another *Redbook, Ladies' Home Journal* or *McCall's*," a reader from California wrote in 1977.[49] Several years earlier, a reader from New York State had described her similar disenchantment with the magazine:

Ms. began as a mixed bag, different articles, different points of view, a magazine of no major story or advocacy. Now I feel . . . that *Ms.* has centered in on just one type of woman: the straight, middle-class lately-become-a-feminist who is unable to have a continuing satisfactory relationship with a man. The readership of women who have beautiful relationships with men or women is not important. The readership of the poor or lower-class women is not important. The readership of black or non-western women is not necessary for success. I feel as if in your efforts to become respectable you've jettisoned your old friends to gain entrance into suburbia.[50]

Of course, it would not be until the late 1970s that *Ms.* would make the explicit move to be more like *Redbook* and its sister publications in order to "gain entrance into suburbia," i.e., to capture the highly competitive advertising dollar. But what these writers in the 1970s already recognized were the forces pulling *Ms.* away from its promise to be an open forum.

While many letter writers focused on the overall composition of the magazine, others pushed *Ms.* to speak more to them and to the women they represented. A writer in 1980, who described herself as a "consistent reader of your magazine," explained that she has been "disappointed by the small amount of articles pertaining to minority women. Why has there been no form of representation of Chicana women in your magazine. We are women also, who are constantly struggling in this male dominated society. I think *Ms.* Magazine would be an excellent medium to educate the public on our struggles. In the future I would like to see more literature about Chicanas and Chicana feminists."[51] Many writers pushed the magazine to be more inclusive of lesbian readers. "You probably are not ignorant of the fact that there has been much criticism of *Ms.* because of your avoidance of a frank approach to Lesbianism," a writer from California wrote in 1975. "Some of us have no doubt that this criticism can affect your future, your position in the women's movement for total liberation from hypocritical attitudes and penalties," she concluded.[52] Another woman, writing in 1976 from Missouri, urged *Ms.* to cover lesbianism but without any sensationalism.

Many lesbians will probably share my hope that *Ms.* will someday deal with an ordinary garden variety Lesbian in its pages, not that it has admitted our existence in recent issues. . . . Where are the stories about those of us who grew up knowing we were Lesbians? Whose coming out was no more dramatic than telling our mothers at age 12 or so. Those of us, who, without turmoil, drugs, male interludes, etc., simply grew up, married other women and lived out our lives peacefully and contentedly among our neighbors. . . . *Ms.* with its apparent editorial attempt to appeal to a balanced cross-section of women seems the most logical place for such a story."

Poignantly, she concludes her letter, "Please DO NOT withhold my name if you use this letter. Closets are for shoes and clothes, not women." [53]

When readers located articles that spoke to their specific identities, they encouraged the editors to include more of the same. In 1978, in response to excerpts from Michele Wallace's *Black Macho and the Myth of the Super-woman*, black women wrote in to voice their agreement and to push *Ms.* to fulfill its promise to include more articles on black feminism. A woman from Rhode Island wrote, "It's about time that we Black feminists were acknowledged and recognized. . . . I am happy to know that *Ms.* will have more articles on Black feminism. The Black woman has been ignored, under represented, misrepresented and misunderstood too long, and I hope Ms. Wallace's book will help to change that. Many people have overlooked the fact that Black women have always been interested in feminism, human rights, and dignity. Let's not forget that Harriet Tubman and Sojourner were two of the first Black feminists." A graduate student in Iowa wrote, "*Ms.*, I've been waiting a long time for a series of articles [on black women] such as you've planned[,] and now you've come through." Indeed, the letters women wrote about Wallace's article—describing their relief at finding someone who saw the world in the same way they did—resembled the letters white women wrote about O'Reilly's "click" article; as one woman from Brooklyn, New York, wrote, "Like Ms. Wallace I am a 26 year old Black woman who is also concerned about the hatred that has developed between our men and women. I see it everyday and for some time felt I was all alone. Thank you for helping me to find I am not." [54]

Not all readers sought for a more inclusive feminist vision, however. Readers of *Ms.* brought to the magazine their ideas of what feminism was and who the typical American was—and sometimes those ideas were cautious, conservative, and even reactionary. Particularly in the first years of *Ms.*, many women argued that the magazine should avoid making any connections between the women's movement and lesbianism. "Lesbian rights may be a legitimate issue for lesbians but shouldn't be foisted on all supporters of the women's movement," one woman complained.[55] In 1977, a reader from Pennsylvania argued, "After two consecutive issues, I have noticed the tendency towards lesbianism. Come on, girls, Homosexuality is on a totally different dimension than is the issue of women's rights. Aren't we, sadly enough, having enough trouble with the passing of the ERA?"[56] Another woman agreed with the Pennsylvania writer: "It is regrettable that the magazine is so openly lesbian-oriented. What people do on their own time is strictly their business, but the lesbian tinge to the woman's movement has not increased its attractiveness or acceptability to the general public. There should be separate lesbian magazines if they would appeal, but I would like to see *Ms.* representative of *all* women interested in improving their status and opportunities. For this reason I hesitated a long time before renewing."[57] Other women argued that by including too many articles on Jews and blacks *Ms.* limited its appeal. "Why not attempt to reach most instead of some?" a woman from Connecticut concluded her letter in 1979.[58]

For these readers, "all" women obviously meant a group exclusive of lesbians, Jews, and blacks. From her early days as a feminist activist, though, when she stood by Kate Millett during media attacks on her for being a bisexual and went on speaking tours with African American activists like Dorothy Pittman Hughes and Margaret Sloan, Gloria Steinem made clear her aversion to divisive tactics, arguing that women needed to stand together to fight sexism.[59] *Ms.* editors and writers had promised to provide an open forum and to push the boundaries of feminism, goals that certainly could not be accomplished by the exclusionary, racist, and homophobic tactics many conservative readers suggested. Editors rarely published blatantly racist or homophobic letters. When they did, readers had a field day responding to them in the following issues, a ritual that worked to further reinforce a shared understanding of feminism as a political perspective that discouraged all forms of oppression.[60]

Ms. never shifted its perspective far enough from a white, middle-class, heterosexual feminism to be more than a token effort at inclusion, however. As late as 1987, readers were "thanking" *Ms.* for including an article on gay marriage. One woman wrote, "I hope it signals more coverage of a much-needed lesbian and bi-sexual voice in *Ms.*"[61] The inability of *Ms.* to construct a feminism that dealt credibly with issues of difference stemmed from its attempt to deal with diversity at the same time it tried to maintain a unified vision of who women were. These contradictory approaches neither pushed the white, middle-class, heterosexual perspective from the foreground nor acknowledged the fact that not all identities were compatible. The woman who wanted *Ms.* to divorce itself from lesbian issues could not easily co-exist with the woman who encouraged *Ms.* to provide more coverage on lesbian issues. Indeed, the problems *Ms.* encountered in its attempt to be a magazine for the women's movement raise numerous questions about who women were and what the movement was.[62] The letters written to *Ms.* force us to abandon any notion of a universally shared experience of womanhood and sometimes suggest there was little common ground among women in the 1970s and 1980s. What is significant in terms of popular culture studies is the way so many women continued to claim this text, despite its limitations. Clearly, *Ms.* spoke to many women's needs and desires to the extent that they were unwilling to give it up without a fight.

Advertising

In *The Legitimation Crisis*, theorist Jurgen Habermas explains how the mass media justify contemporary commodified culture through an invocation of historical relationships—the family, the community, religion, and so on—that actually have been destroyed by the very system of capitalism that underpins U.S. mass media. Likewise, historian George Lipsitz, in *Time Passages*, demonstrates the way television draws on memories of ethnic identity and ties to legitimate itself, despite the imperative within the commercial structure to destroy any identities and ties that compete with the construction of an atomized consumer identity. Yet because the media must draw on these cultural memories to legitimate themselves, they always run the risk of revealing themselves as artificial structures, designed in the interest of the profit maker. Users of the media will often reject the narratives constructed through advertisements, however, because of the great discrepancy and conflict between the cultural memories drawn upon and the consumer message encoded within the narrative. In the case of *Ms.*, the commodified narratives of feminism constructed within the advertisements did not so much conflict with readers' memories of past relationships as they sharply contradicted readers' identification with the promise of a better future offered by the political and social feminist movement.[63]

While readers disagreed over what kind of feminism *Ms.* should advocate, nearly all readers were united in opposition to the advertising. Readers described the ads in *Ms.* as a betrayal and asked, "If we can't expect to avoid such crap in the pages of *Ms.*, what is there left to read?"[64] Ironically, it was the advertising that allowed *Ms.* to reach the huge population it did, to be sold so inexpensively (only $12 for a yearly subscription even in 1987), and to be available in supermarkets and bookstores where more radical journals were unavailable. Besides subsidizing the cost of the mass circulation magazine, advertising also served as a kind of "cultural bridge," traversing the distance between the magazine and the women who might not initially have considered themselves feminists but found *Ms.* in the relatively unthreatening space of the supermarket. Nevertheless, this advertising portrayed women and feminism in a way offensive to most readers, particularly within the context of a magazine that promised to be different from traditional women's magazines. From its first issue, when nearly 8,000 of the 20,000 letters received focused on ads, advertising provoked the majority of readers' critical letters. Many of the ads in this first issue, actually an inset in *New York* magazine, were blatantly sexist. For instance, an ad for a beauty salon read, "Guys Dig Flabby Girls. Guys Blindly in Love." *Ms.* published many of the angry letters and gave a lengthy editorial response as well. After explaining that *New York* magazine had chosen the ads for the preview issue, the editors wrote, "Now that we are responsible for our own advertising, we will do our best to emphasize ads that are a service to women, and reflect the real balance of our lives."[65] They promised to reject obviously offensive or harmful ads but asked the readers for help in less clear-cut cases. This exchange set the precedent for communication between readers and editors. Particularly when readers' critiques focused on advertising policy or selling techniques, *Ms.* responded publicly, a strategy that worked well to encourage readers' identification with the magazine.

Published exchanges between readers and editors, such as the one quoted above, raised the question of corporate control in a public forum and legitimated readers' criticisms. In addition, the *Ms.* text itself, specifically the "No Comment" section, worked to subvert the rather powerful advertising messages. Nearly every month *Ms.* devoted space to one or more sexist advertisements readers sent in, blocked off with the title "No Comment." While readers sent in everything from offensive office memos to copies of billboards, much of the "No Comment" section was taken up by advertisements from mass media magazines, such as the 1984 ad from *Time* magazine for First Citizens Bank telling readers, "Show your wife you love her. Leave her out of your will," or the ad from *Yachting* magazine picturing glamorous blondes on a forty-four-foot yacht, with the caption, "Love Her on the Outside, Love Her on the Inside." Like the "click" and "clunk" letters, the "No Comment" section reinforced a common vocabulary and a sense of community, providing an arena in which readers resisted the ways in which they were encoded in dominant media. In her study of the "No Comment" section, Linda Steiner argues that these pages of reader submissions "provide evidence of a shared map of meaning that enables relatively coherent and stable, if unspoken, responses for the group."[66] Because of this "shared map of meaning," the readers who sent in ads to this section did not have to explain why they found them sexist. They assumed the *Ms.* community would understand. These ads worked as a collective process of oppositional decoding in which readers resisted the dominant meanings encoded in the ads from the mainstream press. As Linda Steiner argues, the "No Comment" ads provided readers with "access and commitment to an alternative, oppositional definition of reality."[67]

Importantly, readers used this feminist perspective on reality not only to critique advertisements from other mass media periodicals but also to question *Ms.*'s own use of commercial texts.[68] An ad published in *Ms.* in 1978 for the Lady Bic Shaver, picturing a tan, white woman from the buttocks down, provides an extremely clear example of how the "No Comment" section worked. The words "Bikini Legs" dominated the page, with smaller copy reminding readers of the challenge of beach life—it was "you and your legs," and they had to be shaved smooth or sleek or you were condemned to a day under water. Over a hundred readers sent in this ad, often with only a slip of paper marked "No Comment." Others analyzed the Lady Bic ad in detail, referring to the skills in deconstruction that they had learned from *Ms.* itself. A woman from Michigan wrote, "Shame on you! . . . Your 'NO COMMENT' section backfired on you, and if many disappointed readers don't send this particular ad among 'NO COMMENT' mail, I'll be surprised." Another woman did send it to the "No Comment" section, but also wrote to editors, because, she said, "I do, after all, have a comment on it." She continued, "Do you think no one will notice and be offended by an ad that is, supposedly, condoned by *Ms.*? That we'll search magazines for offensive ads while ignoring the same in *Ms.*'s pages? (Be yourselves, girls, only shave those legs!) . . . You contradict yourself, *Ms.* I've spent my high-school years reading you and learning from you. So, please, DON'T CHEAPEN YOURSELF, *Ms.*, after teaching *me* not to."[69]

Advertisements evoked heated and angry responses from readers throughout its nearly two-decade history as a commercial magazine. Editors were initially surprised at the vehemence of readers' responses and their keen ability to recognize the way the advertisements either contradicted or, in their words, distorted, the feminist ideas articulated elsewhere in the magazine. In certain cases, however, editors prepared for the onslaught they knew would be arriving from readers. In 1986, despite that preparation, *Ms.* found itself embroiled in a controversy that pitted feminists against feminists when they accepted an ad for Calvin Klein's perfume Obsession. Part of a multi-ad campaign, this ad pictured the body of woman nude from the waist up, being caressed and kissed by a young man. We can see only the woman's body, not her face or even her arms. The caption reads, "OBSESSION" and, in smaller print, "FOR THE BODY." *Ms.* prepared a press release prior to its publication, explaining that the ad was prepared by the thirty-three-year-old Robin Burns and her "mostly female management team." The release stressed that the ad was about "mutual enjoyment, with no force, no dominance." They claimed that it was the man, rather than the woman, who was in a vulnerable position, and that the only "conventional" part of the image was that the woman's face was not shown.[70]

Almost immediately after the April issue hit the newsstand, a reporter from *New York Newsday* called the feminist group Women Against Pornography (WAP) to inquire about their thoughts on the ad running in *Ms.* Apparently, the woman who answered the phone responded that she was "blown away" that *Ms.* would take such an account, which she described as "one long pornographic fantasy."[71] *Newsday* printed her comments without getting WAP's official approval. *New York* magazine also picked up on the apparent fight between Steinem and Women Against Pornography.[72] After Steinem confronted WAP about its accusations that *Ms.* was accepting pornography, Dorchen Leidholdt, one of its cofounders, wrote both *Newsday*, *New York*, and Steinem to clear up the confusion; while WAP did not like the ad, they never wanted to be on record stating that Steinem, or *Ms.* for that matter, had sold out. "At our next general membership meeting, we'll talk about how to deal with reporters who want to stir up trouble between feminists," Leidholdt concluded.[73]

The Obsession controversy illuminates a number of interesting points. First, as usual, *Ms.* was held to a standard higher than its sister publications; no one in the media industry found it worthy to report on other women's magazines who were carrying this ubiquitous campaign. Indeed, the coverage of the supposed fight between WAP and *Ms.* had all the attraction of a cat fight among women for the gossip columns. On a more complex level, we can also see the controversy generated by the Obsession ad as part of the larger debates about female sexuality, or "sex wars," as they came to be known, among feminists in the 1980s. Groups like Women Against Pornography, which voiced the first complaints about the Obsession ad, had articulated powerful arguments against pornography and male dominance within sexuality; they had also generated effective national boycotts and campaigns against advertisers, pornography bookstores, and so on.

By the early 1980s, however, another set of voices began to make themselves heard, arguing that the kind of censorship groups like WAP advocated put them too closely in alliance with New Right organizations and, most importantly, that the nuances of sexual pleasure and sexual danger were too complex to be easily defined as either "bad" or "good." The split among feminists became most clear at the 1982 Barnard College conference "The Scholar and the Feminist IX: Toward a Politics of Sexuality," and in the forums on the conference reported on in the two major feminist journals, *Feminist Studies* and *Signs*, following the acrimonious meeting. In 1986, when *Ms.* ran the Obsession ad, they were in no financial position to refuse any ad. And even if they could have, would they have refused the Obsession ad? Was the portrayal of sexuality inherently antifeminist?[74]

Readers answered this question in no uncertain terms. Within a month *Ms.* had received over 300 letters from readers, including group petitions complaining about the ad; some canceled their subscriptions. "We understand your need for advertising, and have therefore learned to live with full page cigarette ads," one reader wrote. She continued, "We *love Ms.*, and don't want you to whither away financially. But—this Obsession ad is inappropriate—too much of a compromise."[75] Another reader from Michigan explained why she thought *Ms.* had made a blatant mistake in running the ad: "I am enclosing a contribution [the Calvin Klein ad] to your 'No Comment' column. I dare you to run it. . . . At the very least I'd like an explanation of why you accept advertising so clearly inappropriate to feminist goals. If nothing else, surely you could not fail to notice that the face of the semi-nude woman in the photograph is not shown. What better way to objectify woman than to render her faceless. Truly she is the *object* of this man's sexual obsession. *Ms.* Magazine should not be a party to this kind of exploitation."[76] *Ms.* never ran the ad in the "No Comment" section, but the editors did publish two critical letters (one of which was the letter from the Michigan reader, minus the "No Comment" jab). As in other cases where readers forcefully objected to the magazine's content, editors legitimated readers' complaints by publishing a lengthy response. After the two critical letters about the Obsession ad, *Ms.* ran a rather long response from the editors, reiterating the importance of representing a "mutual, freely chosen sensuality of our own." "The next step will be to show a woman, face and all . . . and we are making [your thoughtful letters] available to the advertisers," the response concluded.[77]

For many readers, the visual misogyny in many ads was not the primary source of discomfort. The ads also provided the most tangible evidence that the magazine did not belong to the readers but to those who paid for it—the advertisers. Readers' dissatisfaction with the power of advertisers can be seen most clearly in the letters concerning cigarette and alcohol ads. Unlike the reader who had "learned to live with full page cigarette ads," most readers who wrote to *Ms.* were particularly angry that cigarette and alcohol ads continued to show up in a magazine where editors had promised to refuse to advertise products dangerous to women. And readers also noticed that the inclusion of cigarette ads in the magazine correlated with its lack of coverage about smoking and women. "I've been wondering when *Ms.* was going to write about one of the most relevant health problems affecting us today, the effects of tobacco smoke on humans," a reader wrote in 1979, "but it may just be a question of priorities. Looking at all those full page ads, the message is quite clear: Smoking is the intelligent, sexy thing to do. BULLSHIT! Oh well, I guess it's just good business to alienate me, a mere reader, rather than offend the 'Big Bucks' of the Tobacco Industry."[78] In the early 1970s, one reader received a personal letter from the editors justifying the magazine's acceptance of cigarette ads when it refused ads for other "harmful products" like vaginal deodorant sprays. Unlike the justification used in a later period, which focused almost exclusively on the economic and editorial motivation for accepting cigarette ads, this letter spoke of individual choice and tried to distinguish cigarettes from other products directed to women.

> The warning "The Surgeon General Has Determined That Cigarette Smoking Is Dangerous to Your Health" is printed on all cigarette packs and on every print ad for them. We agree with you: smoking is clearly unhealthy and is a nuisance for non-smokers. But in face of so explicit a warning the choice to smoke or not to smoke should be left up to each individual and that includes women. Once women are apprised of the risks, no one should decide what a woman may or may not do with her body. . . .

> Another point is also worth considering: There is no sexist connotation to most cigarette sales-pitches. Men and women alike are encouraged to find smoking pleasurable, glamorous or sexy. However, the vaginal sprays sell to women on the basis of many women's belief that their natural se-

cretions are unacceptable. Vaginal sprays are an offense to the dignity of women because they all try to exploit our vulnerable self-image. This is why we consider them, in a sense, more harmful.[79]

By the 1980s, the United States' awareness of smoking's addictive quality and of secondhand smoke's dangerous health consequences made rather unpersuasive the earlier *Ms.* defense that smoking was simply an individual choice and secondhand smoke a nuisance. Moreover, in this same period, the American Council on Science and Health reported that magazines that published cigarette ads were less likely to provide any significant coverage on the health risks of smoking. *USA Today*, *The Daily News*, and *Newsweek* identified *Ms.* as guilty of this charge.[80] The *Newsweek* article singled *Ms.* out for particular scrutiny, pointing out that it had never had a full-length feature on women and smoking and that Steinem herself was a smoker. In her response to the *Newsweek* article, Steinem defended the magazine, saying it did indeed "include" these dangers in its other health feature articles. In her own defense, Steinem explained, "I do smoke occasionally as one might an after-dinner cigar, and do not inhale."[81]

Like Steinem's defense that she smoked but did not inhale, *Ms.* attempted to argue that it could accept advertising but not be affected by it. Readers, however, were not convinced by this argument and continued to argue with editors about the representation of women in cigarette ads, the health risks to smokers, and the question of who really was controlling the magazine. Pushed by reader discontent and by the bad publicity surrounding the media reports on *Ms.* and smoking, the magazine decided to publish a special issue on women and addiction in 1987. But readers' criticisms became particularly vocal after this issue was published when *Ms.* chose not to include cigarette or alcohol ads.

In light of readers' response to this special issue, it is important to remember the difficult balance *Ms.* always had to maintain between speaking to its readers and working with its advertisers. For the magazine to succeed, or at the least survive, advertisers could not pay too close attention to the content of the articles, and readers had to ignore, or at least tolerate, the ads that financially supported the magazine. Frequently, however, this was a combination too difficult to sustain, as demonstrated by the publication of the February 1987 issue on women and addiction. In her editorial preface, editor Suzanne Braun Levine explained that the issue contained no cigarette or alcohol ads: "Like most national magazines, we depend on such revenue, but we have never let that affect our decision to publish important new research about women's health. In this case, because of the nature and the scope of this ground-breaking report, we have offered advertisers the courtesy of a choice not to appear in this particular environment. We will welcome them back in future issues and gratefully acknowledge their continuing support."[82] This statement failed to clarify whether *Ms.* gave cigarette and alcohol advertisers the choice *not* to buy space in this issue because their ads would be incongruent in an issue devoted to women and addiction, or because they might not advertise in *Ms.* again if they expected articles to be published attacking their products. Clearly, *Ms.* was attempting to protect itself from both advertisers' boycotts and readers' anger through this "professional courtesy" of allowing cigarette and alcohol advertisers to opt out of this issue.[83]

Many readers found the policy offensive, arguing that these were the products that *Ms.* had originally promised to ban because they were "hurtful" to women. In the May 1987 issue *Ms.* published several pages of letters responding to the addiction issue; one letter focused on the advertising policy. This exchange between reader and editor highlights the tension that existed among economic demands, readers' interests, and editors' negotiations. Rosemary Pitkin from Ithaca, N.Y., in particular, spoke to this conflict:

> I cannot help but wish *Ms.* would let go of *its dependency* on revenue from liquor and cigarette advertising that is so hurtful to the women *Ms.* claims to serve. Your statement that you will "welcome them back in future issues and gratefully acknowledge their continuing support" smack of incongruity. Continuing support of what? Women's dependency? It strikes me that one force that "creates dependence in us" is our willingness to let the economics rather than our own values and integrity define the reality. *Ms.* is in a position to model something different. But, then, change does have its price.

Immediately following this letter, editors responded that this was a dependency over which they had no power; it was not simply a matter of choice to retain cigarette and alcohol advertising but an economic necessity:

> Actually, *Ms.* is *not* in a good position to model something different. As a nonprofit feminist magazine, we can't rely on traditional economic support; we have no corporate publisher and our editorial policy limits our appeal to traditional advertising directed to women. (Food ads usually require an editorial atmosphere of recipes, beauty products require beauty editorials, and so on.) Nonetheless, we're the only women's magazine to do a cover story on women and addiction, and to sacrifice advertising

revenue to do so. We're proud of this fact and of the thousands of reader donations that made it possible.[84]

In speaking about *Ms.*'s policy of refusing to print complementary copy of recipes and beauty editorials, publisher Patricia Carbine explained that she and the other editors were working to eliminate the "double standard" for women's magazines, which "men's magazines did not face." Gloria Steinem reiterated this point in her article "Sex, Lies, and Advertising," in which she spoke about the necessity of removing advertisers' power over the editorial content of women's magazines.[85] What this special issue on addiction demonstrates, however, is the overriding power of corporate demands to shape mass media. That is, women's magazines like *Ms.* faced specific restraints because they could not solicit ads for traditionally feminine products without promising to publish supporting articles. They also faced the demands placed on all commercial media to provide copy conducive to the display of products advertised and to avoid articles that challenge the sales of those products. We must recognize the power of patriarchal capitalism (in contrast to patriarchy by itself, or to capitalism by itself) that existed to construct *Ms.* magazine.

Indeed, readers were astute critics of these limitations, recognizing that the inclusion of cigarette ads in "their" magazine compromised the extent to which they really could consider *Ms.* their own resource. What is particularly striking about the criticisms the editors received about the magazine's advertising policies, and the printed responses readers received from editors, is that readers identified themselves as legitimate critics of *Ms.*, the forum that they hoped would serve as the basis for communication among feminists. Readers' oppositional visions pushed *Ms.* editors to explain its policies and to talk with readers about their shared enterprise. While readers did not actually control the magazine, the dialogue between readers and editors did provide readers with a meaningful claim on the magazine.

Ms. readers raised pertinent and painful questions about the consequences of mass media existence. As one woman from Massachusetts wrote, "While it can be argued that large scale advertising is the only way to support a mass circulation and thus reach more women, at what point do you sell your soul?"[86] Importantly, *Ms.* legitimated readers' dissatisfaction by publishing their letters and by responding to their criticisms in lengthy reports explaining the need for advertising and in asking for readers' suggestions. By promoting the dialogue in this way, publishing three to five pages of readers' letters and two full pages of "No Comment" ads, *Ms.* was able to subvert quietly and gently the commercial matrix in which it existed. The ads that degraded women or that commodified feminism — making women's liberation appear to be synonymous with buying a car or using a credit card — could not be read in the same way in *Ms.* as they were in other magazines. Women continually pointed out that they read *Ms.* in a different way than they did other magazines, as indicated by this comment by a reader from Delaware who asked, "Why can't I just read the articles and skip the ads like I do when I read *Newsweek*?"[87] Indeed, the published readers' letters and the "No Comment" ads created a counterdiscourse to the advertising and elitist narratives of feminism in the magazine. In writing *to* the magazine, readers literally worked to write the magazine itself.

The way that thousands of U.S. women claimed *Ms.* magazine as their own resource speaks to the way this magazine resonated with many of their experiences and identities, to readers' desire to be connected to a "community" of feminists, and to the attractiveness of a magazine that promised to be the voice of the women's movement. The ability of *Ms.* editors to elicit readers' responses and loyalty appears to some critics to be further evidence of the power of mass media to co-opt political and social movements for their own purposes. In exploring the role of *Ms.* within the women's movement, however, what is striking is the way the magazine became a focal point for an unorganized but self-conscious community of feminists who identified with it, pushed it, and criticized it. Readers were active agents, using a commercial, popular culture text and making it as much of their own as possible. Their identification with the magazine laid the groundwork for their high expectations and gave them the legitimacy to criticize it or to give it their approval. Indeed, they claimed the magazine, even as its status as a business enterprise worked against those claims. Throughout the history of *Ms.*, this balance among the editors' perceptions, the advertisers' demands, and the readers' interests was a precarious one. By the end of the 1980s, when *Ms.* faced extensive financial difficulties and was finally sold to an Australian media firm, this balance tipped in favor of the financial imperatives. It is on this transition to a less reader-centered text that the next chapter is focused.

CHAPTER 5

A Change of Skin or a Change of Heart?

Ms. in Transition, 1987–1989

I n the spring of 1987, facing yearly financial losses and extreme competition for advertisers' dollars with other women's magazines, *Ms.*
began to seek an infusion of money, between 10 and 15 million
dollars, from outside investors in order to expand its promotion
capabilities. To solicit more advertising, the key to financial secu-
rity, *Ms.* needed to reach more readers, which was impossible unless
the capital became available to create an extensive marketing campaign. By the end of 1987, *Ms.* had found not an investor but a new
owner, Fairfax, Inc. An Australian media conglomeration, Fairfax
offered to buy *Ms.*, putting two Australian feminists — Anne Summers and Sandra Yates — at the helm as editor and publisher, respectively. Within six months, needing to "liquidize" U.S. assets to maintain control during an attempted financial takeover, Fairfax sold the
magazine again, this time to Summers and Yates themselves, who
created Matilda, Inc. Even with an extensive promotion campaign
and increased circulation, however, Summers and Yates could not
make *Ms.* a financial success. The magazine folded in November
1989, soon to be bought again by Dale Lang, the owner of *Working
Woman* and *Working Mother* magazines, who promised to attempt a
new kind of magazine, advertising-free and reader supported.[1]

This rash of sales illustrates the highly competitive market of
which *Ms.* was a part in the 1980s as well as the international economic context in which corporate takeovers dictated the buying
and selling of companies, organizations, and other assets. Moreover,
these sales — from the first attempt to acquire an outside investor
to the final sale to Lang, Inc., in 1989 — highlight the possibilities
and limitations of creating a feminist resource within a commercial
matrix. This series of sales illuminates the connections among the
ways *Ms.* represented itself, the politics of feminism in the late 1980s,

and the economic context in which the magazine was enmeshed. It is during these last few years of *Ms.* publication that we can see particularly clearly the struggle among the readers, advertisers, and editors for this mass media text.

The transformations that ensued during these years must be understood as part of a cultural milieu that increasingly urged us to believe we were in a "postfeminist" age. Probably first coined publicly by the writer Susan Bolotin in a 1982 *New York Times Magazine* article, "Voices from the Post-Feminist Generation," the term quickly became part of the public discourse to describe women who considered themselves "beyond feminism." "Post-feminist" generally describes those who believe simultaneously that women have won all the necessary changes to make women equal to men in social, economic, political, and cultural spheres (certainly a premature optimism) and that whatever residual problems women do face—the double day, the glass ceiling, sexual harassment—are either caused by the changes the feminist movement wrought, or, perhaps more disturbing, are nonissues concocted by old-fashioned feminists who cannot let go of their irresponsible tirades. While some scholars have argued quite convincingly that the "postfeminist" phenomenon is, as one writer so pointedly put it, simply "sexism by a subtler name," it is generally more complex than that, since it does assume some of the stances of feminism. Films like the 1987 *Baby Boom* or the 1988 *Working Girl*, for instance, may at first appear to be "feminist" until one analyzes the presumptions the films make about women's "natural" maternal instincts or "evil" career women. Popular media by the late 1980s was replete with representations of feminism as an out-of-date trend, in many ways similar to the way that popular culture in the 1920s painted the suffragists of the earlier part of the decade as frumpy and old-fashioned. Reducing women's lives to issues of "lifestyle," "postfeminism" was certainly more amenable to advertisers and a commodity culture than the ideals of change and sisterhood articulated by women's movement activists in the 1970s and 1980s. The struggle over "feminism" and "postfeminism" clearly mark the last years of *Ms.* as a commercial magazine.[2]

A Change of Skin

Part of *Ms.*'s attempt to solicit outside investors in 1987 entailed an extensive publicity campaign, one that would make *Ms.* appeal more strongly to advertisers and to financiers interested in a for-profit magazine. To reach the advertisers who believed *Ms.* to be, in the words of one media industry analyst, "too strident and too focused," *Ms.* worked to distance itself from its roots in the feminist movement and portray itself as vehicle through which to reach potential consumers. As the editor of *Good Housekeeping* expressed it, *Ms.* "has remained a cause in the eyes of a lot of advertising people rather than being a marketing opportunity." *Ms.* redesigned its image for the fall issues in order to remove its "cause" orientation and link it more clearly to the world of "marketing opportunities." "You are going to find more solutions, whereas in the past we spent a lot of time defining problems," explained Carbine in an interview with the *New York Times*. "For the first time, we are going to rate movies and television programs and we are introducing new fashion features such as one called 'Your Own Style.'"[3] The most striking change in image took place on the four transition covers, which each featured the face of some "spirited" woman who "embodied the great burst of optimism among women."[4]

When the editor Suzanne Braun Levine introduced the "*Ms.* of the Future" in the September 1987 issue, she mentioned neither the attempt to solicit more advertisers nor the campaign to attract outside investors. Instead, Levine focused solely on the changes in format that resulted during a reevaluation that took place while editors prepared the fifteenth anniversary issue. In part, her editorial read:

> Who hasn't awakened one day realizing that it is time to cut her long hair short, learn a new skill, or meet some new people? *Something* to fulfill a great need for a change, a kind of impatience that often heralds an exhilarating period of growth. It can strike at any age and is not a reflection of happiness or unhappiness, but is more like shedding a psychic skin and emerging as the same person in a revamped form. That happened to *Ms.* In the process of evaluating our first 15 years for the July/August Anniversary Issue, we realized that in many ways it was time for a change—not of the muscles and bones and heart—but of the skin, the way we present those core issues to the world.[5]

Other than her reference to the "exhilarating period of growth," which suggests (perhaps not intentionally) the expansion expected under commercial ownership, Levine said nothing about any planned structural changes. In this silence and in the assertion that only their "skin" would change, leaving what was substantive and meaningful untouched, *Ms.* diverted attention away from the significance of the connections between its structural and formal changes. She explained their emphasis on "solutions," successful women, and an upbeat feeling as natural attempts to catch up with the aesthetics of the 1980s rather than as marketing attempts to sell the magazine to a potential investor and to advertisers.

Of course, when the editorial came out in the September issue, Levine, or the editorial board of *Ms.* for that matter, did not know for certain that *Ms.* would soon be a for-profit organization. However, four months prior to this September issue, Steinem and Carbine gave an interview for the *New York Times* in which they announced their decision to attract more readers and advertisers and to look for a new owner. In this May 1987 interview they argued that *Ms.* had too little capital to promote itself aggressively to advertisers and to potential readers. A new investor with strong financial backing, they explained, could increase both circulation and advertising. While speaking to the "business world" Steinem and Carbine made the connection between the structural and formal changes clear; they described the new "stylish" *Ms.* as one that would be attractive to a broader range of advertisers and readers.[6]

While the *New York Times* article made *Ms.*'s new image seem to be a purely economic decision, the editorial introducing the changes in format made it seem to be a purely aesthetic judgment. Clearly, though, a combination of aesthetic and economic factors prompted the change. The dominant representations of women in other popular women's magazines dictated that *Ms.* portray a similar "upbeat" feeling if it wished to be in dialogue, or, rather, in competition with them. The economic dependence on advertisers mandated that *Ms.* be in competition with the other women's magazines. Yet because these connections were discounted, *Ms.* worked to make the change in image and the change in economic status seem natural, inevitable, and unrelated.

By suggesting that it was "time for a change — not of the muscles and bones and heart — but of the skin, the way we present those core assets to the world," Levine not only deflected attention from the changed economic structure but also encouraged readers to ignore the semiotic significance of these changes in image. In the words of cultural critic Stuart Hall, Levine attempted to create a "preferred" set of readings in her narrative about the transition issues.[7] Her analogy suggested that by changing the surface of *Ms.*, the content would in no way be tampered with. From its origins, however, *Ms.* paid particular attention to the way it represented itself to the world, and readers certainly took that representation with equal seriousness. For *Ms.* magazine, representation *was* the meaning; to change the cover meant to change the meanings that the magazine constructed. Indeed, it was the "skin" — the covers — that allowed the magazine to maintain a place on the commercial newsstands at the same time it provided an arena in which editors played with, inverted, and challenged the dominant codes of representation on major women's magazines. In the words of John Fiske, the covers allowed for both "evasion" and for "resistance."

When *Ms.* attempted to seek a new investor in late 1987, it turned to the image of the "positive" woman to represent itself. *Ms.* had increasingly relied on this image throughout the 1980s, as it best blended the philosophy of egalitarian feminism with the demands of advertisers. Each of the transitional covers pictured a close-up of some successful woman's face. She smiles and looks directly at us. The covers presented Tracey Ullman, a television comedian (September 1987); Salerno-Sonnenberg, a violinist (October 1987); Cam Starret, a top executive at Avon (November 1987); and Bonnie Allen, a writer for *Ms.* (December 1987). None of the women look like each other, yet their identical poses—the mold of the successful woman—make them appear almost interchangeable. To be in competition with the other women's magazines, *Ms.* chose the representation of women—the "positive woman"—that best masked its "cause" orientation, that distanced itself most fully from victimization, difference, or critique. Indeed, the decision to turn to the image of the successful woman demonstrates the way a capitalist matrix censors not only through explicit rejection of certain images but also—and perhaps more powerfully—through a rejection of all images that do not lend themselves to a consumer ideology.

While these four transition covers rigidify the representation of "positive" women, like all *Ms.* covers they are also marked by a clear negotiation of symbols and codes. While the covers focus on an upbeat image, an interchangeable mold, it is the posture of the women that sets them apart from the covers of magazines like *Vogue, New Woman,* and *Self.* In each of the *Ms.* covers the woman rests her chin on her hands, or, in the case of Salerno-Sonnenberg, on her violin. The significance of this posture becomes clear when we see how it deflects the voyeurism so prevalent in dominant cover photos of women. Both Teresa de Lauretis and Laura Mulvey have written powerfully of the male gaze, of the way photography, cinema, and narrative are constructed so that a masculine subject "captures" a feminine object.[8] These *Ms.* covers resist this male gaze. We see only the straightforward smiling face; the hand obstructs any impulse the viewer might feel to reach in and touch, or grab, or capture the woman. While the nature of photography may still be one of capturing the "subject," the pose of the *Ms.* cover women complicates the viewer's gaze and denies the fulfillment of the photographer's desire to own the photographed.

Some may argue that these *Ms.* women obstruct the gaze simply because they have assumed a masculine posture, becoming, in fact, representations of men. Indeed, in 1986, *Ms.* featured on the cover a very masculine portrait of Richard Gere, positioned in the exact same way as the transition cover women, chin resting on hands. Yet the cover women's lipstick, nail polish, earrings, eyeliner, and smiles all identify them as women. *Ms.* mixed up the signifiers: these women clearly have all the typically "feminine" attributes and accouterments, but they also have the powerful, obstructive "masculine" gesture to defend and support themselves. By combining "masculine" and "feminine" signifiers in an unexpected way, *Ms.* managed to compete with other women's magazines while still maintaining a resistant edge. Even in its latter years when *Ms.* increasingly disassociated itself from an explicit feminist identity, it could still work as a "tarantula" on the commercial newsstands, playing with and questioning dominant images of women. Once *Ms.* was sold to Fairfax, Inc., however, the magazine increasingly deflected its feminist perspectives as it responded to the demands of advertisers.

A Change of Skin and a Change of Heart — Selling Out?

By the fall of 1987, the MFEC and the MFW had decided to sell the magazine to Fairfax Publications, a U.S. subsidiary of the Australian publishing firm John Fairfax, Ltd. Minutes from the board meetings during this time indicate that the foundation actually had been looking for outside investors for a number of years, but thus far it had not found a party both interested in *Ms.* and willing to maintain the magazine's original focus. The MFEC, the minutes pointed out, had accumulated debts totaling $7.1 million, nearly all attributable to the publication of the magazine. *Ms.* had only been able to continue running because of extensive loans, the willingness of some creditors to defer payment, and, above all, the fact that *Ms.* staff had worked for years at pay levels substantially below what they would have received at other periodicals.[9] By the time the offer from Fairfax came in, MFEC had recognized that its only options were to terminate the magazine or to find a buyer, not just an investor.

Agreeing that the terms offered by Fairfax were fair and reasonable, and that Fairfax would continue to run the magazine in a way that would "promote the purposes" of the Ms. Foundation, the MFEC agreed to a sale price of $3.41 million for the magazine. (This sum was actually reduced to $3.01 million after MFEC agreed to return $400,000 at closing to help defer the $7.1 million in debts that Fairfax also assumed with the deal.)[10] Almost immediately, Pat Carbine wrote a letter to Marie Wilson, the president of the Ms. Foundation for Women, donating $400,000 of the profit back to the parent foundation. By 1989, MFEC had donated $1 million back to the Ms. Foundation.[11] The remaining profit went in two directions: part of it went to finance compensation plans for the former staff of the magazine, part of it went to finance the ongoing work of the MFEC.

In recognition of the financial sacrifices that the *Ms.* staff made in order to keep the magazine going, including the absence of a pension plan, MFEC agreed to pay staff members who had worked at *Ms.* longer than five years "certain payments" based on years of service and level of past salary. The four staff members older than sixty were given additional payments of $50,000 each, in recognition of the fact they were nearing retirement age and were less likely to find employment far into the future. Staff members with less than five years of employment at *Ms.* were given severance pay equal to two weeks pay for every year of service.[12] In addition, some of the longtime employees and key figures of *Ms.*, including Ruth Bower, Letty Pogrebin, Pat Carbine, Suzanne Levine, JoAnne Edgar, and Mary Thom, stayed on at MFEC as consultants in order to maintain the work of the foundation and to plan and implement new projects. Gloria Steinem also continued to act as a consultant for MFEC, but she continued to refuse any payment for her services.[13] Indeed, when MFEC decided to sell the magazine, they never intended to conclude the work of the "media arm" of the larger Ms. Foundation for Women. Immediately after the sale of the magazine, the MFEC proposed a number of new projects, including "one-shot" pamphlets and television programs, many of which involved joint-venture involvement with the new publisher of *Ms.* Many of these never came to fruition, due in large part to the legal complexities inherent in proposing joint for-profit and not-for-profit projects.[14] The MFEC continued to provide small grants to a range of feminist media and educational projects, none of which would be eligible for funding under the "survival issues" guidelines of the larger Ms. Foundation for Women. Most visibly, the MFEC also continued its tradition of publishing feminist books, in conjunction with a mainstream publisher. After MFEC sold *Ms.*, for example, it published *I Never Called It Rape: The* Ms. *Report on Recognizing, Fighting and Surviving Date and Acquaintance Rape* by Robin Warshaw in 1988, reprinted in 1994 (New York: HarperCollins, 1988), and *The Ms. Money Book: Strategies for Prospering in the Coming Decade* by Emily Card (New York: E. P. Dutton, 1990).

After the Ms. Foundation for Education and Communication sold the magazine it turned its attention to other, relevant projects in feminist media.

When Fairfax bought the magazine, it was buying a well-known name in American media and at the same time attempting to jettison its roots in feminist activism. What the new publisher and editor of *Ms.* would find, however, was that the ties to the feminist foundation were easier to sever legally than they were in the memories and impressions of readers and advertisers.

By the end of 1987, Anne Summers and Sandra Yates had convinced Fairfax to buy *Ms.* Yates, herself a native of Australia, came to the United States as the president of U.S. Fairfax, Ltd., specifically to launch its new magazine for girls, *Sassy*. Anne Summers, also a native of Australia, had her Ph.D. in government and had worked as a journalist and editor and as the head of the Australian Office of the Status of Women. She was also the author of the awarding-winning 1975 publication *Damned Whores and God's Police*, a feminist history of Australia.[15]

Fairfax's decision to acquire *Ms.* puzzled analysts in the media industry, many of whom suggested that the decision to buy *Ms.* must have been motivated by some sort of altruism. As one analyst expressed it, the sale suggested that "Fairfax is being a bit of a philanthropist. This is not just an investment strategy by Fairfax. The company has got to be a believer in the cause."[16] Considering the lengths *Ms.* had gone to remove itself from its "cause" orientation, this remark spoke to the enduring quality of *Ms.*'s reputation as a resource for the feminist movement. Sandra Yates, however, portrayed the decision to buy *Ms.* as a completely "pragmatic" one: "It's a title that has a lot of potential for growth, given the sufficient resources. That has always been a problem for the people at *Ms.* We feel there is a market for a feminist publication and we will be looking to grow. And it made significant business sense to us."[17] Explaining their plan to increase circulation by 35 to 40 percent (which in turn would help to bring in advertising dollars), Yates said, "I absolutely believe we can make money on *Ms.*"[18] Yates's comments about the magazine emphasized *Ms.*'s "potential for growth" in financial terms, ignoring its history as a feminist resource except as it related to the marketing possibilities of the magazine. Indeed, her comments express most clearly the power of patriarchal capitalism to channel feminism into the needs of the marketplace, to reincorporate the resistance posed by a political and social movement.

Under new ownership in 1987 and 1988, *Ms.* underwent a number of changes, including a transformation in the organization of the magazine staff. Least visible to the public eye, this change was nonetheless quite significant since it indicated a rejection of *Ms.*'s attempt to create a nonhierarchical business organization within the Madison Avenue publishing industry. No longer did the masthead list people in alphabetical order and by area of responsibility only; instead, it listed everyone with a specific title and by specific rank. And as the executive editor and former contributing editor Marcia Ann Gillespie explained it, the decision-making process became much more "rigid" with the new owners in 1988.[19] While she still emphasized the relative openness at *Ms.* compared to other magazines where she had worked, she made a clear distinction between the modes of operation under the two different owners.

The most prominent feature of the Fairfax (and later Matilda) buyout was a concerted effort to reshape *Ms.*'s image. Two of the promotional ads geared to potential advertisers emphasized a portrait of a well-to-do, baby-boomer-age, white woman as the *Ms.* reader. One ad, picturing a thin, well-dressed woman among champagne corks, passports, and credit cards, asked, "What do you call a woman who's made it to the top? Ms." The other pictured a four-photo spread of a white woman casting off her 1960s granny glasses and beaded headband, putting on lipstick, and emerging as an "up-to-date" woman of the late 1980s, complete with permed hair and gold earrings.[20] Moving from a hippy-politico-feminist to a well-coiffed, monied, educated consumer, the *Ms.* reader had grown up, shed her immature politics, and joined the contemporary world and — as the ad inferred — so had *Ms.* This entire campaign constructed the change in image as a matter of keeping up with the times, a natural process of maturation, having nothing to do with the political threat feminism posed to advertisers.

Anne Summers, the new editor-in-chief of *Ms.*, articulated the shift in editorial perspective as equally pragmatic. To Summers, the "basic feminist analysis of the world [had been] worked out many years ago" — now it was a matter of implementing that vision, not adding to it or revising it.[21] She described the new magazine as "less angry, less militant, more focused and, we hope, more successful."[22] Moreover, the magazine was to dwell less on "bona fide" feminist issues: "It's not going to be just stories about child care and affirmative action. We're going to emphasize reporting, politics, and fast-breaking news. It's going to be a more interesting look and a better read."[23] Indeed, the covers continued the trend that had begun prior to the sale of *Ms.*, featuring "successful" women and celebrities. During 1988 and 1989 *Ms.* covers included Cher, Meryl Streep, Bette Midler, Oprah Winfrey, Anita Baker, Cyndi Lauper, Bess Myerson, and Florence Griffith Joyner. In describing the women they chose to feature on the covers, Summers explained, "It's got to be a woman that *Ms.* readers can like, or admire, possibly even identify with, and they're generally women who have made it themselves, they're totally responsible for their own careers. . . . They're not necessarily going to call themselves feminists, but most of them do."[24] And *Ms.* no longer was necessarily going to call itself feminist either. "Our extensive marketing research found that younger women don't like the word 'feminist.' They call it a 1970s word. They agree with the ideas of feminism—from pay equity to reproductive rights—but they don't like that label."[25] The publicity material Fairfax generated about the newest *Ms.* spoke of the "focus groups" they had interviewed in New York, Los Angeles, St. Louis, Chicago, and Washington, D.C.; the women in these groups wanted "honesty, objectivity and reality combined with humanism" in a magazine.[26]

While a *Ms.* editor explicitly refusing the label of feminism for *Ms.* may seem heretical, from the perspective of its nearly two-decade history it seems less shocking. An essential part of the *Ms.* legacy was always to reach out to those who wouldn't necessarily call themselves feminists, to those who believed in feminism's major tenets but did not embrace it as an identity. In fact, *Ms.* had been moving toward this deflection of feminism in its later issues, as it worked to solicit advertisers more aggressively and stay in competition with other women's magazines. But it was not until Fairfax, Inc., and then Matilda, took over that this attempt to avoid "feminism" became an explicit policy, a consciously chosen maneuver to refuse the identity of "feminism" in the name of reaching the most readers. In her interviews and her references to the extensive marketing surveys, Summers portrayed the decision to refuse the title "feminist" as a democratic response to the desires of readers. What this interpretation ignores, however, is the way this refusal of "feminism" resulted from the necessity to attract as many readers as possible, and from advertisers' reluctance to buy space in a magazine they found ideologically offensive, or at least not conducive to their motives. The "democratic" marketplace, worked to eliminate dissenting voices rather than to encourage them.

Indeed, by the late 1980s *Ms.* had moved far from its initial promise to be an "open forum for all women." Throughout its history, *Ms.* had balanced the demands of readers, advertisers, and editors rather precariously; by the time Fairfax, then Matilda, took over, the balance had fallen to the favor of the advertisers. This is not to say that they actually obliged by buying space in *Ms.*, but their threats and demands worked to reshape *Ms.* radically. Moreover, we can see how the balance fell away from readers' favor in the policies instituted by the new editor and publisher in 1988. Summers and Yates shortened the letters section, edited readers' letters more frequently, eliminated the classified section, and abbreviated the "No Comment" section to a quarter page, anchoring it with their own caption rather than leaving it up to reader interpretation. They drastically removed the possibilities for reader interaction — and reader intervention — that had become institutions in the former *Ms.* Speaking about the ways women responded to the new magazine, Summers referred to the "battle" she had with readers, who did not understand the demands of the commercial publishing industry.[27] Ironically, this "battle" had been carefully fostered by the previous editors, who promised the magazine to women as their own feminist resource. If readers did not understand the commercial publishing industry, then Summers clearly did not understand how readers had claimed and challenged this mass media resource that had promised, even if it had not always provided, democratic, oppositional politics and a feminist community.

Repoliticization and Popular Memory

The succession of sales that *Ms.* underwent in the 1980s, as well as the attempt by the new editor and publisher of *Ms.* to recreate the magazine in a form far removed from its political roots, speaks to the power of corporate capitalism to use popular media for its own purposes. *Ms.* had been created in 1972 as a magazine that was to use advertisers' dollars to fund and to popularize the women's movement; by the late 1980s, though, the editorial focus of the magazine refused the identity of "feminist" but used the demographic qualities of the *Ms.* reader — well educated, financially secure, and career oriented — to attract advertisers. Advertisers had, in effect, reincorporated the resistance posed by *Ms.* — as a magazine, an organization, and a readership — into their own needs, channeling the movement into a "market opportunity." Importantly, however, despite the changes made by the new owners, *Ms.* did not become a success; it could not shed its historical aura of feminist politics that, probably from the perspective of the new owners, seemed to haunt the magazine.

Advertisers, of course, feared that *Ms.*'s feminist politics might not really be dead. And they were correct. The same event that repoliticized women across the United States — the Supreme Court's *Webster* decision allowing for some abortion restrictions on a state-by-state basis — also repoliticized *Ms.* President Reagan's appointment of conservative judges to the Supreme Court whittled away women's reproductive rights, culminating in the 1989 *Webster v. Reproductive Health Services.* The *Webster* decision declared as constitutional the state of Missouri's right to restrict abortions in the first trimester, as well as a host of other measures that limited women's reproductive choices that were guaranteed in the 1973 *Roe v. Wade* decision.[28] The decision also repoliticized feminists across the country, as demonstrated by the 300,000 women and men who marched in Washington in opposition to it.

In anticipation of the *Webster* decision, *Ms.* had published its July 1989 issue with the words "IT'S WAR" emblazoned in bold red print across a jet-black cover. Even readers who had rejected the revamped *Ms.* found this a powerful cover and referred to it as a possible direction *Ms.* might go in the future.[29] I witnessed the power of the magazine's cover first-hand at a pro-choice rally I attended in Boston, where one of the major speakers for the day waved the "IT'S WAR" cover throughout her speech. For this speaker, the magazine had reconnected to its political roots, and she found it an excellent resource to illustrate her anger and her determination. The issues following the "IT'S WAR" publication contained pages of letters from readers sharing their frustration, their renewed energy, and their tactics for fighting the *Webster* decision. Advertisers reacted equally powerfully to the "IT'S WAR" cover, and, more generally, to the no-longer-denied political heritage of *Ms.* — they pulled out en masse from future issues. Due to their refusal to advertise in *Ms.* because of its political connections, the December 1989 issue brought in only ten ads, too few for the magazine to publish.[30] Advertisers' ability to shut down this magazine demonstrates that editors were not simply timid in their attempts to mask *Ms.*'s politics; they recognized the reality of advertisers' power to censor media. After the fall 1989 pull-out by major advertisers, the magazine folded, to reemerge in 1990 as a noncommercial magazine.[31]

The final months of *Ms.* history demonstrate the ultimate economic power of advertisers to shape or to break any mass media resource. Even if the demographics of *Ms.* proved "right," the political connotations of the magazine proved too dangerous. Even when the new owners of *Ms.* increased the circulation to over 550,000, the number considered significant enough to attract major advertisers, they still did not respond, finding the political content too controversial.[32] Yet at the same time that the history of *Ms.* illustrates the power of corporate capitalism, it also suggests the power of a magazine to which readers felt strongly connected and that they claimed as their own. In his work *Time Passages*, cultural critic George Lipsitz discusses the ways specific popular culture texts contain sedimented layers of collective memory that evoke the "shared hurts of history" as well as the moments of resistance to those shared burdens.[33] In the case of *Ms.*, the "IT'S WAR" cover evoked not only the shared memory of a powerful historical feminist movement, and the strength of a future feminist movement, but also the collective memory of a magazine that had promised to give voice to and serve the movement.

Imagining a Popular Feminism

Wen Gloria Steinem, Patricia Carbine, and many other dedicated women began *Ms.* in 1972, they envisioned a number of goals for their bold experiment. By staking out territory in the publishing industry, they hoped to provide a training ground for women who otherwise would have no access to jobs in publishing and to reform the unfair advertising policies to which women's (in contrast to general interest) magazines were subject. Moreover, by favoring a nonhierarchical, diverse work environment—in which no one had a title, decision making was dispersed, and workers were encouraged to bring their children to the office—the founders hoped to transform the business of putting out a magazine. Even though the results of this experiment fell far short of the founders' original expectations, *Ms.* always posed a significant challenge to the publishing industry. If the women's movement activists' sit-in at the *Ladies' Homes Journal* provided a one-day threat to the publishers, the existence of *Ms.* worked as an eighteen-year reminder of the demands and goals of the movement and the dedication of the women behind it.

Above all, when the founders of *Ms.* began their experiment, they imagined a magazine that would bridge the boundaries of commercial and political, creating a "popular" feminist periodical. By their very definition, the smaller, alternative, feminist periodicals were marginal texts, both because they could reach only a small percentage of the population and because they figuratively "spoke" only to the audience prepared to hear the message. These smaller periodicals, however, could forcefully articulate the philosophies of the new women's movement and could work to mobilize their readers for action. Commercial women's magazines reached a mass audience, but their foremost purpose was to provide a forum for selling consumer items and an ideology of consumption, or, as Gloria Steinem bitterly declared, they worked primarily as "cash cows" for the publishing industry.[1] Nevertheless, the women's magazine industry represented a powerful institution, one that the *Ms.* founders hoped to tap and use for the movement.

The *Ms.* founders located themselves on the interface of two worlds — the feminist movement and the mainstream magazine industry. *Ms.* magazine became the only representative of the feminist movement on the commercial newsstand, a position that brought with it much power but also extensive responsibility and the burden of "tokenism." By taking the women's magazine — which had perfected the female address, the hailing of women as a group — and blending with it the oppositional politics of feminism, *Ms.* offered an arena through which women could create a broad-based constituency and a unified movement for personal, cultural, and political change. Yet *Ms.* faced the dilemma at the heart of all feminist endeavors — how to speak to and mobilize women as a group while maintaining an attentiveness to difference, to the heterogeneity of women's lives, experiences, and identities. In essence, *Ms.* needed to create a credible version of a feminist "we." The editors attempted to do this by articulating an overarching theme of sisterhood, a culture shared by all women, and by promising an "open forum" policy, which suggested the magazine would solicit and publish various viewpoints and the voices of a wide range of women, including readers.

Internal contradictions and unforeseen consequences of the feminist philosophies articulated by *Ms.* editors and staff, however, undermined this attempt to create a mass media magazine that could mobilize women as a group at the same time respecting differences among women. The emphasis on sisterhood provided strong legitimacy for a mass-based movement among women, but, when spoken from the perspective of someone white, heterosexual, and economically privileged, it often obscured power differentials and cultural incompatibilities among women. The equal, if not more powerful, focus on personal transformation and the women's movement as a humanist revolution also subverted *Ms.*'s potential to articulate an inclusive feminism. While the stress on personal growth spoke to many women's changing identities, it also redirected the movement from being about collective, cultural change to being about individual self-improvement and economic success. Moreover, this focus on personal growth dovetailed with a consumer ethic, in which atomized individuals solved their problems through their purchases, through their participation in a commodified culture.

Significantly, the bulk of new women's magazines published in the late 1970s and into the 1980s ignored the discussion of sisterhood, picking up solely on this emphasis on self-improvement and personal transformation, ideas that complemented a consumer magazine. In 1991, for the third anniversary of *Lear's*, an upscale magazine for the "woman who wasn't born yesterday," editor Frances Lear praised women's "phenomenal growth in self-esteem" and emphasized the "lifelong process by which a person increasingly becomes the whole and complete person God intended her to be."[2] Clearly, this editorial focused entirely on the individual, with no vision of a collective, cultural transformation. As *Ms.* faced growing competition for advertisers' dollars from new women's magazines like *Lear's*, and had to articulate a feminist vision in a culture dominated by the conservative politics of the 1980s, the editors and staff increasingly turned to this emphasis on personal growth and individual success. By the late 1980s, editor Suzanne Levine complained that they were spending most of their time "imitating their imitators."[3]

By claiming a position on the commercial newsstand, *Ms.* could push and challenge the institution of the mainstream women's magazine, but that same commercial position also thwarted the magazine's potential to work as a powerful resource within the women's movement. The need to present the *Ms.* reader as an ideal consumer — for the advertiser's benefit — eventually forced the editors and staff to deflect attention from the politics of sisterhood and to attract attention to the politics of individual advancement and success. In a sense, *Ms.* had to prove to advertisers that it could be a "cash cow" even though its primary audience wanted *Ms.* to be a forum for the feminist movement. Both Steinem and Carbine have spoken forcefully about how demands for complementary copy and supportive editorial atmosphere are placed on women's magazines but not on more general interest magazines like *Time*, *Newsweek*, and *Sports Illustrated*. Both regret that they could not destroy this "double standard," as Carbine referred to it, facing women's magazines. While the history of *Ms.* demonstrates the power of this "double standard," it also points to the larger problem confronting anyone attempting to use commercial media for a political movement. Commercial media demand an atmosphere conducive to a consumer ethic; they want to create a culture of commodities, not a culture of politics and social transformation, which may either ignore, or perhaps even resist, a culture based on the purchase of goods. Above all, commercial media strive to avoid the controversial and the political, anything that dares to take a position for change; the sensationalism of "career moms" and "career infertility" might work to sell products, for instance, but a feminist analysis of those issues would not.

The history of *Ms.* points to the fundamental incompatibility of commercialism and social movements.

Conversely, however, the history of *Ms.* also points to the ways that advertisers draw from the power of social movements. Advertisers must speak to the needs, desires, and dreams of actual and potential consumers if they are to succeed. Feminism—the dream for equality, for fairness, for justice, for a world that values women and women's myriad contributions to society—is a powerful set of beliefs that advertisers have always latched onto, from the early advertisements for typing machines and washing machines that promised to "liberate" women, to the contemporary ads for fast food that vow to free women from dinnertime responsibilities. While advertisers may have found parts of the feminist dream conducive to marketing, however, they needed to ignore or whittle away other parts less amenable to their purposes. The history of *Ms.* demonstrates the process by which advertisers were able to commodify feminism.

This conclusion, however, is significantly complicated when one takes into account the roles that readers played in the history of the magazine. As a mass circulation periodical, *Ms.* reached thousands and thousands of women, many who were predisposed to the ideas of feminism, but many who had little previous connection to the movement. Indeed, *Ms.* broke through much of the literal as well as figurative isolation of women living in nuclear families, in secluded communities and suburbs, and more generally in the alienating and disempowering culture of patriarchy. The lengthy letters section, publishing personal stories and critiques of the magazine, provided women with a "free space" in which to articulate their concerns, their changed perceptions of the world, and their needs.[4] Importantly, the letters section transformed private talk into public discourse, allowing women to create a montage of feminist voices and to rehearse their arguments and critiques for an audience outside *Ms.* Once they connected to the magazine, readers did not easily abandon it, for it promised them oppositional politics and a democratic forum. Using the language of the women's movement as well as the editors' marketing promises, readers resisted the commodification and narrowing of feminism in *Ms.* that they observed as the magazine moved into the 1980s. Readers claimed this text as their own resource.

That *Ms.* reemerged in 1990 in a revamped form—advertising-free and completely subscriber-supported—demonstrates the continued determination by activists across the country to fulfill the promises originated by the founders. After the canceled issue in December 1989, Dale Lang, Inc., owner of *Working Woman* and *Working Mother*, bought the magazine, and Robin

Morgan, longtime activist and former contributing editor of *Ms.*, accepted the position of editor. Publishing an even more extensive letters section than the old *Ms.* as well as lengthy articles expressing a wide range of views and voices, the new *Ms.*—referred to as a "magabook" by Morgan—promised to become a useful forum for debate and communication among feminists.[5] With no advertisers to please, no need to blend with the other magazines on the newsstands, and no need to mask its politics, *Ms.* could now name feminism explicitly, allowing it the freedom to construct an oppositional politics, to work unambiguously for the resurgence of the women's movement in the 1990s.

Inevitably, however, we must ask ourselves what had been lost with the demise of the "old" *Ms.* In sharp contrast to the "old" *Ms.*, the new magazine is expensive ($40 a year), has limited distribution, and seeks to reach those already considering themselves feminists. Most significantly, one can no longer find *Ms.* at the grocery store, the airport, or on most commercial newsstands. This lack of availability signals a number of implications for the role of the new *Ms.* Ironically, even as the new *Ms.* has the freedom to construct a more inclusive feminism, attentive to the voices of women of color, lesbians, and poor women, its absence from the commercial arena prevents it from reaching all but those women who have the knowledge and the money to subscribe to it or to find it in alternative bookstores.[6] Moreover, without mass distribution, we do not find *Ms.* next to copies of *Vogue* or *New Woman*; thus, although *Ms.* can now construct oppositional images of women with little constraint, it is no longer on the popular, commercial battlefield, pushing and playing with the discursive boundaries of some of the most dominant image- and meaning-makers of our culture—women's magazines. Finally, without the need to attract a mass audience, *Ms.* can assume a feminist perspective rather than working to construct one. While this gives the magazine considerable room to create more complex feminist analyses, it also removes its responsibility to speak to women who do not identify themselves consistently as feminists, or even as political. Considering these consequences, we must then question whether *Ms.* can any longer work as a "tarantula on a banana boat," reaching those women who otherwise would be unconnected to the movement.[7]

Above all, the legacy of the *Ms.* experiment calls us to reimagine "the popular," and, more specifically, what a popular feminism might look like in the twenty-first century.[8] At this point, I think it would be useful to return to the definitions I introduced in the beginning of this book. By "feminism," I referred to the commitment to improving women's lives and to ending gender domination. By "popular" I referred both to a feminism that is wide-spread, common to many, and to one that emerges from the realm of popular culture. In the late twentieth century in the United States, commercial media predominantly defines what is experienced as "popular culture." "Popular feminism," then, would mean a shared, widely held cultural and political commitment to improving women's lives and to ending gender domination that is both articulated and represented within popular culture.

By now, the history of *Ms.* should make it clear that my definition of feminism is deceptively easy, as "who women are" and what constitutes "gender domination" are as contested as what we might consider "improvement" in women's lives. *Ms.*, of course, negotiated the muddy waters of feminism by paying homage to a sisterhood that frequently glossed over differences among women or by valorizing individual women's lives. Certainly, neither one of these strategies worked adequately to create a popular feminism. One might be tempted, considering the multiple identities and multiple concerns that shape women's lives, as well as the problems that plagued *Ms.*, to concede that a shared feminism is impossible. I strongly urge us not to, however. Rather, I would suggest that we need to work to a new vision of sisterhood, one in which an emphasis on "sameness" and a belief in a common oppression is replaced with an emphasis on shared commitment to ending all oppressions.

At its best, *Ms.* worked to foster this kind of unison in diversity, particularly in the way that it encouraged dialogue, interaction with readers, and the voices of many women. At its worst, *Ms.* spoke more for the concerns of advertisers than for those women across the nation it promised to speak for and to. This, of course, is because the magazine not only had to struggle to create a common feminism but also to articulate it within the realm of commercial media. What had seemed so promising about the early *Ms.* was that it offered to construct an oppositional politics within this popular setting; yet, as the history of the magazine demonstrates, the commercial matrix sharply curtailed its ability to be explicitly political. Now outside the commercial setting, the new *Ms.* appears to have lost its "popularity," its ability to speak to and mobilize a wide range of people. The elitism of the alternative rather than the censorship of the commercial now constrains *Ms.*

Ironically, the history of this magazine makes me simultaneously pessimistic that any kind of hybrid like *Ms.* can succeed and insistent that we need more experiments like *Ms.* I am pessimistic because the history of *Ms.* makes clear the fundamental incompatibility of commercialism and feminism. The imperatives of the marketplace and the desire for a truly participatory, democratic, pluralistic feminist movement are mutually exclusive. Only a feminism based solely on individual upward mobility can coexist with a commercial magazine, and, even then, advertisers will strive to find sites less political and more amenable to their purpose of selling consumer goods and, equally important, a consumer ideology. Considering this fundamental incompatibility, then why am I insistent that we need more experiments like *Ms.*? In late-twentieth-century culture, the realm of popular culture—of commercial culture—is the most powerful arena in which ideas are created and circulated. To abdicate this space means that feminists will not have access to this important terrain. In retrospect, the most revolutionary quality of *Ms.* in the 1970s and 1980s was its power to be a magazine on the commercial racks that dared to say "feminism." As we move into the twenty-first century, facing increased poverty among women, welfare "reform," racial and ethnic inequities, and the ongoing struggles to retain the legal, cultural, and economic gains women made earlier in the movement, we need more "tarantulas" like *Ms.* Hybrids like *Ms.* will not cure our problems, but they provide crucial sites of intervention we dare not give up.

NOTES

INTRODUCTION

1. This was true from its origins to its final commercial issues. See, for instance, Wayne, "Australia Concern to Buy *Ms.*," D1, D3, and "*Ms.* Says G'day to New Owners."

2. "Personal Report from *Ms.*," January 1973, 97.

3. Circulation and readership statistics are drawn from yearly circulation information *Ms.* reported to the U.S. Postal Service.

4. Historians Evans and Echols have demonstrated the way young women involved in the Civil Rights movement and the New Left made the "personal" the "political" through consciousness-raising groups and takeovers of male-dominated alternative organizations. Others have focused more specifically on the growth of mainstream women's political organizations, like the National Organization for Women and the National Women's Political Caucus. Still others have emphasized the links between social movement organization, feminist consciousness, and state and national politics. See Evans, *Personal Politics* and *Born for Liberty*, esp. chs. 12 and 13, and Echols, *Daring to Be Bad*. For an overview of the U.S. women's movement in the 1970s, see Wandersee, *On the Move*. For a collection of essays on the links between the state and women's changing consciousness, see Katzenstein and Mueller, *Women's Movements of the U.S. and Western Europe*.

5. Ferree and Hess, *Controversy and Coalition*, 7.

6. Katzenstein, "Comparing the Feminist Movements," 3.

7. Mansbridge, "What Is the Feminist Movement?" 29.

8. Zillah Eisenstein, *Radical Future of Liberal Feminism*, 6.

9. Lipsitz, *Time Passages*, 13–14.

10. Carroll, *It Seemed Like Nothing Happened*, 35–36.

11. For a useful introduction to the influence of poststructuralist theory on historical and cultural studies, see Scott, *Gender and the Politics of History*, especially 1–14. Kozol's *Life's America*, a study of *Life* magazine during the 1950s, is an excellent example of scholarship that explores the intersections among the construction of ideology and social, cultural, and economic contexts.

12. See, for instance, Lewis, *Gender Politics and MTV*, and Radway, *Reading the Romance*.

13. "Personal Report from *Ms.*," January 1973, 114.

14. Douglas, *Where the Girls Are*, 14.

15. This phrase comes from Cassell, *Group Called Women*. Cassell discusses at length the centrality of constructing gender consciousness to the second wave of feminism.

16. Wandersee, *On the Move*, 174, 169.

17. Rich, *On Lies, Secrets, and Silences*, 14.

18. Kristeva quoted in Moi, *Sexual/Textual Politics*, 154, 156; Fiske, *Reading Popular Culture*, 6; Radway, *Reading the Romance* and *Feeling for Books*.

19. Christopher, " 'Ms.'-Givings over Celebration," 37.

20. See Althusser, "Ideology and Ideological State Apparatuses," and Barrett, *Women's Oppression Today*, for a discussion of the importance of exploring the connections between ideology and material conditions.

21. A number of excellent articles have been published that describe these various approaches as well as the need to combine them in order to understand how popular culture texts work within U.S. culture. See, for instance, Lipsitz, " 'This Ain't No Sideshow,' " 147–61; Long, "Feminism and Cultural Studies," 427–35; Schwichtenberg, "Feminist Cultural Studies," 202–8; and Steeves, "Feminist Theories and Media Studies," 95–135.

22. Dismissive or negative perspectives include ones by authors such as Maurine Christopher and Ellen McCracken. *Ms.* has published many of its own historical chronicles, including Mary Thom's *Letters to Ms.* and *Inside Ms.*

CHAPTER ONE

1. Dekkers, "Periodicals," 19.

2. Lorde, *Sister Outsider*, 110.

3. For a more in-depth look at the historical events outlined in this chapter, see Castro, *American Feminism*; Davis, *Moving the Mountain*; Evans, *Born for Liberty*; and Wandersee, *On the Move*. Some recent scholarship is beginning to question this convention of dating the roots of 1960s feminist activism to the two strands of legislative activism by an older cohort of professional women in the early 1960s and radical activism by a cohort of mostly college-educated younger women in the late 1960s. Daniel Horowitz, for instance, traces the roots of Betty Friedan's activism to her radical leftist activism of the 1940s and 1950s, and suggests that his findings urge a reconsideration of the early stages of feminist activism. See Horowitz, "Rethinking Betty Friedan," 1–42.

4. Evans, *Born for Liberty*, 277.

5. Ibid., 291.

6. Echols, *Daring to Be Bad*, 38.

7. Some scholars have argued that Carmichael made the "prone" comment in jest, referring to the infamous sexual liaisons throughout the organizations (see King's *Freedom Song*, 450–42). Whatever Carmichael's intent, however, his comment has come to represent the sexism within those organizations, and, more broadly, within the Civil Rights, student Left, and Black Power movements.

8. Polatnick, "Diversity in Women's Liberation Ideology," 679–706.

9. Wandersee, *On the Move*, 97–101.

10. Evans, *Born for Liberty*, 293.

11. Ibid., 287.

12. Castro, *American Feminism*, 189–91; Evans, *Born for Liberty*, 288.

13. Tuchman, "Symbolic Annihilation of Women," 5.

14. Joreen, "Voice of the Women's Liberation Movement," 112.

15. Castro, *American Feminism*, 187–89.

16. Freeman, in *Politics of Women's Liberation*, 112–13, discusses the trivialization and distortion of the women's movement in the mass media. Gitlin, in *Whole World is Watching*, 161, discusses the celebrity-making power of the media in terms of the women's liberation movement. Cohen's *Sisterhood*, which details the "stories" of Betty Friedan, Kate Millett, Germaine Greer, and Gloria Steinem (and pictures them on the front cover), provides an excellent example of this celebrity-focused journalism.

17. Heilbrun, *Education of a Woman*, 170–72; Steinem, *Outrageous Acts*, 17–18, and "The City Politic."

18. The first pathbreaking study of the history of U.S. feminist periodicals, and still one of the most comprehensive, is Mather's three-part series, "History of Feminist Periodicals." See also the chapter on the feminist press in Kessler's *Dissident Press* and the chapter on the feminist press in Marzolf's *Up from the Footnote*. This quote was taken from "Women's Free Press," 1.

19. Quoted in Beasley and Gibbons, *Women in Media*, 116–18.

20. Kirchwey, "Woman's Magazine and Why," 356.

21. Howard, "*Ms.* and the Journalism of Women's Lib," 44; Steinem, *Outrageous Acts*, 3.

22. Castro, *American Feminism*, 228.

23. Heilbrun, *Education of a Woman*, 218.

24. "A Birthday Book," #88s-17, Box 24, *Ms.* Magazine Records.

25. Harris interview; Carbine interview.

26. O'Reilly, "Whatever Happened to 'Ms.'?" 39.

27. "Feminist Forum," 104.

28. "Personal Report from *Ms.*," July 1972.

29. "How *Ms.* Magazine Got Started," 266.

30. Pogrebin interview.

31. Heilbrun, *Education of a Woman*, 218.

32. Echols, *Daring to Be Bad*, 266, 354.

33. Howard, "*Ms.* and the Journalism of Women's Lib," 44.

34. "For the Liberated Female," 52.

35. "Publicity: *Ms.*," #88s-17, Box 42, *Ms.* Magazine Records.

36. Winship, *Inside Women's Magazines*, 1–15.

37. Examples are from *Ms.*, January and October 1973.

38. Conversation with Susan Niles at the School of American Research, Santa Fe, New Mexico, October 1990.

39. For a discussion of Durga/Kiva, see Grimal, ed., *Larousse World Mythology*, 225, 268, and *Encyclopedia of World Mythology*, 34, 44, 64–65.

40. "What's a Ms.?," 4, 113.

41. Pogrebin, "Down with Sexist Upbringing," 25.

42. This, more than any other issue, was Steinem's product. While she used the input from others working on the issue, she made the decisions as to what went into the first full issue dated Spring 1972, and most of the articles were authored by women or men whom she already knew.

43. Pogrebin, "Down with Sexist Upbringing," 18–19.

44. *Ms.*, Spring 1972, 113.

45. Ibid., 5.

46. Cott, *Grounding of Modern Feminism*, 171–75.

47. Harris interview.

48. "Staff M–Z," #90s-5, Box 41, *Ms.* Magazine Records.

49. Lorde, *Sister Outsider*, 110.

50. Carbine interview.

51. Freeman, "Origins of the Women's Liberation Movement," 792–811; Martin, "Rethinking Feminist Organizations," 184–85; Smith, "Women's Movement Media and Cultural Politics," 280.

52. Kathy Ferguson, *Feminist Case against Bureaucracy*; Acker, "Hierarchies, Jobs, Bodies," 139–58; Morgen, "Work Culture in a Feminist Women's Health Clinic"; Taylor and Whittier, "Collective Identity in Social Movement Communities."

53. Rothschild-Whitt, "Collectivist Organization," 513.

54. "*Ms.* Makes It," 52.

55. Carbine interview.

56. "*Ms.* Makes It," 51–52.

57. Lyons interview.

58. Mainardi and Sarachild, "*Ms.* Politics and Editing," 168.

59. Lyons interview.

60. Peacock interview.

61. Levine interview.

62. Thom interview.

63. Breasted, "Move Over, 'Cosmo,' " 10.

64. Lyons interview.

65. Ibid.; Carbine interview.

66. Carbine interview.

67. O'Reilly, "Whatever Happened to 'Ms.'?" 40.

68. Harris interview.

69. "Feminist Forum," 104.

70. "*Ms.* Makes It," 51, and "Two Sides of the Woman Reader's Coin," in "Publicity: *Ms.*," #90s-5, Box 42, *Ms.* Magazine Records.

71. Of course, arguing that politics had no place in the marketplace ignored the fact that an "apolitical" consumer orientation constitutes a politics of its own.

72. Breasted, "Move Over, 'Cosmo,' ", 12.

73. Howard, "*Ms.* and the Journalism of Women's Lib," 54.

74. Conversation with New York advertising executive Richard Farrell, New York, N.Y., August 2, 1990.

75. "H" File, #90s-5, Box 6A, *Ms.* Magazine Records.

76. Howard, "*Ms.* and the Journalism of Women's Lib," 44.

77. Dekkers, "Periodicals," 19.

78. Howard, "*Ms.* and the Journalism of Women's Lib," 43.

79. Dekkers, "Periodicals," 19.

80. Pederpark, "I Want Everyone to Know," 29.

CHAPTER TWO

1. Levine interview.

2. Evans, *Born for Liberty*, 290.

3. Ibid., 300. For an excellent study of feminist academic journals, see McDermott, *Politics and Scholarship*. For a wide-ranging examination of the growth and status of feminist organizations in the 1970s, 1980s, and 1990s, see Ferree and Martin, *Feminist Organizations*.

4. Echols, *Daring to Be Bad*, 139–286.

5. Davis, *Moving the Mountain*, 435.

6. Evans, *Born for Liberty*, 305.

7. For a further discussion of the Houston conference, see Wandersee, *On the Move*, 175–96, and Castro, *American Feminism*, 199–200; Evans, *Born for Liberty*, 306.

8. Levine interview.

9. For a discussion of both "semiotic resistance" and "evasion," see Fiske, *Reading Popular Culture*, 9–10.

10. For a discussion of the use of national rhetoric in the first wave of feminism, see Evans, *Born for Liberty*, 145–74. See Wandersee, *On the Move*, ch. 2, for a discussion of women and electoral politics. For a discussion of 1970s feminist historical documentaries that focus on the 1940s, see Farrell, "History with a Vengeance." Quotation from Edgar, " 'Wonder Woman' Revisited," 52.

11. For a further discussion of the significance of covers and marketing, see McCracken, *Decoding Women's Magazines*, 14.

12. Letters, July 1973, 4.

13. Levine and Lyons interviews.

14. The huge outpouring from readers can be found in, Carton 4, Folder 93, *Ms. Magazine Letters*.

15. For a range of responses to these covers, as well as reports of stores and libraries refusing to display these issues, see, Carton 5, Folders 146 and 150, *Ms.* Magazine Letters.

16. For a further discussion of boycotts by advertisers, see Steinem, "Sex, Lies, and Advertising," 18–28.

17. Carbine interview.

18. "Personal Report from *Ms.*," January 1973, 97.

19. Ibid., July 1972, 7.

20. See Klein, *Gender Politics*, for a discussion of the connections between women's consciousness and political action.

21. In *American Feminism*, 65, Castro refers to *Ms.* primarily as "egalitarian." Echols, in *Daring to Be Bad*, 268, also alludes to *Ms.* as part of the "liberal" wing of the movement.

22. See Evans, *Born for Liberty*, esp. 54–56.

23. Morgan, "Rights of Passage," 77.

24. Sarachild, "Consciousness-Raising," 144–49.

25. Echols, *Daring to Be Bad*, 84.

26. Ibid., 87.

27. Sarachild, "Consciousness-Raising," 147.

28. Tillmon, "Welfare Is a Women's Issue," 116, 111.

29. Mainardi and Sarachild, "*Ms.* Politics and Editing," 168.

30. "Guide to Consciousness-Raising," 18.

31. Pogrebin, "Rap Groups," 104.

32. Morgan, "Rights of Passage," 74.

33. Pogrebin, "Motherhood," 49.

34. "Special Issue on Men," 47.

35. Peacock interview.

36. "Guide to Consciousness-Raising," 22.

37. "H" File, #90s-5, Box 6A, *Ms.* Magazine Records.

38. Willis, "Economic Reality and the Limits of Feminism," 90.

39. Morgan, "Rights of Passage," 75.

40. Evans and Boyte, *Free Spaces*.

41. Letters, February 1973, 7.

42. For a further discussion of the evocation of male and female "cultures" throughout various institutions of contemporary life, see Tavris, *Mismeasure of Woman*.

43. Letters, February 1973, 7.

44. Riley, *"Am I That Name?"* In *Grounding of Modern Feminism*, Cott explores with much precision the contradictions and paradoxes inherent in the woman movement just as it became termed "feminism" in the 1910s and 1920s. In particular, she demonstrates the way the premise of unity on which feminism rested disintegrated as activists pressed for individual rights for women.

45. Steinem, "Sisterhood," 48.

46. Steinem, "Women Voters Can't Be Trusted," 50.

47. Steinem, "Pornography—Not Sex,," 43–44.

48. Letters, July 1972, 42.

49. Steinem, "It's Your Year," 45.

50. *Ms.*, Spring 1972, 113.

51. Marie Ratagick, Nancy Sirkis, and Susan Berman, "Two American Welfare Mothers," 74; National Black Feminist Organization, 97; Susan Braudy, " 'We Will Remember' Survival School: The Women and Children of the American Indian Movement," 77; Michele Wallace, "Black Macho and the Myth of the Superwoman," 45; Angela Davis, "Joanne Little: The Dialectics of Rape," 74.

52. "Personal Report from *Ms.*," July 1972, 7.

53. Pogrebin, "Down with Sexist Upbringing," 18–19.

54. Joan Larkin, "Coming Out: 'My Story Is Not about All Lesbians,'" 72; Charlotte Bunch, "Forum: Learning from Lesbian Separatism," 60; Del Martin and Phyllis Lyons, "Lesbian Mothers," 78.

55. For a range of responses to the "click" article, see *Ms.* Magazine Letters, especially Cartons 1 and 2.

56. The contradictions within *Ms.* rhetoric between an emphasis on a shared culture among women and an emphasis on individual rights forms the crux of a major debate among feminists, for it seems impossible to argue one without refuting the other. To assert the essential sameness between men and women is to deny any specific gendered bonds, and vice versa. In addition, if the object of a political and social movement is to reach a state of full humanity, then any culturally based female superiority would deconstruct. If, however, we argue that the female culture is biologically based, then we back ourselves into a corner of biological determinism, which had been our original focus of criticism. Even taken separately, the concepts of individual liberty and of sisterhood have been strongly critiqued within the feminist movement. Feminist scholars involved in poststructuralism emphasize the difference "within" as well as "among" women; that is, the assertion of individual rights and full humanity assumes a fixed, "real" identity that does not exist except in our construction of it. We are instead made up of multiple and ever-changing identities that we use according to our specific needs and context. For an excellent collection of essays on the differences within women, see Nicholson, *Feminism/Postmodernism*. While the assertion of individual humanity ignores differences *within* women, argue other feminists, the emphasis on sisterhood obscures differences *among* women, most notably women of color. See hooks, *Feminist Theory*, 44.

57. "Alix at *Ms.*," 51.

58. All editors' quotes from the "housewife" debate are from "Housewives," #88s-17, Box 87, *Ms.* Magazine Records.

59. Jane Lazarre, "Jane Broderick," 83.

60. Memo dated April 27, 1977, from Carbine to *Newsday* editor, #90s-5, Box 107, *Ms.* Magazine Records.

61. Steinem, "Sisterhood," 49.

62. As Spelman argues in *Inessential Woman*, a significant problem within feminist politics is the assumption that all women's relationship to the oppressor — men — is the same.

63. "Guide to Consciousness-Raising," 18.

64. Martin and Lyons, "Lesbian Lovers," 74.

65. Olsen, *Silences*, and Rich, *On Lies, Secrets, and Silences*.

66. Willis, "Economic Reality and the Limits of Feminism," 91.

67. Redstockings, "Redstockings Challenge," 32.

68. Echols, *Daring to Be Bad*, 139–202.

69. Carton 3, Folder 62, *Ms.* Magazine Letters.

70. Willis, "Statement from Willis," 7.

71. "Everything You Wanted to Know about Advertising," 58.

72. "Personal Report from *Ms.*," July 1972, 7.

73. Ibid.

74. Levine interview.

75. Ferree and Hess, *Controversy and Coalition*.

76. *Ms.*, January 1974.

77. Ibid., January 1973.

78. Phillips, "Magazine Heroines."

79. Dougherty, "*Ms.* Publisher Spreads the Word," 71; Carbine interview.

80. "The Ms. Most," 3, #90s-5, Box 22, *Ms.* Magazine Records.

81. Ibid., 6.

82. Ibid., 12, 20, 9.

83. Ibid., 20.

84. "Foundations and Women Still Have a Long Way to Go," 13, and "How *Ms.* Magazine Got Started," 266, 269.

85. "Ms. Foundation," #90s-5, Box 98, *Ms.* Magazine Records.

86. Steinem, "What is a New *Ms.*?" 4.

87. Kort, "Ms. Foundation Helps Bring Feminism to Bear," 11. For legal reasons, the *Free to Be* project also spawned a new foundation, the Free to Be Foundation (FTB), whose fund-raising was earmarked for feminist children's projects around the nation; it existed under the legal umbrella of the Ms. Foundation, however, which continued to distribute all funds.

88. "Ms. Foundation," #90s-5, Box 98, *Ms.* Magazine Records.

89. Kort, "Ms. Foundation Helps Bring Feminism to Bear," 12.

90. "MFW 3/81; Grants analysis for 77–80," #90s-5, Box 112, *Ms.* Magazine Records.

91. "MFW 4/82," #90s-5, Box 112, *Ms.* Magazine Records.

92. "Foundations and Women Still Have a Long Way to Go," 13.

93. Memo from Margaret Sloan to "*Ms.* collective," "Staff M–Z," #90s-5, Box 42A, *Ms.* Magazine Records.

94. Levine, Thom, and Pogrebin interviews.

95. Peacock, Freeman, and Pogrebin interviews; Heilbrun, *Education of a Woman*, 249; Edgar interview.

96. Memo from Jolly Robinson to *Ms.* staff, Patricia Carbine Files, "M–Z Staff," #90s-5, Box 42A, *Ms.* Magazine Records.

97. Freeman, "Tyranny of Structurelessness," 77.

98. Lyons and Peacock interviews.

99. Ibid.; Willis, "Statement from Willis," 7.

100. Lyons interview.

101. "Patricof Report 1978," #90s-5, Box 110, *Ms.* Magazine Records.

102. Memo from Patricia Carbine, Suzanne Levine, and Gloria Steinem to *Ms.* staff, July 1, 1975, Patricia Carbine Files, "P–S," #90s-5, Box 42, *Ms.* Magazine Records. The memo stated that there would be no raises due to increased expenses and newsstand problems. It continued, "For people with good reason to discuss a loan, you know we'll try to work something out."

103. Peacock and Edgar interviews.

104. Levine and Edgar interviews.

105. Carbine interview.

106. Smith, "Women's Movement Media and Cultural Politics," 278–98.

1. Castro, *American Feminism*, 226.

2. Van Gelder manuscript, #88s-17, Box 44, *Ms.* Magazine Records.

3. Lyons interview.

4. Katzenstein, "Feminism within American Institutions," 27–54. For an exploration of comparable worth, see Evans and Nelson, *Wage Justice*. In *Born for Liberty*, 310, Evans reports that "despite active opposition by the Reagan administration, by 1987 more than forty states and seventeen hundred local governments had taken major steps toward implementing a comparable worth policy to raise the wages of female-dominated job classes."

5. Congress extended the deadline to June 30, 1982; see Davis, *Moving the Mountain*, 391. See also Berry, *Why ERA Failed*, and Mansbridge, *Why We Lost the ERA*.

6. Wandersee, *On the Move*, 182.

7. Evans, *Born for Liberty*, 305.

8. See Faludi, *Backlash*, for a full examination of the media backlash against women in the 1980s.

9. Memo from Karen Nussbaum to the Ms. Foundation for Women; "NEH Stop Funding Artistic Circuses," *New York Times*, and "MFW 3/81," #90s-5, Box 112, *Ms.* Magazine Records.

10. "One-Parent Families Singled Out for Trouble," 13. See also Ehrenreich, *Hearts of Men*.

11. "One-Parent Families Singled Out for Trouble," 13, 14. For a discussion of deindustrialization in the 1970s, see Bluestone and Harrison, *Deindustrialization of America*. For an exploration of the continuing gender gap in income and wages in 1988 and 1989, see "Economy in Numbers," 23.

12. Bisbee, "Top Ms. Aims to Hit Up Hub for Big Bucks," 11.

13. Steinem, "What is a New *Ms.*?" 4.

14. "Personal Report: Reader Alert!," back page.

15. "Patricof Report 1978," 3, #90s-5, Box 110, *Ms.* Magazine Records.

16. Miller, "*Ms.* Magazine Ten Years Later," 18.

17. Ibid.

18. "Patricof Report 1978," 40, #90s-5, Box 110, *Ms.* Magazine Records. The introduction of the report, 1–2, explained that between September and December 1978, the Patricof Corporation "conducted a thorough examination of the historical, current, and projected operations of *Ms.* magazine to develop a detailed, factual base on which to project *Ms.*'s potential performance in the segment of the magazine industry in which it operates."

19. Ibid., 8.

20. Ibid., 9–10, 40.

21. Ibid., 39, 7, 8, 41.

22. Ibid., 47–48, 50–51.

23. Ibid., 19, 8–9.

24. Ibid., 68, 8–9, 53.

25. Memo from Pogrebin to Carbine and Steinem, January 8, 1979, 10, #90s-5, Box 110, *Ms.* Magazine Records.

26. Memo from Steinem and Carbine to the stockholders of *Ms.* Magazine Corporation, August 10, 1979, "MFEC," #92s-49, Box 1, *Ms.* Magazine Records.

27. 1979 Proposal submitted by the Ms. Magazine Corp. to the Ford Foundation, "MFEC," #92s-49, Box 1, *Ms.* Magazine Records.

28. Steinem, "What is a New *Ms.*?" 6.

29. Memo from Rochelle Korman to MFEC Board, January 22, 1980, "MFEC," #92s-49, Box 1, *Ms.* Magazine Records.

30. Steinem, "What is a New *Ms.*?" 7.

31. Direct mail letter from 1980, "MFEC," #92s-49, Box 1, *Ms.* Magazine Records.

32. Steinem, "What is a New *Ms.*?" 7.

33. Miller, "*Ms.* Magazine Ten Years Later," 18.

34. Ibid.

35. Letters, January 1978.

36. Lyons and Peacock interviews.

37. Kaplan, "Feminist Criticism and Television," 221.

38. For a discussion of how the media blackout by radical feminists allowed Steinem to become the movement's spokesperson, see Echols, *Daring to Be Bad*, 209–10. See Gitlin, *Whole World is Watching*, 146–79, for a discussion of the way the media turned leaders from the New Left into celebrities.

39. Memo from Pogrebin to Carbine and Steinem, January 10, 1980, 2, #90s-5, Box 110, *Ms.* Magazine Records.

40. McDermott's work *Politics and Scholarship* is an excellent study of what happened when feminist thinking moved into the academy, exploring in particular the discourse of the three major feminist journals, *Signs*, *Feminist Studies*, and *Frontiers*.

41. Letter from Catharine Stimpson to Martha Nelson and Ruth Sullivan, March 14, 1981, #90s-5, Box 75, *Ms.* Magazine Records.

42. Questionnaire from Joan Huber, Department of Sociology, University of Illinois, 1980, #90s-5, Box 75, *Ms.* Magazine Records.

43. Correspondence between Susan Sands and *Ms.*, 1981, #88s-17, Box 113, *Ms.* Magazine Records.

44. Questionnaire from Joira Ferguson, Department of English, University of Nebraska-Lincoln, 1980, #90s-5, Box 75, *Ms.* Magazine Records.

45. Rejected Mss., 1985/86, JoAnne Edgar, #88s-17, Box 17, *Ms.* Magazine Records.

46. Letter from Steinem to Bunch, Spring 1980, #88s-17, Box 56, *Ms.* Magazine Records.

47. Letter from Edgar to Bunch, April 24, 1980, #88s-17, Box 56, *Ms.* Magazine Records.

48. Memo from Martha Nelson to Ruth Sullivan, March 14, 1981, #90s-5, Box 75, *Ms.* Magazine Records.

49. Gorney, "Gloria," 22.

50. Steinem, "What is a New *Ms.*?" 14.

51. "Personal Report: Reader Alert!," back page.

52. "Ninth Birthday Personal Report (and Urgent Alert)," 12, 14.

53. "Patricof Report 1978," 7, #90s-5, Box 110, *Ms.* Magazine Records.

54. Memo from Pogrebin to Carbine and Steinem, January 8, 1979, 2, #90s-5, Box 110, *Ms.* Magazine Records.

55. 1985 Promotional Brochure, #88s-17, Box 33, *Ms.* Magazine Records.

56. Ibid.

57. Promotional letter from Steinem to advertisers, 1985, #88s-17, Box 33, *Ms.* Magazine Records.

58. Memo from Lisa Cardile to Helen Barr, January 15, 1986, #88s-17, Box 33, *Ms.* Magazine Records.

59. Campus Life Promotional Material, n.d., #88s-17, Box 33, *Ms.* Magazine Records.

60. Promotional Material for April 1985 Travel Issue, #88s-17, Box 33, *Ms.* Magazine Records.

61. See, for instance, Ballaster et al., *Women's Worlds*, 16–42, 126–68, and Winship, *Inside Women's Magazines*.

62. "One Step Forward," December 1980, 108.

63. "Women Friends," September 1981, 104; "Nurturing Fathers," February 1982, 102; "Women in Sports," May 1983, 147; "Women Blue Collar Workers," June 1984, 37; "Men and Affection," August 1984, 149.

64. Quoted in "One Step Forward," April 1981, 99.

65. "Selling of the Nurturing Father," in "One Step Forward," February 1982, 102.

66. See Lipsitz, *Time Passages*, for a full discussion of capitalism's simultaneous destruction and valorization of traditional cultural forms.

67. For a further discussion of the media's need to solicit the readers/consumers with the best demographic profile, see Marc, *Demographic Vistas*.

68. Memo from Marie Wilson to MFW board members, September 23, 1985, "Ms. Foundation 1986," #92s-49, Box 2, *Ms.* Magazine Records.

69. Steinem, "What is a New *Ms.*?" 6.

70. Rosemary Bray, "Ms. Foundation: Dollars to the Grassroots," June 1986, 29.

71. These problems were discussed in the "End of the Decade Strategic Planning Document," "Ms. Foundation, 88–89," #92s-49, Box 2, *Ms.* Magazine Records.

72. Letter from Bolen to Angelou, "MFW 10/87," #88s-17, Box 83, *Ms.* Magazine Records.

73. "Established Funders Still Shortchanging Women and Girls," *Responsive Philanthropy*, Spring 1986, 1.

74. "Women Create New Movement: Dollars, Diversity Prime Concerns: 28 Funds Around the Country Targeting Women and Girls," *Responsive Philanthropy*, Spring 1986, 1.

75. Minutes of Annual Meeting of Board of Directors of the MFW for April 3 and 4, 1982, "MFW 8/82," #90s-5, Box 112, *Ms.* Magazine Records.

76. Memo from Aileen Hernandez to Board members, November 23, 1981, "MFW 12/81," #90s-5, Box 112, *Ms.* Magazine Records.

77. Memo from Director to Board members, November 22, 1981, "12/1–5/85 MFW," #90s-5, Box 115, *Ms.* Magazine Records.

78. 1982 Memo, "Dec. 1–5, 1985," #90s-5, Box 115, *Ms.* Magazine Records.

79. Memo from Jean Hardisty to Board and Staff, May 14, 1985, "6/1–2/85 MFW," #88s-17, Box 83, *Ms.* Magazine Records.

80. Letter from Rochelle Korman to Marjorie Fine Knowles, November 11, 1982, "MFW 12/82," #90s-5, Box 112, *Ms.* Magazine Records.

81. Letter from Rochelle Korman to Julia Scott, Director of MFW, November 19, 1982, "Folder 12/1–5/85," #90s-5, Box 115, *Ms.* Magazine Records.

CHAPTER FOUR

1. Rich, *On Lies, Secrets, and Silences,* 14.

2. Unpublished letters written to *Ms.* from 1972–80, with the exception of the letters written after the first issue, are collected at the Schlesinger Library at Radcliffe College. I looked solely at the published letters from 1981–89. Mary Thom's *Letters to Ms.* is a useful collection of published letters.

3. Letter from reader, September 1975, Folder 60, Carton 2, *Ms.* Magazine Letters.

4. "Personal Report from *Ms.,*" January 1973, 96.

5. For two excellent review articles of feminist cultural studies, see Schwichtenberg, "Feminist Cultural Studies," 202–7, and Long, "Feminism and Cultural Studies," 427–31. Fiske's *Reading Popular Culture* is a useful source for an introduction to British cultural studies. Radway's *Reading the Romance* is an excellent example of a work that combines institutional, textual, and reader analyses to provide a complex understanding of romance reading in the United States.

6. For Hall's discussion of the encoding and decoding processes, see his "Encoding/decoding," 128–38.

7. M. M. Bakhtin, *Dialogic Imagination.* I am also indebted to Mae G. Henderson for her insightful comments on the distinctions between Gadamer's and Bakhtin's notion of a dialogic, although I read Bakhtin's theory as allowing for both adversarial and harmonious dialogue and conversation. See Henderson, "Speaking in Tongues."

8. Editor Mary Peacock explained that Steinem generally would write the "Personal Reports," then pass them around to the editorial staff for comments and additions (Peacock interview).

9. "Personal Report from *Ms.,*" July 1972, 5, 7.

10. "Mothers Are People," May 1973, 102–3.

11. "Personal Report from *Ms.,*" July 1972, 7, 6.

12. "A Happy Birthday from *Ms.,*" July 1973, 83.

13. Ibid., 89.

14. "Personal Report from *Ms.,*" July 1972, 6.

15. "Unforgettable Letters from Battered Wives," December 1976.

16. See, for instance, "Dear Sisters," *Ms.,* December 1973, 76.

17. Renewal letter from Steinem to Subscribers, n.d. [1975], Folder 48, Carton 2, *Ms.* Magazine Letters.

18. "Personal Report from *Ms.,*" June 1974, 73.

19. Horkheimer and Adorno, *Dialectic of Enlightenment,* esp. 168–208; Lears, *No Place of Grace*; Ewen, *Captains of Consciousness*; Jameson, *Political Unconscious,* 288.

20. Memo from Ingeborg Day to "Ms. Family," January 2, 1973, #90s-5, Box 42A, *Ms.* Magazine Records.

21. "Letters Report," November 1977, #90s-5, Box 106, *Ms.* Magazine Records.

22. Carbine interview.

23. Jameson, "Reification and Utopia in Mass Media," 144.

24. Letter from reader, October 3, 1977, Folder 204, Carton 6, *Ms.* Magazine Letters.

25. Ibid., November 3, 1975, Folder 65, Carton 3.

26. Letters from readers, August 28, 1973, and June 9, 1974, Folder 8, Carton 1, ibid.

27. Freeman quoted in Davis, *Moving the Mountain*, 113.

28. Evans, *Personal Politics*, and Echols, *Daring to Be Bad*, both provide excellent historical accounts of how consciousness-raising groups worked within the early movement. Echols also discusses the demands placed on the early groups to accommodate increasing numbers of women. For a sociological discussion of consciousness-raising, see Ferree and Hess, *Controversy and Coalition*, esp. 63–64.

29. Letter from editor to reader, December 5, 1972, Folder 2, Carton 1, *Ms.* Magazine Letters.

30. Letter from reader, August 1973, Folder 2, Carton 1, ibid.

31. Ibid., July 1, 1974, Folder 5.

32. Ibid., February 1, 1975, Folder 36, Carton 2.

33. Letters, March 1986, 12.

34. Ibid., July 1986, 8–10.

35. O'Reilly, "Housewife's Moment of Truth."

36. Letter from reader, November 19, 1973, Folder 8, Carton 1, *Ms.* Magazine Letters.

37. Ibid., November 1975, Folder 65, Carton 3.

38. Letters, May 1986, 8.

39. Ibid., June 1974, 49.

40. Letter from reader, n.d. [1973], Folder 2, Carton 1, *Ms.* Magazine Letters.

41. Ibid., August 21, 1975, Folder 59, Carton 2.

42. Ibid., n.d. [1975], Folder 34, Carton 1.

43. Ibid., n.d. [1973], Folder 3.

44. Ibid., March 29, 1974, Folder 7.

45. Ibid., n.d. [1978], Folder 204, Carton 6.

46. Ibid., n.d. [1975], Folder 142, Carton 5.

47. Jameson, "Reification and Utopia in Mass Media," 144.

48. Letters, January 1978.

49. Letter from reader, September 4, 1977, Folder 142, Carton 5, *Ms.* Magazine Letters.

50. Ibid., June 22, 1974, Folder 20, Carton 1.

51. Ibid., April 29, 1980, Folder 228, Carton 7.

52. Ibid., October 2, 1975, Folder 62, Carton 3.

53. Ibid., March 3, 1976, Folder 75.

54. Ibid., January 1979, Folder 187, Carton 6.

55. Ibid., June 1, 1975, Folder 48, Carton 2.

56. Ibid., September 29, 1977, Folder 142, Carton 5.

57. Ibid., n.d. [1977], Folder 150.

58. Ibid., January 1979, Folder 186, Carton 6.

59. Heilbrun, *Education of a Woman*, 165.

60. See, for instance, the letters published in the September 1976 issue in reply to Gerald Wildermuth's musings on his attempts to fight feminism. These are also printed in Thom's *Letters to Ms.*, 190–93.

61. Letters, May 1987, 8.

62. Two excellent works that deconstruct the notion of "woman" and "women" are Riley, *"Am I That Name?"*, and Butler, *Gender Trouble*.

63. Habermas, *Legitimation Crisis*, and Lipsitz, *Time Passages*, esp. 71–72.

64. Letter from reader, n.d. [May 1978], Folder 204, Carton 6, *Ms.* Magazine Letters.

65. "Personal Report from *Ms.*," July 1972, 7.

66. Steiner, "Oppositional Decoding as an Act of Resistance," 6.

67. Ibid., 12.

68. Only ads from outside *Ms.* were ever published in *Ms.*, until the advertising-free *Ms.* published a two-page spread of offensive *Ms.* ads in its premier 1990 issue.

69. Letters from readers, June 1978, Folder 204, Carton 6, *Ms.* Magazine Letters.

70. Release, March 29, 1986, #88s-17, Box 33, *Ms.* Magazine Records.

71. Ben Kubaskik, Susan Mulcahy, and Anthony Scaduto, "Inside New York," *New York Newsday*, March 10, 1986.

72. *New York*, April 14, 1986.

73. Letter from Dorchen Leidholdt to Gloria Steinem, April 5, 1986, #88s-17, Box 33, *Ms.* Magazine Records.

74. For an overview of the "sex wars," see McDermott, *Politics and Scholarship*, 113–19. Many books emerged in this period that chronicled the central debates over female sexuality, including Snitow, Stansell, and Thompson, eds., *Powers of Desire*, Vance, *Pleasure and Danger*, and Samois, *Coming to Power*.

75. Letter from reader, n.d. [March 1986], #88s-17, Box 33, *Ms.* Magazine Records.

76. Ibid., March 29, 1986.

77. Letters, July 1986, 10.

78. Letter from reader, January 1979, Folder 186, Carton 5, *Ms.* Magazine Letters.

79. Letter from *Ms.* staff to Sherry Davis, n.d. [1970s], #90s-5, Box 42A, *Ms.* Magazine Records.

80. "Tobacco ads are in, smoking warnings out," *USA Today*, June 17, 1986, 4D; Beverly Stephen, "No Butts about It, Women Have Come a Little Too Far," *Daily News*, November 21, 1985, 44; Jean Seligmann et al., "Women Smokers: The Risk Factor" *Newsweek*, November 25, 1985, 76–78.

81. Letter from Steinem to *Newsweek*, November 19, 1985, #88s-17, Box 33, *Ms.* Magazine Records. In *Media Monopoly*, 172, Bagdikian reported that around 1980 Whelan offered to write on the growing incidence of tobacco-related health problems in women. Ten women's magazines, including *Ms.*, refused.

82. Levine, "New Words, New Understanding," February 1987, 35.

83. Carbine interview.

84. Letters, May 1987, 8.

85. Carbine interview. Steinem, "Sex, Lies, and Advertising," 18–28.

86. Letter from reader, May 1978, Folder 204, Carton 6, *Ms.* Magazine Letters.

87. Ibid., February 1979, Folder 186.

CHAPTER FIVE

1. For a chronicling of these changes in ownership, see Fabrikant, "Turnaround Sought at *Ms.* Magazine," 37; Wayne, "*Ms.* Magazine is Being Sold," D1; La Ganga, "Revised *Ms.* to Publish," D7.

2. Bolotin, "Voices from the Post-Feminist Generation," 31; Stacey, "Sexism by a Subtler Name?," 338–56. Two excellent discussions of postfeminism and the backlash in the popular media include Walters's "Postfeminism and Popular Culture," in *Material Girls*, 116–42, and McDermott's "On Cultural Authority," 668–84. For a discussion of the way 1920s women viewed the suffragists of the previous generation, see Cott, *Grounding of Modern Feminism*.

3. Fabrikant, "Turnaround Sought at *Ms.* Magazine," 39.

4. Levine, "*Ms.* of the Future Is Here," 5.

5. Ibid.

6. Fabrikant, "Turnaround Sought at *Ms.* Magazine," 137, 139.

7. While published letters during this period do not indicate resistance to these preferred readings, we can see readers developing another set of readings in published articles and in my interview with a group of readers. Hall discusses his notion of "preferred readings" in "Encoding/decoding," 128–38.

8. De Lauretis, *Alice Doesn't*, 57, and Mulvey, "Visual Pleasure and Narrative Cinema," 14–28.

9. Minutes of MFEC and MFW Meeting, October 16, 1987, "MFW 87–88," #92s-49, Box 1, *Ms.* Magazine Records.

10. Minutes of MFW, October 16, 1987, "MFW 87–88," #92s-49, Box 1, *Ms.* Magazine Records.

11. Memo from Carbine to Wilson, Ex. Director of MFW, June 30, 1989, "MFEC Board," #92s-49, Box 2, *Ms.* Magazine Records.

12. Minutes of MFW, October 25, 1987, "MFW 87–88," #92s-49, Box 1, *Ms.* Magazine Records.

13. Memo from Levine to Carbine; Steinem, Bower, and Pogrebin, February 10, 1988, and Memo from Caplin and Drysdale (attorneys) to MFEC Board, March 31, 1988, both in "MFEC Board," #92s-49, Box 2, *Ms.* Magazine Records.

14. Memo from JoAnne Edgar to MFEC Board, December 22, 1987, "MFEC Board," #92s-49, Box 2, *Ms.* Magazine Records.

15. Hester Eisenstein's *Gender Shock* provides a useful comparison between Australian and U.S. feminism in its second wave.

16. Wayne, "Australia Concern to Buy *Ms.*," D3.

17. Ibid.

18. "*Ms.* Says G'day to New Owners," 57.

19. Gillespie interview.

20. For a description and brief discussion of these promotion ads, see Winegar, "New *Ms.* Appears Slicker," 1E, and Laurence Zuckerman, "From Upstart to Mainstream," 72.

21. Lathrop, "Demographic Dilemma," 13.

22. Hamilton, "New Blood for *Ms.* Magazine," E1.

23. "New *Ms.* from Down Under," 13.

24. Lathrop, "Demographic Dilemma," 15.

25. Hamilton, "New Blood for *Ms.* Magazine," E1.

26. Fairfax Promotional Materials, n.d., #88s-17, Box 24, *Ms.* Magazine Records.

27. Summers interview.

28. Castro, *American Feminism*, 212–14.

29. Lathrop, "Demographic Dilemma," 12.

30. Allemang, "*Ms.* Gives It a Miss," C11.

31. I discuss the newest *Ms.* in the final chapter.

32. See Reilly, "*Ms.* to Be Published without Ads," for a discussion of the *Ms.* demographics.

33. Lipsitz, *Time Passages*, 93.

CHAPTER SIX

1. Steinem, "Sex, Lies, and Advertising," 19.

2. Lear, "Third-Anniversary Blessing," 140.

3. Levine interview.

4. For a discussion of the concept of "free spaces," see Evans and Boyte, *Free Spaces*.

5. Goodman, "*Ms.* is Back," 14A. The current editor is Marcia Gillespie. On May 29, 1996, Dale Lang announced he would sell Lang Communications, which owned the newest *Ms.*, to MacDonald Corporation. The sale appeared to have been precipitated by ailing financial condition of two of Lang's assets, *Working Mother* and *Working Woman* magazines; *Ms.* appeared to be in the black financially. Changes that MacDonald would make to *Ms.* were at that point unclear (see Laurence Zuckerman "Publisher of *Ms.* Will Sell Magazine Group to Investors," C5).

6. Editor Marcia Gillespie spoke quite powerfully about the implicit racism and classism of all print media, in comparison to electronic media (i.e., television), and the inherent elitism of the new *Ms.* (Gillespie interview).

7. In the *Women's Review of Books*, Deborah Solomon responded negatively to the first four issues of the new *Ms.*, arguing that the editors limited the magazine's reach by assuming a shared perspective among all women and by restricting its sales to alternative book stores and only a few mainstream marketing arenas like Dalton's. Solomon criticized the new magazine's rejection of a mass media audience or mass media look, pointing out that *Ms.* should attempt to reach those who are "skillfully navigating the brightly colored aisles, making informed, and sometimes unexpected, choices" if it wishes to reach a national audience. What Solomon never explicitly discusses, but what her mention of the "brightly colored aisles" suggests, is how the eradication of advertisements denies an element of pleasure for readers, even as it removes a major obstacle to publishing an explicitly feminist text ("New and Improved?" 9–10).

8. Two excellent studies of other sites of "popular politics" include D'Acci's *Defining Women* and Rose's *Black Noise*.

BIBLIOGRAPHY

BOOKS, ARTICLES, AND UNPUBLISHED PAPERS

Acker, J. "Hierarchies, Jobs, Bodies: A Theory of Gendered Organizations." *Gender and Society* 4, no. 2 (June 1990): 139–58.

Albrecht, Lisa, and Rose M. Brewer, eds. *Bridges of Power: Women's Multicultural Alliances.* Philadelphia: New Society Publishers, 1990.

Allemang, John. "*Ms.* Gives It a Miss." *Toronto Globe and Mail* November 3, 1989, C11.

Althusser, Louis. "Ideology and Ideological State Apparatuses," *Lenin and Philosophy and Other Essays.* Translated by B. Brewster. London: New Left Books, 1971.

Bagdikian, Ben. *The Media Monopoly.* Boston: Beacon Press, 1990.

Bakhtin, M. M. *The Dialogic Imagination: Four Essays.* Edited by Michael Holquist. Austin: University of Texas Press, 1981.

Ballaster, Ros, Margaret Beetham, Elizabeth Frazer, and Sandra Hebron. *Women's Worlds: Ideology, Femininity and the Woman's Magazine.* London: Macmillan, 1991.

Barrett, Michelle. *Women's Oppression Today: Problems in Marxist Feminist Analysis.* London: Verso, 1980.

Beasley, Maurine, and Sheila Gibbons. *Women in Media: A Documentary Sourcebook.* Washington, D.C.: Women's Institute for Freedom of the Press, 1977.

Berry, Mary Frances. *Why ERA Failed.* Bloomington: Indiana University Press, 1986.

Bisbee, Dana. "Top Ms. Aims to Hit Up Hub for Big Bucks." *The Boston Herald,* June 14, 1987, 11–13.

Bluestone, Barry, and Bennet Harrison. *The Deindustrialization of America: Plant Closings, Community Abandonment, and the Dismantling of Basic Industry.* New York: Basic Books, 1982.

Bolotin, Susan. "Voices from the Post-Feminist Generation." *New York Times Magazine,* October, 17, 1982, 31.

Breasted, Mary. "Move Over, 'Cosmo,' Here Comes 'Ms.'!" *Saturday Review,* July 15, 1972, 5–12.

Butler, Judith. *Gender Trouble: Feminism and the Subversion of Identity.* New York: Routledge, 1990.

Carabillo, Toni, Judith Meuli, and June Bundy Csida. *Feminist Chronicles: 1953–1993.* Los Angeles: Women's Graphics, 1993.

Carroll, Peter N. *It Seemed Like Nothing Happened: America in the 1970s.* New Brunswick: Rutgers University Press, 1990.

Cassell, Joan. *A Group Called Women: Sisterhood and Symbolism in the Feminist Movement.* New York: David McKay Company, 1977.

Castro, Ginette. *American Feminism: A Contemporary History.* Translated by Elizabeth Loverde-Bagwell. New York: New York University Press, 1990.

Christopher, Maurine. " 'Ms.'-Givings over Celebration." *Advertising Age,* July 13, 1987, 36–37.

Cohen, Marcia. *The Sisterhood: The True Story of the Women Who Changed the World.* New York: Simon and Schuster, 1988.

Coward, Rosalind. *Female Desires: How They Are Sought, Bought, and Packaged.* New York: Grove Press, 1985.

Cott, Nancy F. *The Grounding of Modern Feminism.* New Haven: Yale University Press, 1987.

Czitrom, Daniel J. *Media and the American Mind: From Morse to McLuhan.* Chapel Hill: University of North Carolina Press, 1982.

D'Acci, Julie. *Defining Women: Television and the Case of Cagney and Lacey.* Chapel Hill: University of North Carolina Press, 1994.

Davis, Flora. *Moving the Mountain: The Women's Movement in America Since 1960.* New York: Simon and Schuster, 1991.

Dekkers, Onka. "Periodicals." *off our backs,* September 1972, 19.

de Lauretis, Teresa. *Alice Doesn't: Feminism, Semiotics, Cinema.* Bloomington: Indiana University Press, 1984.

———. "Feminist Studies/Critical Studies: Issues, Terms and Contexts." In *Feminist Studies/Critical Studies,* edited by Teresa de Lauretis, 1–19. Bloomington: Indiana University Press, 1986.

Dougherty, Phillip H. "*Ms.* Publisher Spreads the Word." *New York Times,* November 20, 1975.

Douglas, Susan. *Where the Girls Are: Growing Up Female with the Mass Media.* New York: Random House, 1994.

Echols, Alice. *Daring to Be Bad: Radical Feminism in America 1967–1975.* Minneapolis: University of Minnesota Press, 1989.

"Economy in Numbers: Gender Gaps Galore." *Dollars and Sense,* December 1992, 23.

Ehrenreich, Barbara. *The Hearts of Men: American Dreams and the Flight from Commitment.* Garden City, N.Y.: Anchor Press, 1983.

Eisenstein, Hester. *Gender Shock: Practicing Feminism on Two Continents.* Boston: Beacon Press, 1991.

Eisenstein, Zillah R. *Radical Future of Liberal Feminism.* Boston: Northeastern University Press, 1981.

Encyclopedia of World Mythology. New York: Galahad Books, 1975.

Evans, Sara. *Born for Liberty: A History of Women in America.* New York: The Free Press, 1989.

————. *Personal Politics: The Roots of Women's Liberation in the Civil Rights Movement and the New Left.* New York: Vintage Books, 1979.

Evans, Sara M., and Harry C. Boyte. *Free Spaces: Sources of Democratic Change in America.* New York: Harper and Row, 1986.

Evans, Sara M., and Barbara J. Nelson. *Wage Justice: Comparable Worth and the Paradox of Technocratic Reform.* Chicago: University of Chicago Press, 1989.

Ewen, Stuart. *Captains of Consciousness: Advertising and the Social Roots of the Consumer Culture.* New York: Basic Books, 1975.

Fabrikant, Geraldine. "Turnaround Sought at *Ms.* Magazine." *New York Times,* May 9, 1987, 37–39.

Faludi, Susan. *Backlash: The Undeclared War against American Women.* New York: Crown Publishers, 1991.

Farrell, Amy Erdman. "History with a Vengeance: Feminist Historical Documentaries of the 1970s." Paper presented at the National Women's Studies Association Conference, Akron, Ohio, June 1990.

————. " 'Like a Tarantula on a Banana Boat': *Ms.* Magazine, 1972–1989." In *Feminist Organizations: Harvest of the New Women's Movement,* edited by Myra Marx Ferree and Patricia Yancey Martin. Philadelphia: Temple University Press, 1995.

"Feminist Forum." *Newsweek,* November 8, 1971, 104.

Ferguson, Kathy. *The Feminist Case against Bureaucracy.* Philadelphia: Temple University Press, 1984.

Ferguson, Marjorie. *Forever Feminine: Women's Magazines and the Cult of Femininity.* London: Heinemann, 1983.

Ferree, Myra Marx, and Beth B. Hess. *Controversy and Coalition: The New Feminist Movement.* Boston: Twayne Publishers, 1985.

Ferree, Myra Marx, and Patricia Yancey Martin. *Feminist Organizations: Harvest of the New Women's Movement.* Philadelphia: Temple University Press, 1995.

Fiske, John. *Reading Popular Culture.* New York: Unwin Hyman, 1989.

"For the Liberated Female." *Time,* December 20, 1971, 52.

"Foundations and Women Still Have a Long Way To Go." *The Grantsmanship Center News,* January/February 1978, 13.

Freeman, Jo. "The Origins of the Women's Liberation Movement." *American Journal of Sociology* 78, no. 4 (1973): 792–811.

————. *The Politics of Women's Liberation.* New York: Longman, 1975.

Friedan, Betty. *The Feminine Mystique.* New York: W. W. Norton, 1963.

Gitlin, Todd. *The Whole World Is Watching: Mass Media in the Making and Unmaking of the New Left.* Berkeley: University of California Press, 1980.

Goodman, Ellen. "*Ms.* is Back, as a 'Magabook.' " *Star-Tribune* (Minneapolis-St. Paul), August 10, 1990, 14A.

Gorney, Cynthia. "Gloria." *Mother Jones* 20 (November/December 1995): 22–24.

Grimal, Pierre, ed. *Larousse World Mythology.* New York: Hamlyn Publishing Group Limited, 1965.

Habermas, Jurgen. *The Legitimation Crisis.* Boston: Beacon Press, 1975.

Hall, Stuart. "Encoding/decoding." In *Culture, Media and Language*, edited by
    S. Hall, D. Hobson, A. Lowe, and P. Willis, 128–38. London: Hutchinson, 1980.
———. "Notes on Deconstructing the Popular." In *People's History and Socialist
    Theory*, edited by Raphael Samuel, 227–40. London: Routledge and Kegan
    Paul, 1981.
Hamilton, Mildred. "New Blood for *Ms.* Magazine." *San Francisco Examiner*,
    February 7, 1988, E1.
Heath, Stephen, and Gillian Skirrow. "Interview with Raymond Williams." In
    Studies in Entertainment: Critical Approaches to Mass Culture, edited by Tania
    Modleski. Bloomington: Indiana University Press, 1986.
Heilbrun, Carolyn. *The Education of a Woman: The Life of Gloria Steinem*. New
    York: The Dial Press, 1995.
Henderson, Mae G. "Speaking in Tongues: Dialogics, Dialectics, and the Black
    Woman Writer's Literary Tradition." *Changing Our Own Words: Essays on
    Criticism, Theory, and Writing by Black Women*, edited by Cheryl A. Wall.
    New Brunswick: Rutgers University Press, 1989.
hooks, bell. *Feminist Theory: From Margin to Center*. Boston: South End Press, 1984.
Horkheimer, Max, and Theodor W. Adorno. *Dialectic of Enlightenment*. Translated
    by J. Cumming. New York: Herder & Herder, 1972.
Horowitz, Daniel. "Rethinking Betty Friedan and *The Feminist Mystique*: Labor
    Union Radicalism and Feminism in Cold War America." *American Quarterly*
    48, no. 1 (March 1996): 1–42.
"How *Ms.* Magazine Got Started." In *The First Ms. Reader*, edited by Francine
    Klagsbrun, 262–79. New York: Warner, 1973.
Howard, Pamela. "*Ms.* and the Journalism of Women's Lib." *Saturday Review*,
    January 8, 1972, 43–45.
Jameson, Frederic. *The Political Unconscious: Narrative as a Socially Symbolic Act*.
    New York: Cornell University Press, 1981.
———. "Reification and Utopia in Mass Media." *Social Text* (Winter 1979): 130–48.
Joreen. "Voice of the Women's Liberation Movement." In *Women in Media:
    A Documentary Source Book*, edited by Maurine Hoffman Beasley.
    Washington, D.C.: Women's Institute for Freedom of the Press, 1977.
Kaplan, E. Ann. "Feminist Criticism and Television." In *Channels of Discourse*,
    edited by Robert C. Allen. Chapel Hill: University of North Carolina Press,
    1987.
Katzenstein, Mary Fainsod. "Comparing the Feminist Movements of the U.S. and
    Western Europe: An Overview." In *The Women's Movements of the U.S. and
    Western Europe: Consciousness, Political Opportunity, and Public Policy*, edited
    by Mary Fainsod Katzenstein and Carol McClung Mueller. Philadelphia:
    Temple University Press, 1987.
———. "Feminism within American Institutions: Unobtrusive Mobilization in the
    1980s." *Signs* 16, no. 1 (Autumn 1990): 27–54.
Katzenstein, Mary Fainsod, and Carol McClung Mueller, ed. *The Women's
    Movements of the U.S. and Western Europe: Consciousness, Political
    Opportunity, and Public Policy*. Philadelphia: Temple University Press, 1987.

Kessler, Lauren. *The Dissident Press: Alternative Journalism in American History.* Beverly Hills: Sage Publications, 1984.

King, Mary. *Freedom Song: A Personal Story of the 1960s Civil Rights Movement.* New York: Morrow, 1987.

Kirchwey, Freda. "A Woman's Magazine and Why." *The Suffragist* 9, no. 1 (January/February 1921): 356.

Klein, Ethel. *Gender Politics: From Consciousness to Mass Politics.* Cambridge, Mass.: Harvard University Press, 1984.

Kort, Michele. "Ms. Foundation Helps Bring Feminism to Bear." *The Grantsmanship News*, January/February 1978, 11–13.

Kozol, Wendy. *Life's America.* Philadelphia: Temple University Press, 1994.

La Ganga, Maria L. "Revised *Ms.* to Publish, but Without Ads." *Los Angeles Times*, March 5, 1990, D7.

Lathrop, Jan. "The Demographic Dilemma: *Ms.* Sells Out." *Feminist Voices: A Madison Area News Journal* 2, no. 6 (July/August 1989): 13–15.

Lear, Frances. "Third-Anniversary Blessing." *Lear's*, March 1991, 140.

Lears, T. J. Jackson. "A Matter of Taste: Corporate Cultural Hegemony in a Mass Consumer Society." In *Recasting America: Culture and Politics in the Age of Cold War*, edited by Lary May, 38–60. Chicago: University of Chicago Press, 1989.

———. *No Place of Grace: Antimodernism and the Transformation of American Culture, 1880–1920.* New York: Pantheon Books, 1981.

Lewis, Lisa A. *Gender Politics and MTV: Voicing the Difference.* Philadelphia: Temple University Press, 1990.

Lipsitz, George. "The Struggle for Hegemony." *Journal of American History* 75, no. 1 (Spring 1988): 146–50.

———. " 'This Ain't No Sideshow': Historians and Media Studies." *Critical Studies in Mass Communication* 6 (December 1989): 427–35.

———. *Time Passages: Collective Memory and American Popular Culture.* Minneapolis: University of Minnesota Press, 1990.

Long, Elizabeth. "Feminism and Cultural Studies." *Critical Studies in Mass Communication* 6 (December 1989): 427–35.

Lorde, Audre. *Sister Outsider.* Trumansburg, N.Y.: Crossing Press, 1984.

McCracken, Ellen. *Decoding Women's Magazines: From Mademoiselle to Ms.* New York: St. Martin's Press, 1993.

McDermott, Patrice. "On Cultural Authority: Women's Studies, Feminist Politics, and the Popular Press." *Signs* 20, no. 3 (Spring 1995): 668–84.

———. *Politics and Scholarship: Feminist Academic Journals and the Production of Knowledge.* Urbana: University of Illinois Press, 1994.

Mainardi, Patricia, and Kathie Sarachild. "*Ms.* Politics and Editing: An Interview." In *Feminist Revolution*, edited by Redstockings, 167–69. New York: Random House, 1975.

Mansbridge, Jane. "What Is the Feminist Movement?" In *Feminist Organizations: Harvest of the New Women's Movement*, edited by Myra Marx Ferree and Patricia Yancey Martin, 27–34. Philadelphia: Temple University Press, 1995.

———. *Why We Lost the ERA*. Chicago: University of Chicago Press, 1986.

Marc, David. *Demographic Vistas: Television in American Culture*. Philadelphia: University of Pennsylvania Press, 1984.

Martin, Patricia Yancey. "Rethinking Feminist Organizations." *Gender and Society* 4 (1990): 182–206.

Marzolf, Marion. *Up from the Footnote: A History of Women Journalists*. New York: Hastings House Publishers, 1977.

Mather, Anne. "A History of Feminist Periodicals." Parts 1–3. *Journalism History* 1, no. 3 (Autumn 1974); 1, no. 4 (Winter 1975); 2, no. 1 (Spring 1975).

Miller, Pam. "*Ms.* Magazine Ten Years Later: Readership Continues to Build." *Christian Science Monitor*, December 29, 1981, 18.

Millett, Kate. *Sexual Politics*. Garden City, N.Y.: Doubleday, 1970.

Moi, Toril. *Sexual/Textual Politics*. New York: Methuen, 1985.

Morgan, Robin, ed. *Sisterhood Is Powerful: An Anthology of Writings from the Women's Liberation Movement*. New York: Vintage Books, 1970.

Morgen, Sandra. "Work Culture in a Feminist Women's Health Clinic." Paper presented at Feminist Organizations: Harvest of the New Women's Movement, Washington, D.C., 1992.

"The *Ms.* Biz." *Newsweek*, October 15, 1973, 70.

Ms. Magazine Letters. Arthur and Elizabeth Schlesinger Library on the History of Women. Radcliffe College. Cambridge, Massachusetts.

Ms. Magazine Records. Sophia Smith Collection. Smith College. Northampton, Massachusetts.

"*Ms.* Makes It." *Time*, December 25, 1972, 51.

"*Ms.* Says G'day to New Owners." *Time*, October 5, 1987.

Mulvey, Laura. "Visual Pleasure and Narrative Cinema." In *Visual and Other Pleasures*. Bloomington: Indiana University Press, 1989.

"A New *Ms.* from Down Under." *New York*, October 12, 1987, 13.

Nicholson, Linda J., ed. *Feminism/Postmodernism*. New York: Routledge, 1990.

Olsen, Tillie. *Silences*. New York: Dell Publishing Company, 1978.

"One-Parent Families Singled Out for Trouble." *Dollars and Sense*, September 1983, 13.

O'Reilly, Jane. "Whatever Happened to 'Ms.'?" *New York*, July 26, 1972, 39.

Pederpark. "I Want Everyone to Know That I Love Lean, But He Wouldn't Never Give Me None." *Northwest Passage* 7, no. 9 (August 18–September 10, 1972): 29.

Polatnick, M. Rivka. "Diversity in Women's Liberation Ideology: How a Black and a White Group of the 1960s Viewed Motherhood." *Signs* 21, no. 3 (Spring 1996): 679–706.

Phillips, E. Barbara. "Magazine Heroines: Is *Ms.* Just Another Member of the *Family Circle*?" In *Hearth and Home: Images of Women in the Mass Media*, edited by Arlene Daniels, Gaye Tuchman, and James Benet. New York: Oxford University Press, 1978.

Radway, Janice A. *A Feeling for Books: The Book-of-the-Month Club, Literary Taste, and Middle-Class Desire.* Chapel Hill: University of North Carolina Press, 1997.

―――. *Reading the Romance: Women, Patriarchy, and Popular Literature.* Chapel Hill: University of North Carolina Press, 1984.

Redstockings. "Redstockings Challenge." *off our backs*, July 1975, 8–9.

Reilly, Patrick M. "*Ms.* to Be Published Without Ads in Attempt to Save the Magazine." *Wall Street Journal*, October 13, 1989.

Rich, Adrienne. *On Lies, Secrets, and Silences: Selected Prose 1966–1978.* New York: W. W. Norton and Company, 1979.

Riley, Denise. *"Am I that Name?" Feminism and the Category of "Women" in History.* Minneapolis: University of Minnesota Press, 1988.

Rose, Tricia. *Black Noise: Rap Music and Black Culture in Contemporary America.* Hanover: Wesleyan University Press, 1994.

Rothschild-Whitt, J. "The Collectivist Organization: An Alternative to Rational-Bureaucratic Models." *American Sociological Review* 44 (1979): 509–27.

Samois. *Coming to Power: Writings and Graphics on Lesbian S/M.* Boston: Alyson Publications, 1987.

Sarachild, Kathie. "Consciousness-Raising: A Radical Weapon." In *Feminist Revolution*, edited by Redstockings, 144–49. New York: Random House, 1975.

Schudson, Michael. *Advertising, the Uneasy Persuasion: Its Dubious Impact on American Society.* New York: Basic Books, 1986.

Schwichtenberg, Cathy. "Feminist Cultural Studies." *Critical Studies in Mass Communication* 6 (June 1989): 202–8.

Scott, Joan Wallach. *Gender and the Politics of History.* New York: Columbia University Press, 1988.

Smith, Marilyn Crafton. "Women's Movement Media and Cultural Politics." In *Women in Mass Communication: Challenging Gender Values*, edited by Pamela J. Creedon. Newbury Park: Sage Publications, 1989.

Snitow, Ann, Christine Stansell, and Sharon Thompson, eds. *Powers of Desire: The Politics of Sexuality.* New York: Monthly Review Press, 1983.

Solomon, Deborah. "New and Improved?" *The Women's Review of Books* 7 (April 1991): 9–10.

Spelman, Elizabeth V. *Inessential Woman: Problems of Exclusion in Feminist Thought.* Boston: Beacon Press, 1988.

Stacey, Judith. "Sexism by a Subtler Name? Postindustrial Conditions and Postfeminist Consciousness in Silicon Valley." In *Women, Class, and the Feminist Imagination: A Socialist Feminist Reader*, edited by Karen V. Hansen and Ilene Philipson, 338–56. Philadelphia: Temple University Press, 1990.

Steeves, Leslie. "Feminist Theories and Media Studies." *Critical Studies in Mass Communication* 4 (June 1987): 95–135.

Steinem, Gloria. "The City Politic: 'After Black Power, Women's Liberation.' " *New York*, April 7, 1969.

―――. *Outrageous Acts and Everyday Rebellions.* New York: Holt, Rinehart and Winston, 1983.

Steiner, Linda. "The History and Structure of Women's Alternative Media." In *Women Making Meaning: Feminist Directions in Communication*, edited by Lana F. Rakow, 121–43. New York: Routledge, 1992.

———. "Oppositional Decoding as an Act of Resistance." *Critical Studies in Mass Communication* 5 (March 1988): 1–15.

Tavris, Carol. *Mismeasure of Woman: Why Women Are Not the Better Sex, the Inferior Sex, or the Opposite Sex*. New York: Simon and Schuster, 1992.

Taylor, V., and N. Whittier. "Collective Identity in Social Movement Communities: Lesbian Feminist Mobilization." In *Frontiers in Social Movement Theory*, edited by C. Mueller and A. Morris. New Haven, Conn.: Yale University Press: 1990.

Thom, Mary. *Inside Ms.: Twenty-Five Years of the Magazine and the Feminist Movement*. New York, Henry Holt and Company, 1997.

———, ed. *Letters to Ms.* New York: Henry Holt and Company, 1987.

Tuchman, Gaye. "The Symbolic Annihilation of Women by the Mass Media." In *Hearth and Home: Images of Women in the Mass Media*, edited by Gaye Tuchman, Arlene Kaplan Daniels, and James Benet, 3–38. New York: Oxford University Press, 1978.

Vance, Carole S. *Pleasure and Danger: Exploring Female Sexuality*. Boston: Routledge and Kegan Paul, 1984.

Walters, Suzanna Danuta. *Material Girls: Making Sense of Feminist Cultural Theory*. Berkeley: University of California Press, 1995.

Wandersee, Winifred. *On the Move: American Women in the 1970s*. Boston: Twayne Publishers, 1988.

Wayne, Leslie. "Australia Concern to Buy *Ms.*" *New York Times*, September 24, 1987, D1, D3.

———. "*Ms.* Magazine is Being Sold for Second Time in Six Months." *New York Times*, March 18, 1988, D1.

Williamson, Judith. *Consuming Passions: The Dynamics of Popular Culture*. London: Marion Boyars, 1986.

———. *Decoding Advertisements: Ideology and Meaning in Advertisements*. London: Marion Boyars, 1978.

Willis, Ellen. "Statement from Willis." *off our backs*, September–October 1975, 7.

Winegar, Karin. "New *Ms.* Appears Slicker: Some Say It's Less Militant." *Star Tribune* (Minneapolis/St. Paul), April 2, 1988, 1E.

Winship, Janice. *Inside Women's Magazines*. New York: Pandora Press, 1987.

"Women's Free Press." *Know News Bulletin*, January 1973, 1.

Zuckerman, Laurence. "Publisher of *Ms.* Will Sell Magazine Group to Investors." *New York Times*, May 29, 1996, C5.

———. "From Upstart to Mainstream." *Time*, December 12, 1988, 72.

MS. ARTICLES CITED

Jane O'Reilly. "The Housewife's Moment of Truth." Spring 1972, 54–59.

Letty Cottin Pogrebin. "Down with Sexist Upbringing." Spring 1972, 18–20.

Gloria Steinem. "Sisterhood." Spring 1972, 46–49.

Johnnie Tillmon. "Welfare Is a Women's Issue." Spring 1972, 111–16.

"What's a Ms.?," Spring 1972, 4, 113.

JoAnne Edgar. " 'Wonder Woman' Revisited." July 1972, 52.

"Guide to Consciousness-Raising." July 1972, 18–23.

Letters. July 1972, 40.

Del Martin and Phyllis Lyons. "Lesbian Lovers." July 1972, 74.

"Personal Report from *Ms.*" July 1972, 4–7.

"Personal Report from *Ms.*" January 1973, 96–97.

Gloria Steinem. "Women Voters Can't Be Trusted." February 1973, 50.

Letters. February 1973, 7.

Letty Cottin Pogrebin. "Rap Groups: The Feminist Connection." March 1973, 80–83.

"Mothers Are People — A *Ms.* Family Album." May 1973, 102–3.

Letty Cottin Pogrebin. "Motherhood." May 1973, 49–51.

Gloria Steinem. "If We're So Smart, Why Aren't We Rich?" June 1973, 37–38.

Ellen Willis. "Economic Reality and the Limits of Feminism." June 1973, 90–93.

Jo Freeman. "The Tyranny of Structurelessness." July 1973, 76–78.

"A Happy Birthday from *Ms.*" July 1973, 83–84.

Letters. July 1973, 4.

"Dear Sisters." December 1973, 76–78.

"Personal Report from *Ms.*" June 1974, 72–75.

"What It's Like to Be Me: Young Women Speak for Themselves." compiled by Curtis
    Ingham. June 1974, 45–49.

"Everything You Wanted to Know about Advertising and Were Not Afraid to Ask —
    Personal Report from *Ms.*" November 1974, 56–59.

Gloria Steinem. "It's Your Year." January 1975, 45.

Robin Morgan. "Rights of Passage." September 1975, 77–78.

"Special Issue on Men." October 1975, 47.

Gloria Steinem. "Cheer Up!" July 1976, 47.

"Unforgettable Letters from Battered Wives." December 1976.

Gloria Steinem. "Pornography — Not Sex, But the Obscene Use of Power." August
    1977, 43–44.

Letters. January 1978.

"Personal Report: Reader Alert!" July 1978, back page.

Gloria Steinem. "What is a New *Ms.*?" November 1979, 4.

"A Ninth Birthday Personal Report (and Urgent Alert)." July 1981, 12–16.

"Personal Report: *Ms.* at 11." July 1983, 103–5.

Minnie Bruce Pratt. "Who Am I If I'm Not My Father's Daughter? A Southerner
    Confronts Racism and Anti-Semitism." January 1984, 72–73.

Lindsy Van Gelder. "Carol Gilligan: Leader for a Different Kind of Future." January
    1984, 37–40.

Alice Walker. "When a Tree Falls." January 1984, 48–55.

Letters. March 1986, 12.

Letters. May 1986, 8.

Letters. July 1986, 10.

Suzanne Braun Levine. "New Words, New Understanding." February 1987, 35.

Letters. May 1987, 8.

Suzanne Braun Levine. "The *Ms.* of the Future Is Here." September 1987, 5.

Gloria Steinem. "Sex, Lies, and Advertising." Premier Issue 1990, 18–28.

INTERVIEWS

All interviews were conducted by the author unless otherwise specified.

Carbine, Patricia. New York, N.Y., August 1, 1990.

Edgar, JoAnne. Carlisle, Pa., July 1, 1993 (phone interview).

Freeman, Jo. Carlisle, Pa., September 23, 1992 (phone interview).

Gillespie, Marcia. New York, N.Y., August 2, 1990.

Harris, Elizabeth Forsling. New York, N.Y., June 8, 1990.

Levine, Suzanne Braun. St. Paul, Minn., August 8, 1990 (phone interview).

Lyons, Harriet. New York, N.Y., August 1, 1990.

Peacock, Mary. New York, N.Y., June 8, 1990.

Pogrebin, Letty Cottin. Carlisle, Pa., February 1, 1994 (phone interview).

Steinem, Gloria. New York, N.Y., August 2, 1990.

Summers, Anne. Interview by Mollie Hoben. Minneapolis, Minn., November 17, 1989.

Thom, Mary. New York, N.Y., August 2, 1990.

INDEX

Lyons, Harriet, 11, 41, 43, 96, 140. *See also* Editors; Staff

Lyons, Phyllis, 15, 73, 74

McCall's (magazine), 5, 27. *See also* Carbine, Patricia

McDermott, Patrice, 212 (n. 74)

MacDonald Corporation, 214 (n. 5)

Madge the hairdresser, 56

Majority Enterprises, 27

Male gaze, 183, 184

Mansbridge, Jane, 3

Martin, Del, 15, 73, 74

Martin, Patricia, 38

Mass media: and feminism, 21–23, 201 (n. 16), 208 (n. 38); implicit racism and sexism of print, 214 (n. 6). *See also* Commercial media; Popular culture

Matilda, Inc., 40, 179

Methodology, 10–14

Midler, Bette, 56, 116, 187

Millett, Kate, 23, 68, 168; *Sexual Politics*, 19

Miss America Beauty Pageant, 19, 23, 64

Monroe, Marilyn, 43, 56

Moral Majority, 113

Morgan, Robin, 63, 66–67, 68, 80; *Sisterhood is Powerful*, 19. *See also* Editors; Staff

Morgen, Sandra, 39

Mother Jones (magazine), 107

Mount Vernon/New Rochelle (New York), 19

"Ms.": as term, 32–33

Ms. Foundation for Education and Communication (MFEC), 10, 132; creation of, 110–14; sale of *Ms.*, 184–85. *See also* Ms. Foundation for Women

Ms. Foundation for Women (MFW), 10, 40, 111, 206; creation of, 89–93; board, 90; in the 1980s, 103–4, 132–37; and diversity, 133–35; legal issues, 135–37; profits from sale, 185. See also *Free to Be*; Ms. Foundation for Education and Communication

"*Ms.* Guide to Consciousness-Raising," 65–68

Ms. magazine: importance of history, 1–2; as discursive site, 2; as resource, 2; tensions within, 3–5, 10; as service magazine, 6, 30–31; as crossover magazine, 6, 60, 191–92; as "open forum," 6–7, 59; "golden age" view, 9; reformist vs. revolutionary, 14–16; origins, 15–48; as organization, 36–44, 93–99, 186–87; concepts of self-help and sisterhood, 61–62, 192; diversity, 72–79; promotional material, 86–87, 127–30, 145; financial problems, 105, 126, 179; becomes nonprofit, 111–14; textual transitions, 114–18, 179–80, 187–89; sale price, 184; advertising-free *Ms.*, 194–95, 212 (n. 68); histories of itself, 200 (n. 22). *See also* Academic feminism; Advertising; Covers; Editors; Letters; Preview issue; Readers; Staff

The Ms. Money Book (Card), 185

Ms. Scholarly Board of Advisers, 120

Ms. Woman of the Year, 31

Mulvey, Laura, 183

Myerson, Bess, 187

National Abortion Rights Action League, 51

National Endowment for the Humanities, 102

National Federation of Business and Professional Women's Clubs, 52

National Network of Women's Funds, 133. *See also* Foundations

National Organization for Women (NOW), 2, 17–18, 33, 49, 50, 51, 85, 199 (n. 4)

National Press Club News Conference, 139

National Right to Life Committee, 102

National Women's Political Caucus (NWPC), 17–18, 26, 50, 199 (n. 4)

National Women's Studies Association, 50

GENDER AND AMERICAN CULTURE ·

Yours in Sisterhood: Ms. *Magazine and the Promise of Popular Feminism,*
    by Amy Erdman Farrell (1998)
We Mean to Be Counted: White Women and Politics in Antebellum Virginia,
    by Elizabeth R. Varon (1998)
*Women Against the Good War: Conscientious Objection and Gender on the American
    Home Front, 1941–1947,* by Rachel Waltner Goossen (1997)
Toward an Intellectual History of Women: Essays by Linda K. Kerber (1997)
*Gender and Jim Crow: Women and the Politics of White Supremacy in North Carolina,
    1896–1920,* by Glenda Elizabeth Gilmore (1996)
*Delinquent Daughters: Protecting and Policing Adolescent Female Sexuality in the
    United States, 1885–1920,* by Mary E. Odem (1995)
U.S. History as Women's History: New Feminist Essays, edited by Linda K. Kerber,
    Alice Kessler-Harris, and Kathryn Kish Sklar (1995)
*Common Sense and a Little Fire: Women and Working-Class Politics in the United
    States, 1900–1965,* by Annelise Orleck (1995)
How Am I to Be Heard?: Letters of Lillian Smith, edited by Margaret Rose Gladney
    (1993)
Entitled to Power: Farm Women and Technology, 1913–1963, by Katherine Jellison
    (1993)
Revising Life: Sylvia Plath's Ariel Poems, by Susan R. Van Dyne (1993) ·
Made From This Earth: American Women and Nature, by Vera Norwood (1993)
Unruly Women: The Politics of Social and Sexual Control in the Old South,
    by Victoria E. Bynum (1992)
The Work of Self-Representation: Lyric Poetry in Colonial New England,
    by Ivy Schweitzer (1991)
Labor and Desire: Women's Revolutionary Fiction in Depression America,
    by Paula Rabinowitz (1991)
*Community of Suffering and Struggle: Women, Men, and the Labor Movement in
    Minneapolis, 1915–1945,* by Elizabeth Faue (1991)
All That Hollywood Allows: Re-reading Gender in 1950s Melodrama, by Jackie Byars
    (1991)
Doing Literary Business: American Women Writers in the Nineteenth Century,
    by Susan Coultrap-McQuin (1990)

Ladies, Women, and Wenches: Choice and Constraint in Antebellum Charleston and Boston, by Jane H. Pease and William H. Pease (1990)

The Secret Eye: The Journal of Ella Gertrude Clanton Thomas, 1848–1889, edited by Virginia Ingraham Burr, with an introduction by Nell Irvin Painter (1990)

Second Stories: The Politics of Language, Form, and Gender in Early American Fictions, by Cynthia S. Jordan (1989)

Within the Plantation Household: Black and White Women of the Old South, by Elizabeth Fox-Genovese (1988)

The Limits of Sisterhood: The Beecher Sisters on Women's Rights and Woman's Sphere, by Jeanne Boydston, Mary Kelley, and Anne Margolis (1988)